Bob Allan, John Dix

The Sportsman in Ireland

Bob Allan, John Dix

The Sportsman in Ireland

ISBN/EAN: 9783742899187

Manufactured in Europe, USA, Canada, Australia, Japa

Cover: Foto ©ninafisch / pixelio.de

Manufactured and distributed by brebook publishing software (www.brebook.com)

Bob Allan, John Dix

The Sportsman in Ireland

THE
SPORTSMAN IN IRELAND

BY

A COSMOPOLITE

A NEW EDITION
WITH ILLUSTRATIONS BY P. CHENEVIX TRENCH

EDWARD ARNOLD
Publisher to the India Office
LONDON   NEW YORK
37 BEDFORD STREET   70 FIFTH AVENUE
1897

"My gun was now in requisition."

INTRODUCTION

This volume, which has been selected to form the third in the "Sportsman's Library," is a condensed edition of a work published in two volumes in 1840. Its authorship has been the occasion of a singular blunder. It is attributed by Cushing in his *Dictionary of Initials and Pseudonyms* (New York, 1885) to John Dix, afterwards Ross. This writer was denounced by Mr. Moy Thomas in the *Athenæum* (5th December 1857, and 23rd January 1858) as an unscrupulous literary forger, and his pretensions were challenged further in *Notes and Queries* (4th series, ix. 294, 365; x. 55). Among a number of pseudonyms, Dix or Ross wrote under that of "A Cosmopolitan," which doubtless led Mr. Cushing to confound him with "A Cosmopolite." Mr. Frederic Fane, of Moyles Court, Ringwood, informs me that "Cosmopolite" was really Serjeant Allen, as he believes of the Irish Bar.

Of the book Mr. Fane adds: "It gave such a delightful description of the then wilds of Kerry, and especially of Waterville and the Blackwater of that county, that I at once betook myself to that part of Ireland, to which I have been faithful now for more than fifty years, rarely missing, year by year, a sojourn in the West—to me a Paradise."

There is a good deal in the original edition unsuitable to the character of the present series, in which it is intended to reproduce only the best sporting literature of the past. In his preface the author had not a word to say about the varied scenes of fishing and shooting which he describes with such admirable vivacity; he dwelt only on political and ecclesiastical questions of a highly controversial character, and on the remedies which he considered desirable in the interests of the people. This preface, therefore, has not been reprinted in preparing a new edition, and those chapters and passages dealing with political and ecclesiastical controversy have been left out also.

It has been a matter of greater regret that some chapters at the end of the second volume, describing Cosmopolite's "Summer Route through the Highlands of Scotland," have had to be sacrificed, in order to bring the work within the scope of a single volume. The only part of the Highlands which he traversed was the region lying between Loch Fyne and Loch Lomond, and the reader may rest assured that the best of the author's exploits took place in Ireland. It is hoped that Mr. Trench's drawings will help to give a vivid impression of Irish sport as it was sixty years ago. The illustrations in the original edition were no more than poor, with the exception of two which have been reproduced for the present one (pp. 1 and 110).

The scheme of Cosmopolite's tour in Ireland was somewhat similar to that undertaken by Colonel Thornton in Scotland fifty years previously, but the scale of his preparations was very different from that of the opulent Yorkshireman. It will be seen, too, that whereas Colonel Thornton, when he left his own camp, did so to pay visits to the various county magnates living near his route, Cosmopolite, on the other hand, contented himself with such accommodation as he could find in humble inns and farmhouses, varied occasionally by hospitality freely offered by the poorer gentry and clergy of the west.

From a modern point of view the use of the "incomparable bait," described on p. 28, is exceedingly reprehensible; but at that time the use of salmon-roe had not been declared illegal, and it is curious that Cosmopolite claims to have been the first to make its dangerous attractions known to Irish anglers.

INTRODUCTION

The natural advantages offered by Ireland to the salmon and trout angler are almost incomparable—quite so, if easy access and a moderate climate are taken into account. Compared with other parts of the United Kingdom the extent of naturally *good* fishing water is in far greater proportion than in England, Scotland, or Wales. Irish lakes and streams produce, as a rule, trout of far greater weight and of finer quality than those of the sister island; while Irish rivers are as favourable for salmon and sea trout as those of any country in the world. On the other hand, it must be confessed that in no other country have the angling resources suffered more grievously from mismanagement, excessive net-fishing, and river pollution. In the last-named respect, the general absence of manufactures might be supposed to save the fisheries from the lamentable devastation which has overtaken so many fair streams in northern England and Scotland; but this has been fully balanced by the effects of the pernicious habit of steeping flax, whereby hundreds of miles of admirable trout-fishing has been totally destroyed. When it is considered what enormous rents men are willing to pay for good fishing, surely it must be reckoned worthy the attention both of the legislature and of private owners to take measures for the restoration of such an abundant source of wealth. It has been known for long that good salmon angling would command plenty of customers; but the later refinements of trout-fishing, especially the use of the dry fly, have attracted great numbers of people to a sport which fifty years ago nobody thought of paying for. Many of the Irish trout streams, if they got fair play and were protected from flax pollution, crosslines, and other destructive practices, would produce trout superior to and more numerous than those of the southern English chalk streams. As a rule, these streams are admirably suited to dry fly fishing.

Some politicians may consider such a subject as too trivial for their attention; others may regard with indifference, or even with prejudice, anything that, in their view, would only serve to put money into the pockets of Irish landlords. But that would be only a small part of the effect of the restoration of Irish angling waters. Anglers must live as well as other people, and pay for their living. It is true that the owners of lakes and streams would benefit in the first instance, just as they have done in Scotland by the development of the sporting resources of that country. But the benefit does not stop with the landlords; it would be impossible to calculate to what extent the poorest districts in Scotland have been enriched by the presence, year after year, of wealthy strangers attracted thither by sport. One other consideration remains. Great Britain is a vast workshop, working at high pressure; the playgrounds are limited in extent, though the numbers of those for whom healthy recreation is indispensable are annually increasing. For one angler of thirty years ago there are it would be hard to say how many now. The advantage of restoring to Ireland the qualities she naturally possesses of entertaining anglers, would be a mutual boon to the two countries; and the man, be he statesman or sportsman, who gives the movement a successful start, would deserve the gratitude of workers in the British hive, not less than of the struggling population of poor Ireland.

HERBERT MAXWELL.

Monreith, 1897.

CONTENTS

CHAPTER I

The Sportsman's Resolve—The Slow Coach—The Irish Packet—Passengers—Irish Family—View of Ireland—The British Legioner—His History—The Mutiny—The Spokesman—The Punishment—The Return—Arrival in London—The Stipendiary Magistrate—Arrival at Cork—Appearance of the Coast—Dreary Prospect to some . Page 1

CHAPTER II

Cork—The Harbour—Splendour and Misery—Imperial Hotel—High Charges—The Assizes—Irish Eloquence—Want of Dignity and Decorum—Irish Judges and Counsel—An Irish Case—Mike and the Cows—Theatre at Cork—The Castle Spectre—An Acting Manager—An Evening Party—Punch-drinking—Three-Card Loo and the Ladies—Female Talent and Accomplishments—Beauty of the Women—Advice to Sportsmen—Departure from Cork . . Page 12

CHAPTER III

Start from Cork—Wild Character of the Country—An Irish Coachman—Sporting Prospects—Warning to Improvers—Pike *versus* Salmon—Arrival at Macroom—Ominous Demonstrations—A False Alarm—Inn Accommodations—An Irish Waiter—Extravagant Charges—Poverty and Desolation—Taste for Mud—Commencement of Operations—A Native Sportsman—Irish Blarney—Directions for Trolling—Incomparable Bait . . . . . Page 20

CHAPTER IV

Advice to Sportsmen—Mode of Conveyance—An Irish Pony and his Food—Delight of the First Cast—Failure and Success—Irish Astonishment—An Irish Sign—Native Hospitality—A Sportsman's Dinner—Natural Magic—Lake Inchgeelah—Directions for Fishing in this Lake—Hints to Anglers and Sportsmen in general—Character of the Kerry Peasantry—An Invitation to Dinner—Irish Servants—An Odd Establishment—An Irish Kitchen—Irish Hospitality—Wine and the Ladies—Whiskey and the Gentlemen—An Irish Dinner Party—The Sporting Major—Longbow-ism—An Irish Angler's Exploit—Sporting Extraordinary—A Dance—Prospective Sport with the Major

Page 29

CHAPTER V

Characteristic Scenery—Encampment of the Whitefeet Rebels—Romantic Escapes and Dangers of an Irish Gentleman—Irish Hospitality—The Lake of Inchgeelah—Delicious Treat—Difficult Road—Inn of the Desert—Splendid View—Irish Ingenuity—History of an Irish Fisherman—His Devoted Affection—Heroic Self-devotion—Death of his Betrothed—His Filial Affection—Character of the Irish Peasantry—Sporting renewed—A Double Bite—Start for Killarney—The River Flesk—Noble View—Coltsman Castle—Sporting Notices—Killarney—A Perfect Gentleman!—Ill-effects of English Generosity on the Poor of Killarney . . . . Page 41

CHAPTER VI

Arrival at Killarney—Strange Costume—Street Annoyances and Beggars—Character of the Inhabitants of Killarney—Lord Kenmare and the Lakes—Inn Accommodation—Doherty, the Fly-maker—The Lions of the Lakes—The Major—Impudence and Imposition—Advantage of Private Lodgings—Price of Provisions—Impositions of Innkeepers—Hints to Anglers at Killarney—The Major's Narrative—Hoaxing—A Fighting Tailor—The Major's Revenge . . . Page 53

CHAPTER VII

First Day on the Lake—Ross Castle—Splendid View—Accidental Sport—A Disappointment—The Evil of Sight-gazing—Scarcity of Salmon in the Lakes—Island of Innisfallen—An Impromptu Breakfast—Beauties of the Island—The Monastery—Coasting—Famous Sport—The Eagle's Nest—Extraordinary Echoes—The Pass—The Lower Lake—Residence of Mr. Hyde, Rector of Killarney—Trouting—Directions for Bait—How to astonish the Natives—Wonderful success of Salmon-roe—Lord Kenmare's Cottage—An Angler's Dinner—Turk Lake—Its Monster Trout—Angling Exploit of Lady Headley—The Major in his Glory—Enormous Trout—More Hints to Sportsmen at Killarney
Page 62

CHAPTER VIII

The Rivers—Residences of James and John O'Connell—Lord Kenmare—The Gap of Dunloe—Major Mahony—Beaufort Bridge—Residence of Mr. Mullins, Member for Kerry—The River Laune—Excellent Sport—Izaak Walton—The Major incredulous—Sporting extraordinary—A Cure for Everything—Killarney Scandal—Lord Headley—The Irish Agents—A Stag-Hunt in the Lake—Extraordinary Scene of Irish Jollity—Timber-Hunting in the Bogs—Extinct Animals—Unpopularity of Lord Kenmare—Reasons for it—Beauties and Merits of Killarney as a Watering Place . . . . Page 74

CHAPTER IX

Kenmare—Blackwater—Liberality of the Rev. D. M——.—Irish Cunning and Roguery—O'Rourke, the Salmon-Poacher—Story of O'Rourke and the Magistrate—Gaffing at the Falls—The Poacher in Exile—The Flood—Singular Habits of the Salmon—Ascent of the Hills—A Sudden Storm, and its consequences—Perils and Escapes—Fatal Catastrophe at Clydah—The whole of the Cattle and Inhabitants destroyed by a Flood . . . . . Page 82

CHAPTER X

A Mountaineer — Harvest-Hunters — Kerry Agents — Influence of the Catholic Clergy — Causes of that Influence — Safe Travelling in Ireland — Temper of the Irish Peasantry — Means for Improving their Condition — Abundance of Wild Fowl — The Secret — Return to Killarney — Kellorglin — Lake Carraght — Wales's Inn — Fishery on the Carraght River — Lob-Trout — Fishing in Lake Carraght — Disappointment — Seal-Shooting — Castlemaine Bay — Birthplace of Daniel O'Connell — Arrival at Cahirciveen . . . Page 91

CHAPTER XI

Cahirciveen — Comfortable Inn — John O'Connell — Portrait of the Liberator — Mountain Hunting — A Sportsman's Breakfast — The Mass — State of Crime in Kerry — Party Feuds — The Lawlors and Cooleens — A Smasher — The River Inny — Waterville Lake — Courtesy of Mr. Butler — Live Lamb for Dinner — Produce of the Weirs — A Deathbed Scene . . . . . . Page 113

CHAPTER XII

Enormous Eagle — Fishing in Waterville Lake — Morning-Breakfast — Island Burial-Ground — Funeral — A New Friend — The White Strand — Anecdote of the Duke of Wellington — Round Tower — Mullet-fishing — An Extempore Fishing Yacht — The Knight of Kerry — Colony of Fishermen — Fishing Arrangements — A Night's Fishing — An Unexpected Prize — Paddy Shea — The Perfection of Sport — A Great Haul — Cormorant Soup — Threatening Weather — Irish Superstition — A Storm — Courage of the Irish Fishermen — Dangers and Escapes — A Dance — An Event — Dangers of the Irish Coast — Frightful Scene of Shipwreck — A suspicious Visit — Irish Smugglers . . Page 127

CHAPTER XIII

Visit to Waterville—New Mode of Angling—Mistake about the Potato Diet of the Irish—Cobbett right as to its Mischievous Effects—Drive to Tralee—Miserable State of the Peasantry—Prevalence of Scrofula and Consumption—Fine Mountain Scenery—Castlemaine—The River—The White Trout—The Lob Trout—Fine Shooting Station for Sea-Fowl and Grouse—Sporting Exciseman—Folly and Rapacity of Irish Landlords—The Surgeon's Tale—The Murderers—A Mysterious Character—Irish Court of Justice—The Trial—The Defence—The Cross-Examination—The Verdict—The Mystery explained—Three pleasant Weeks—O'Connell as a Landlord—His Occupation at Derrynane—His Devotion to the Peasantry—The Dancing-Master in Ireland—Advantages of Ireland over the Continent—Cheapness and Security of the Living—Farewell to Cahirciveen—Departure for Dingle—Wild-Fowl Shooting—Fishing at Dingle—Hospitality of the Resident Gentry—Trout-fishing and Grouse-shooting—Causes and Remedy of Irish Discontent—An Irish Wake—The Irish Howl—A Victim of the "Good People"—A Fairy Tale . . . . Page 148

CHAPTER XIV

To the Shannon—Mountain Scenery—Profusion of Wild Fowl and Hares—Listowel—Extempore Dinner—Cheap Travelling—Excellent Sport—Primitive Cooking—Mill Street—Extraordinary Cheapness of Living—Extreme Wretchedness of the Inhabitants—First View of the Queen of Irish Rivers, the Shannon—Athlone—Ballinasloe Fair—Onions and Eels—Athlone Bridge—Lough Ree—The Shannon—Splendid Tract of Country—Suitable Harbour for Shipping . . . Page 160

CHAPTER XV

Galway—Mr. Keogh—Fishing in Lough Corrib—First Failure of the Infallible Bait—Its Causes—A New Acquaintance—The Monastery—

Claddagh—Its Antiquity—Forms of Marriage—Dress of the Females—Respect paid to the Dead—Prevalence of the Cholera—Benevolence of the Rev. Father Fay—Protestants and Catholics—History of James Lynch Fitzstephen, the Mayor of Galway . . . Page 179

CHAPTER XVI

Fishing in Lough Corrib—Enormous Trout—The Weirs—Perch and Pike—Productiveness of the Weirs—Arrival of the Major—Difficulty of getting a Fishing-Boat—Independence of the Fishermen—Herring Fishery—The Mayor of the Claddagh—The Prior—The Priesthood—Preparations for Sport . . . . . Page 192

CHAPTER XVII

Dress of a Sportsman — Embarkation — Wild-Fowl — Appearance of a Grampus — A Haul — The Conger and Dog-fish — The Herring—"Heads, heads, nothing but heads!"—Accident to the Major—A Splendid Halibut—A Sea-Dinner—Islands of Arran—Costume of the Arran Peasantry—Cordial Reception—A Dance—A Beauty—Amorous Propensity of the Major—Smuggling—Coast of Connemara—Magnificent Scenery—Return to Galway . . . Page 201

CHAPTER XVIII

Superstition of the Fishermen—Execution of Lynch for the Murder of his Wife—General Sympathy for the Murderer—The Priest—His Disclosure of the Circumstances of the Murder—Villainy of R——
Page 215

CHAPTER XIX

Departure from Galway—Coasting—The Coal-Fish, or Bace —Aground on Roundstone Flats—The Harbour—Protestant Clergyman—The Major's Reminiscences in America—Catching a Sea-Serpent with a Shoe . . . . . . Page 225

CHAPTER XX

Connemara—Serving a Writ—Mr. Martin's Permission to Fish—Rags, Rags, everywhere Rags!—Character of the Inhabitants—Departure—Bad Roads—Desolation of Connemara—Cong—The Subterranean River and the Lady White Trout—Mountain Accommodation—A Strange Adventure in the Gorge—Its Satisfactory Result—Bog River Fishing—The Wilds of Lough Mask—The Desert Lands and their Proprietors—The Major's Run and Catastrophe—The Prize   Page 234

CHAPTER XXI

The Friar's Visit—The Monster of the Mountains—The Mystery Solved—The Whiskey Store—The Unparliamentary—Traversing a Bog—Process of Grabbling—A Brood of Otters—Castlebar—Wretched State of the Inhabitants—Annual Subscriptions—Ludicrous Adventure of Owen—Following a Salmon—Decency on Entering a Town   Page 262

CHAPTER XXII

A Curse against Preserves—Reasons for condemning them—A Slap at the Peers—Apology and Reconciliation—An Irish Tory—After-Dinner Argument on Popular Education—Challenge—Preparations for a Meeting—Satisfactory Arrangement—An Old Acquaintance—The Spanish Legioner—His Last Trip—The Shipwreck—How to Qualify for Exciseman—Belfast—Manufactures at Belfast—Last Evening in Ireland—Leave-taking   .   .   .   .   .   Page 283

ILLUSTRATIONS

	PAGE
"My Gun was now in Requisition"	Frontispiece
Connemara—Ballinahinch	Facing 1
"Car, your Honour?"	,, 12
"Here I Purchased my Tackle"	. 18
"With some Difficulty we Landed him"	Facing 30
"The Wind blew—the Torrents descended"	30
"A Pike had taken my Trout"	. 50
"Among them was one Doherty"	Facing 56
"Here, indeed, the Major was Great"	,, 70
The River Laune	,, 76
"I raised him in my Arms"	,, 88
"Freed from Restraint, we saw him once more"	. 107
The Birthplace of O'Connell	Facing 110
"The Cry of the Lad Warns them to Watch"	,, 114
Night Sport	,, 137
"Good Cooking, any way"	,, 171
Prepared for a Night Out	. 176
"I was Close to the Bridge"	Facing 192
Leaving the Claddagh	. 202
The Island Dance	Facing 212
An Irish Street Piper	,, 214
"I Shook off the Butt"	,, 245
"The Monster Floundered on the Shore"	,, 256
"I Looked at the Major"	274

CONNEMARA – BALLINAHINCH.

THE SPORTSMAN IN IRELAND

CHAPTER I

The Sportsman's Resolve—The Slow Coach—The Irish Packet—Passengers—Irish Family—View of Ireland—The British Legioner—His History—The Mutiny—The Spokesman—The Punishment—The Return—Arrival in London—The Stipendiary Magistrate—Arrival at Cork—Appearance of the Coast—Dreary Prospect to some.

Who that has heard of the resources and beauties of the Emerald Isle—who that has listened to the torrents of abuse levelled against those who are at once termed her patriots and her destroyers, her liberators and enslavers—who that has heard of the trackless mountains, the rushing torrents, the splendid rivers unsullied by a line, or of the wild birds that are undisturbed on her desolate coasts; the honest generosity of character, the hospitable feelings, yet, albeit, the murderous villany, the bloodthirsty relentlessness of her children—who that has only *heard* of all these, but will determine at once to be convinced of the truth or falsehood of the accounts put forth—will at once seize his rod and his gun, and, delivering himself up to fortune, make his journey unite the pleasure of wild sports with the philosophy of statistical observation?

I, at all events, will for one; and, ere I revisit the artificial shore of my birth, the Irish as they are, and not as political partisans would paint them, shall be known to me.

My preparations were simple; and let me entreat all those who follow me to make their own so.

In the first place, let no London fly or rod maker impose on them by the delicate manufacture of their wares, but by all means let the gun-maker have his chance; take a good double-barrel, powder, and casts for bullets, and leave the rest to fortune and my direction; also a good woollen suit, one change for dress, a mackintosh, a well-strapped wallet—for there is much in its being well strapped.

These are all that can be required by or desirable to those who would really make the tour of a sportsman through Ireland. Every desirable comfort will follow in its proper place; and it should not be forgotten that the greatest inconvenience of travelling is the travelling with too many conveniences. But, as I hate people who would have to make their arrangements all tending inevitably to embarrass their progress and restrict their independence, we will suppose the usual horn-blowing has taken place, the usual number of now despised coachmen have been fee'd, and that we find ourselves half asleep and half awake at Bristol.

We judge of the distance of places by the time consumed in reaching them; in fact, time *is* distance, and Bristol is a heavy journey. Bristol itself is a sort of a *slow coach*. It has, by its paltry efforts at inordinate gain in the harbour dues, wrapped itself up in a dignified independence, while all other ports have surpassed its accommodations, and withdrawn its trade. Even the Great Western does not help it: we must still be bugled down, and cramped in four insides. But we are there.

And this is the Irish packet? you need not answer—I perceive it is. Those shoeless wretches, shivering under the March blasts, and crouching midst the packages for a momentary protection—the surly officers who have just presented them with their *free* passage to their native land; the hopeless gaze of that suffering mother, who deprives herself of her ragged shawl that she may shelter her still more suffering infant; all these proclaim the destination of the vessel. Midst the hoarse orders of the bluff commander she moves in stately grandeur down the river, and carries with her the farewells, the hopes, the happiness of many!

It is needless to describe the Clifton Rocks. I perceive the pencils of the lady passengers are at work, while the obsequious gentlemen surrounding them gaze on the performances, and admire the wonders of nature, but more those of art.

The massive rocks of the extended scene give rise to general hilarity, and the ever-varying range on each side calls forth the admiration of the Creator's works.

But the sea-breeze now breaks on us. The hitherto stately vessel yields to the coming tide. Now shawls and cloaks are in requisition, and the sketches are left for future finishing and future encomiums. Less is heard of the beauty of surrounding objects, and more of personal comfort.

The cabin is sought by some, where fires, books, and all the comforts which the gaudy packet can afford, are at hand. The sea rises—the scudding squalls dash over the angry spray —there is more silence and more self among the previously gay and joyous crowd on the front deck; each looks to himself, while the storm increases, and the rains descend.

Let us survey the deck. Not one of the many, now wrapped in all the comforts which art can supply, has condescended to do so. Each passenger has selected his bed, and made his inquiries for dinner; but where is to be *your* bed—where *your* dinner, ye homeless, hapless wanderers—cursed in your birthplace—whose crime is that you are the offspring of a doomed land! a land, beauteous to the eye, fertile in its resources, yet whose shipless harbours yawn in hospitality without a guest— upon whose shores the wild sea howls, and the angry billows alone unite to break the silence of a gloomy solitude!

See that father and mother, with their helpless race of children; behold them shivering in the bleak March blast, and now and then submitting to the spray which dashes over their half-covered limbs! That child, squalid and bare, crouching beneath the mother's scanty rags; behold her! She is human—those blue eyes seem to speak intelligence; she looks wistfully, beseechingly, yet modestly. It is for food she asks. Inquire their little history: it is the history of all. That father is strong, active, and not deficient in intelligence. You see he does not want feeling for those dependent on him; he has covered the children with his grey frieze coat, and bears the falling rain with a manly defiance. Unable to discharge the heavy imposts of his landlord and the tithe, he has been expatriated; he has sought what he imagined was the golden land; he has sought the English coast. Prejudice and the poor-laws have been his unconquerable foes. Employment was nowhere to be found; and, after a year's travelling from place to place, during which the hedge and the sheep hovel have been his only covering, and the covering of his wife and little ones, he has at length been found guilty of being destitute, and condemned to—his native country. The surly officer, whom you saw speaking to him at Bristol, was employed to ship him and his family safely off by the packet. Their sea-store was supplied, their passage was paid. The bundle, which the enduring woman has hanging from her arm, contains potatoes; they have been already cooked, and you will see the father frequently distributing a portion among his trembling children—God help them! But their native land is now in sight. A joyous exclamation is heard among some—it is among the cabin passengers. Each runs to gain a glimpse of land—of Ireland—the place of our destination.

All are pleased, except only the miserable family whose patient endurance of the long sea passage, whose hunger the lowest of human food has barely appeased;—from them, and those who surround them, no sound of delight is heard. The countenance of the oppressed father, as he shiveringly looks down upon his children, is marked by a stern misery;—his native land is indifferent to his view; it almost excites horror. For him, alas! and his, no home is there prepared;—he has no spot whereon to lie! no store, from which the wants of his little ones shall be supplied! To him, his native shores present only the barren rocks of desolation and despair.

The morning broke; and who that has voyaged by steam or coach does not shrink at the remembrance of the peeping morn of March? The face of the ocean presents a cold cheerlessness, which even the sluggish sunrise does not dispel; its rays seem rather to render still more visible the ravages of watchfulness or inebriety. Every face is without a smile; the features are paralysed; even the mind is benumbed and depressed, and misery looks still more miserable.

The lower deck of the steamer was the parade of those who had known no other couch during the night. The wretched family I had before observed were still crouching under the packages; the father standing, in silent suffering, over them!

Among these involuntary watchers I observed a sprightly and good-looking young man, whose nether person a pair of soldier's duck trowsers, and whose upper man a simple white flannel jacket protected from the searching cold of the breaking morning. A foraging cap was stuck *à la militaire* on one side of his head. He was determinedly energetic in his promenade, and bore the inconvenience of his slight covering and the absence of all comfort with a cheerful philosophy. I could not but admire his independent and erect form; and, on entering into conversation with him, I soon found that he had not from habit braved so well the cold of the past night. On the contrary, he assured me that he had felt it severely, as he had but lately arrived from a warmer climate, and did not remember the necessity of thicker clothing. Perhaps if his attention had been directed to the probable severity of the night, and the prudence of provision against it, it might not have made much difference in his arrangements, as he happened just then to be without one farthing in the world, or a single additional garment. The good humour with which he made this reply encouraged me to pursue my inquiries as to his history.

"I was tolerably well born, your honour, though I could not live without work. I did work till I found rent too high and produce too small to get on with. I was 'noticed'; that is, served with tithe process for my little ground; and, rather than submit to the extortionate villain who had hired the tithes of the clergyman, whom I had never seen, and who indeed lived somewhere in France, I sold what little I possessed and went to Dublin. Here I found instant employment offered me, which required me to assist the Queen of Spain, under General Evans. The terms were easily settled, as they were at first all on my own side. We were promised ten pounds on our arrival in Spain—a fortune in my own country; and, in addition to this liberal donation, there was the prospect of promotion and other advantages. Of course, I and the rest never doubted but that all these promises would be realised; and with light hearts, little clothes, and no money, to the number of fifty, we were shipped from Kingstown.

"Our passage was rough, and rougher the fare,—the captain of the transport declaring that he had no allowance for provisions on our account; or, at least, that he doubted whether he should be ever paid for any. He exhorted us therefore to be content, and consider ourselves happy in the enjoyment of the meagre fare his liberality allowed. I believe all this to have been false—that the captain had received for our provisions a considerable sum; but thinking, as I found many have since, not even excepting your London magistrates, that our employment was altogether illegal, he would be justified in cheating us to any extent short of absolute starvation.

"On our arrival in Spain, we found ourselves just in time to be sent on picquet duty. Arms were thrown on our shoulders;— those who had jackets were well off; as the midnight air, acting on empty and sea-sick stomachs, as well as on the uncovered skin, is by no means calculated to awaken the soul to deeds of heroism.

"However, at four in the morning we were relieved, and found good straw in an outhouse prepared for our reception.

In the morning, the jacket I now wear, and these trowsers (they are rather thin) were presented to me, with fourpence for my day's rations. I now inquired for my ten pounds bounty. This, I was assured, had been expended for my benefit—that is, it had been applied to the purchase of my clothing and arms;—and as, without these, a soldier is nothing, nor likely to obtain promotion, no objection could be made to so wise, just, and judicious an outlay.

"Our piece of hardest service was the taking a fort, well fortified by Don Carlos; and, after a severe battle, we were successful. Several of my fellow recruits fell in this terrible engagement. The storming lasted several hours, and, during its continuance, we who were fresh found ourselves always in the front.

"At last, on returning to the town where our quarters were assigned, myself and my companions went (about thirty of us remaining) to the superior officer; and, without the least intention of giving offence or of breaking discipline, inquired for our rations and pay. We were stopped by a serjeant, who seemed to have been well enough fed. He told us that our conduct was disorderly—that our rations and pay were the same, and would continue the same, as the Spanish regiments engaged. Now this pay was fourpence per day, instead of eightpence, which we had bargained for on enlistment at Dublin. We returned to our quarters, and one and all agreed to lay down our arms.

"I was unfortunate—for my comrades fixed upon me, being the most learned of the party, as spokesman on the occasion. Not that they lacked eloquence when they spoke of their indignation at the state of hunger and destitution into which we had been so unjustly deluded;—nor did they fail to promise that in all I should say on these subjects they would with life stand by me. I don't know how it is—but I somehow think that being spokesman, though a post of honour at the time, does not always bring any very great advantage after the occasion has passed by and the object settled.

"Somehow, I think, one is likely to get into scrapes by being made head man. At all events, I think it is so in the army, and especially that under the English General in Spain; for I found that my comrades, being chiefly of the lowest order of poor fellows, soon began to perceive what they did not perceive when they elected me spokesman—that fourpence was better than nothing. Certain it is, they at once yielded to the persuasions of some of the officers; while I and ten others, being seized and manacled by a guard of our own corps, those who had been the loudest among us in their complaints and protestations of perseverance in their demands were conveyed to prison.

"Prison in England is not much;—it affords comfortable lodging, good air, and *something* to eat. In fact, to us Irishmen an English prison is a tolerable asylum. But a prison in Spain is a different matter altogether. We were put into cellars, one quart of meal and water was our food, no covering of any kind, and nothing but the indulgence of the jailor afforded us a little straw.

"In this plight were we left for a whole week; till, perhaps, from the representation of the jailor, who must have perceived we could not last long in that condition, we were visited by a Spanish officer who spoke English; and who came, he said, from her most Christian Majesty the Queen. He was very well instructed in English. He assured us (a fact we were before ignorant of) that we had been guilty of so enormous a crime that nothing but our lives could atone for it; but that, in case we were disposed to make a full confession of our sins, and humbly sue to her Majesty for pardon, she might be induced to extend mercy to us.

"Hereupon I told him, without difficulty or hesitation (at that moment getting a peep, through the door which was open, of the beautiful daylight, and also of some black bread which had been brought by the officer's attendant), that, on behalf of myself and fellow-sufferers, I would make any apology her Majesty pleased; and that, if she would give us something to eat, and a chance of getting home to our native island, there was no kind of sorrow and repentance which should stop us from either.

"We were liberated, and I was not long in finding that the extraordinary grace of her Majesty, and the kind non-interference of the English Commander, who never appeared in the business, were owing to the exertions of the British Consul, who had peremptorily demanded our discharge. This we learned from the English Consul himself, who, on our discharge, sent for us, expressed his commiseration at the plight we were in, and regretted his inability farther to relieve us than in giving us fourpence each, and commending us to a merchant vessel, the captain of which gladly took us to work our passage home.

"I need say nothing of our voyage. We landed on the southern coast of England, and were not long in making our way to London, where we had been informed our claims would be heard. We had too much pride to beg; though, God knows, we needed all things; but, in our walk (about fifty miles) we were upheld with the hope that, by application to the Spanish Minister, we should obtain our arrears of pay. Many a morning saw us at his door; but every one of them saw us also sent off by his servant, who at last threatened prison and the police. We were still soldiers, and had the pride of soldiers; so we would no longer run that risk, though we had been four days without either food or shelter. I suppose our appearance —you see I am not too corpulent now—attracted attention, and a benevolent gentleman advised us forthwith to prefer our demands on the Spanish Ambassador, before a magistrate; and he was kind enough to direct us where to go. We now surely thought all was right—that we should be relieved and redressed. We marched in good order into a dark room, where two elderly gentlemen with bald heads were very comfortably seated. It was a police office. The magistrates were not such as we have in Ireland—gentlemen appointed to do what they please with the poor, and who send any man to jail because he is a Catholic;

—they were regularly paid magistrates who heard our story. After I had finished (for I was still spokesman), I was accosted in a very angry manner by the most elderly of the two gentlemen.—'What right had you in Spain?—you had no business to enlist—it was wholly illegal, and we will do nothing for such fellows but this: send you to the treadmill as rogues and vagabonds. Officer, if you find any of these fellows in the open air, after night, take them into custody, and I will commit them all—turn them out!'"

I could not believe that such language to a band of injured, starving, and unoffending men could have been used by a London magistrate. The very helpless condition of these poor men would and ought, as I imagined, to have forbidden the gross perversion of the law against them, if humanity had no share in the decision. My supposition was ill-founded; for, on afterwards consulting the newspapers, I found that this language had been used—had been passed over without comment—and that the paid perverter of law was still an officer of the executive!

He continued: "I, last night, reached Bristol, much reduced in pride, as I made no scruple of begging my way. I slept in an outhouse, not being desirous of the treadmill, which would have been my destination if found in the streets. I, yesterday, got a pass from the mayor to my own country, having given a solemn promise never again to return to the free and hospitable shores of England. I have done with being spokesman, and return to Ireland still poorer than I left it. Those are the shores of a land I love, but in which I have no home! What I can have to do with that land, or that land with me, I know not;—thither the English law sends me, and there I suppose I must dwell, if a life of beggary be dwelling. No landlord will receive me on his estate—no farmer employ me—for they are both overburthened already; and to whatsoever district I shall direct my steps, the answer will still be—'We cannot support our own people—go to your native town'—Sir, we are too many, or have too little to do."

With the advance of day came the splendid views of coast scenery which everywhere distinguish Ireland, and especially the entrance to the Cove of Cork. Iron-bound as this coast is, yet the avenues which here and there are observable between the abrupt and occasionally terrific rocks of varied hues, heightened by the glare of the sun, present patches of that deeply verdant surface, the characteristic of the beauteous isle; and as the rapid movement of the well-appointed vessel continues to vary the position, new beauties are as continually opening.

The dashing and roaring of the sea, against the dark and hollow masses that form the entrance to the Cove, are distinctly heard; and now, the suddenly smooth water informs us that we have entered the haven; while the banks on each side, and the rock itself which opposes its noble front to the angry ocean, become speckled with habitations as it were of a fairy land, each spot tipped with the brilliancy of the sun.

Hundreds of boats are seen pressing all canvas towards the vessel. The coast is lined with inhabitants, all anxious to know what the majestic mass now slowly forcing her way up the shallow river contains. Fathers for their children—children for their homes—are panting with expectation and long-anticipated happiness; and I must add, there are the multiplied sighs of wretches who have nought but the dreary prospect of ending their few remaining days in the land which gave birth to them and their uninterrupted sorrows.

CHAPTER II

Cork—The Harbour—Splendour and Misery—Imperial Hotel—High Charges—The Assizes—Irish Eloquence—Want of Dignity and Decorum—Irish Judges and Counsel—An Irish Case—Mike and the Cows—Theatre at Cork—The Castle Spectre—An Acting Manager—An Evening Party—Punch-drinking—Three-Card Loo and the Ladies—Female Talent and Accomplishments—Beauty of the Women—Advice to Sportsmen—Departure from Cork.

"Car, your honour, car? here! here is a car, your honour. Oh, don't be after listening to Murdock, there! Out of the way, ye spalpeen—sure, didn't the gentleman spake to me first? that's my fare, anyhow."

Fifty voices at once, from as many ragged good-tempered fellows who surround the passage leading from the steamer's side, sufficiently prove that we have changed the country.

The cars thus numerously offered bear all the marks of a people who are not impeded in their progress by any unnecessary attention to outward show. The accumulated dust and filth of years covers the vehicle; and lest there should be any discrepancy of appearance, the harness, horse, and man, are all of a colour, and *that* the natural one—I mean the colour of the earth, in its most impalpable form. A sportsman, however, suffers no annoyance from these accidental changes; and I was not long in reaching the hotel at Cork.

It would be unjust not to say anything of this splendid city—for splendid it is; though I cannot spare much space for the topography of those places which afford nothing more than the

"CAB, YOUR HONOR?"

amusements to be derived from other well-populated and extensive towns.

The harbour is excellent, and is formed by the embouchure of the river Lee. At first view of the magnificent range of buildings, one is tempted to ask if this be the misery of Ireland? Shops fitted up in the most attractive style; abundant population, and all bearing the appearance of the utmost prosperity—the appearance, I say, and that is the drawback; for, though affectedly fine, the eye cannot fail to rest on the crowds of desolate creatures, worn by disease or age, who, at every corner, assail the passer-by for charity.

The Imperial is a good hotel, but partakes of the characteristics to which I have elsewhere referred. Indeed, generally, the traveller will find that, amidst other things which have been adopted from England, inn-charges have not been forgotten; and, if we doubted the extent of any acquaintance a *maître d'hôtel*, in Ireland, may have with English civility and attention, it would be at once conceded, when the bill is presented, that he was on intimate terms with the book department of the Clarendon. To be well treated, and charged unreasonably, may be forgiven, but it is execrable to be starved and fleeced; and, although " marble chimney-pieces, not expressly mentioned in the bill, inflame it most confoundedly "—it is mortifying to find the swelling exist, where the marble chimney-piece does not.

Cork, on my arrival, was in an excited state; the assizes had just commenced, and I lost no time in making my way to the court-house, anxious to hear some of that extravagant eloquence, for which the Irish bar is so celebrated.

On my entrance, I was at once struck by the apparent want of decorum of the scene. Nothing can be more offensive to an English lawyer, than that absence of dignity and order, which is everywhere observable in a court of justice in Ireland. The counsel, wigless, gownless — without any mark whereby they could be distinguished from attorneys, visitors, witnesses, or thieves; but all appeared huddled together round the judge, who, in a plain scratch, looks commonplace enough. There is a familiarity among all parties that would startle the pride of an English lawyer, and may have led to the Milesian joke, of a suitor stopping the judge, on his way to the court-house, and imploring him "to do justice in *his* favour."

Something has been said of Irish eloquence. I had an opportunity, here, of judging of the style which seems to have been universally adopted by the bar of this country. There is no difficulty in perceiving that it differs from that which the calmer feelings of the English, and the phlegmatic constitution of our juries, have fostered. The mercurial temperament, and naturally romantic tone, which are generally ascribed to the Irish character, pervade even the commonplace matters of mere legal considerations. It is not impossible that the ornamental flourishes, adopted in such disquisitions, may be designed to cover ignorance of the abstract question, or to hide errors in practice. Nor are the Irish alone in that.

I believe no persons in the world are more constitutionally addicted to ideality than the Irish; and, when the superiority of their country is the subject, the warmth of conviction which they evince shows how little they stop to examine, how little disposed they are, to let reason have her influence. It has been said, that this devotion to the imaginative produces, not unfrequently, great errors among gentlemen who have been induced to leave their native isle. So far, indeed, has the power of fancy not unfrequently carried them, that they at last have arrived at the conviction of their being possessed of estates, the fee simple of which existed nowhere but in their own productive minds.

However the imagination may be cultivated by the bar in Ireland, it is quite certain that among the laity nothing seems to excite more ingenuity than litigation; nor is it uncommon to find, among the lower orders, although utterly ignorant of all other things, some who are adepts in the art of legal quibbling. It was my lot to hear one case tried at the assizes, at Cork. The corollary I afterwards learned. Patrick O'Sullivan sued Mike

Moriarty for the value of three cows, sold to Mike during the lifetime of the plaintiff's (O'Sullivan's) father. To the declaration, stating that Mike had had the cows, Mike could offer no plea. True it was that Mike had had the cows—true he had killed them, or sold them, or eaten them—but by no means under contract of debt; and yet a defence, under the circumstances, would have been impossible.

Mike took advice, and let the action go by default. But the facts were amusing, if not quite creditable to the plaintiff's morality. O'Sullivan, during his father's life, had stolen the cows, and bartered with Mike to kill and sell them, allowing him (the stealer) certain profits and certain portions. These were paid. Lamentations, deep and loud, were made by the elder O'Sullivan, for the loss of his cows, which had been his chief fortune and support. He published hand-bills for their recovery, but no cows came back.

None joined in the pursuit of the culprit with more apparent ardour than the son of the loser. The old man died. He bore his loss hardly, and perhaps his death was hastened by the grief arising from it. Whereupon the son, now heir, brought his action for the recovery of the value of the cows, well knowing that recrimination was impossible on the part of the defendant, who paid the money, and who declareth on the oath of an honest Irishman, that Patrick O'Sullivan is the greatest rogue 'tween Donaghadee and Tig na Vauria.

Cork has a theatre, which, being open during the assizes, led me to contemplate the state of the histrionic art in the sister isle. The play was The Castle Spectre, and it was somewhat droll to hear the broad Irish accent with which the old English Baron expressed his loves and his dream. He was a man of about four feet, either way; and if you had put him on his side, he would have acted with as much locomotion and agility.

I inquired who the Roscius was, and by what accident he was pressed into the service of the first tragedy. The answer was satisfactory—the same vanity exists here as in other places.—The old English Baron was enacted by the manager!

Let me do justice to the hospitality of my Cork friends to whom I had letters of introduction. One whom I had not the pleasure to find at home, but for whom I left my letter, sent down to my inn a warm request that I would join the evening party, which he expected that day at his house.

The invitation was so warm and unaffected that I accepted it, and was introduced to about forty gentlemen, who were not, as would be said at Oxford, *wining* but *punching*. It was true I had greatly the advantage of this party, in having temperately taken my quiet dinner alone. The sudden transition from the ennui and gloomy loneliness in which an Englishman "abroad" is inclined to indulge, to a noisy, joyous party, who had advanced already to the fourth tumbler, will be supposed to have been productive of some impression; and, when I entered, I found the glasses jingling from violent blows on the table: the party, one and all, having arrived at that method of expressing their approbation of a speech which had just been delivered.

"Hurra! bravo! sir—glorious country where the whiskey is the only drink!—let me entreat you—not a headache in a hogshead—most happy to see English gentlemen in Ireland—we want but free intercourse to set aside all prejudices."

"Who says we stand in need of intercourse? Sir, no offence to you—you are an Englishman, proud of your country—we are Irishmen, and, till the English learn to drink whiskey instead of the miserably washy wine, there can be no intercourse, and the union must be dissolved."

"Union dissolved!" exclaimed another voice. "By the powers, when I see that day I'll not be alive!"

"Alive or dead, you'll soon see the day! O'Connell for ever! who says no?"

"O'Connell for ever!" was re-echoed through the room. The very name was sufficient to set all in an uproar. Our host now proposed an adjournment; but the subject was not to be so passed; agitation had begun, and this was the signal. Every man had his opinion on the subject, and every man thought he had a right to express it, and exhibited the utmost impatience to do so.

The whiskey was now mixed, and disposed of in greater haste; it was evident the row would begin; five or six gentlemen were at once on their legs, all speaking at the extent of their voices, and each appearing impressed with the notion that he was the only party commanding attention. Glasses began to dance, chairs to slip from under their disputants, and, amid the complete uproar, I could only distinguish these facts — that O'Connell was the greatest villain alive, and the only prop and stay of his country!

Cards were handed across,—till our host opened the door, and in the loudest tone invited the gentlemen to the drawing-room. Many followed: and there we found the ladies, deeply engaged in the mysteries of three-card loo, and indeed with tolerable stakes. There were no introductions or ceremonies, nor did the gentle part of the audience feel at all disturbed by the riot which occasionally, as the door was opened, burst on our ears.

I was seriously alarmed, and expressed my feelings to my host, who assured me that twenty gentlemen would in all probability exchange cards, yet that was a ceremony which was too common to be alarming, and too harmless to be fraught with any considerable consequences. "In fact," said he, "out of a hundred challenges we find few duels; the gentlemen are only desirous of proving the truth of their positions, and nothing can tend so satisfactorily to do so as the passing of a card. With the whiskey the ardour will evaporate, and the same parties will meet again to-morrow, in all probability with a like result."

On our entrance into the drawing-room there was no appearance of alarm among the ladies. Every accomplishment was there in requisition, which the riotousness of the party from the dining-room did not interrupt or disturb. We are deceived by the representation of those who have attempted to depict the manners of the Irish fair. Although my rambles did not afford me many opportunities of testing my opinion, yet those that did occur to me confirm me in the belief that Irish ladies are

I HERE PURCHASED MY TACKLE.

generally more accomplished, and exhibit more talent in acquirement than may generally be found among the English higher classes. Their manners are gentle and unaffected, with a dash of hilarity which renders them infinitely more fascinating. They are beautiful to a proverb; and it is not true that the moment your eye rests on a lady, she immediately responds—

"port, if you please"—nor that the second look induces the declaration that "she will ask papa."

Cork must be set down, upon the whole, as the most flourishing town in Ireland. Its buildings, especially those residences on the banks of the river towards the island called the Cove, are in English taste, and bespeak close connection with the sister country. The continual intercourse, now established by means of steam-packets, has tended greatly to improve the taste and manners of the inhabitants of all those towns situated on the English side; and although much may be found to admire in this city, it must be observed that it still exhibits all the prosperity and wretchedness, all the elegance and the squalid poverty, which seem everywhere associated in Irish towns.

I here purchased my tackle. I recommend the angler to choose a good *tie rod*, and a large reel that will contain 150 yards of stout hemp line, well twisted. It should be soaked in oil and bees-wax, well melted; then stretched and reeled. The cost of this, which is the only line fit for use among the rocky rivers he will have to traverse, will be one shilling. Select, also, in Cork, a few flies of various sizes and colours, which will be found well made and of the right kind. With these, a good gun, a pound of the *best tobacco* (the most acceptable return that can be made for the civility of a mountaineer), I took coach to Macroom, a distance of thirty miles.

CHAPTER III

Start from Cork—Wild Character of the Country—An Irish Coachman—Sporting Prospects—Warning to Improvers—Pike *versus* Salmon—Arrival at Macroom—Ominous Demonstrations—A False Alarm—Inn Accommodations—An Irish Waiter—Extravagant Charges—Poverty and Desolation—Taste for Mud—Commencement of Operations—A Native Sportsman—Irish Blarney—Directions for Trolling—Incomparable Bait.

From Cork, 27 miles; from Killarney, 28 miles; from Mill Street, 11 miles.

Fishing stations, Lake Inchgeelah, 5 miles; and the rivers Toom, Lee—the latter running close by the town.

ARMED with all the appliances of sport, I mounted the coach from Cork to Macroom. The ride presented a desolate country, composed alternately of bog and rocky mountain, with little wood, which becomes less and less as the journey is pursued into the interior of the country. Even one mile from Cork, no trace appears of the neighbouring refinement. Poverty of the extremest kind is exhibited in habitations scarcely one degree above the damp cave of the wild beast; furze being used for doors, and turf for the roof. Here and there a solitary and staring creature, half of whose body is covered with a mass of rags, which are blown about by the wind—the other half perfectly uncovered—leads the traveller to imagine that he has taken some sudden leap from all that is civilised into a new and hitherto undiscovered country. No inn on the road breaks the monotony of the scene, or relieves the gloominess of the way. The coachman, with a large glazed hat, a home-made whip, and blue sailor's jacket, is the only person who interrupts the depressed tone which the mind is apt, under such circumstances, to assume. He indeed keeps up a continual conversation with his horses—reasons with them—threatens them. "Ah, by the powers!—come up there now—d'ye start at that!—faith you've seen it before, many a day.—Ah! ah! there I caught you—don't be too forgiving now—bear malice agin me, and remember it.—Ah! you're too forgiving, any way—catch a glimpse o' that, ye spalpeens—come along here now—faith you'll have a stop at the rise."

The road follows the river Lee for some miles, and then crosses the river Bride, a tributary to the Lee. Although the latter river does not present any chance of good trout-fishing, the Bride, which is of a more declivitous character, will repay the angler, especially if he watches the opportunity of rainy weather.

Owen's Inn will be found a tolerable station for the Bride; though I should not advise any lengthened stay at any place short of Killarney, as all the streams are of an uncertain character, and require to be visited at the exact moment to ensure success—I mean the subsiding of a flood. The beauty of this river consists in its varied falls—some of ten or fifteen feet; but the country through which it flows has the air of terrible desolation. Here and there may be observed patches of corn; but the general view presents little but bog and mountain.

But, to the sportsman, the wildness of the mountains—the unhedged expanse, on which nothing appears but the thinly scattered cots of the humble labourer—the sparkling and rapid river, now sullenly smooth, now dashing down precipices and dividing its streams into deep and gurgling eddies — inspire feelings of delightful anticipation.

The river Lee, into which the Bride falls, was once highly celebrated for its fine trout and salmon. Now, alas! it swarms with pike; the salmon have greatly diminished, and trout have become almost extinct.

It is remarkable that, as yet, the whole county of Kerry, to which we are progressing, does not contain a single pike; and, till within these twenty years, there was not one known in the noble river Lee. Its source, the Lake Inchgeelah, is a noble expanse of water, and was once the resting-place of immense shoals of salmon, and white trout. Latterly they have disappeared, and from a cause which should, and I trust will, operate as a warning to all who live in the neighbourhood of rivers not yet infested with the destructive pike. The injury done to the inhabitants of this part of the country, —through whose property flows the river Lee, once so prolific in excellent food, and from whose wild waters even the poorest could once make an easy addition to their humble meal,—is irreparable. It appears that a gentleman who had built a house on its banks, not far from Cork, among other ornaments sank a pool, which discharged itself into the river. Not content with the abundant supply of salmon and trout which the stream afforded, he was desirous of surprising his neighbours by the possession of a fish until then unknown in this part of the country. With a view of obtaining this distinction, he sent for some pike, which with great difficulty were brought fifty miles, and placed in his despicable pond. The natural consequence ensued: the banks, during a flood, gave way, and the pike were at once precipitated into the river. Here food was so abundant amidst the trout and young salmon, that, since this accident, such has been the increase of pike, that they now occupy every hole in the Lee. The troller, however, may find good sport, and it is not the least recommendation of this river that its banks are open to all comers; so that, from Lake Inchgeelah, a distance by the river of fifty-six miles, there will be found no obstruction to the humblest sportsman.

In following this river down, the only difficulty would be

the want of accommodation, which could only be procured in the wretched cabins of the peasantry near the road, which crosses and re-crosses the river many times between Cork and Macroom. It is not now unusual to find pike of from thirty to forty pounds weight in the least frequented parts,—in the long reaches, or wherever the fall of the stream is sluggish.

The rising smoke in that low corner of the opening valley now warns us of our approach to our station, Macroom. The cabins become more numerous along the side of the road, though not better in their construction. On approaching the town, we had attracted one or more of the inmates of every cabin; and, by the time we had entered the town, we had an escort of at least two thousand persons, men, women, and children, who had collected by degrees as the coach passed. I was somewhat alarmed at the assembly, which increased at every yard of our progress. The moment the sound of the coach was heard, out poured the inhabitants of every cabin.

On our entering the broad, open space, in the middle of the town, the crowd closed on us, and nothing could be seen but a sea of heads. English and Irish exclamations were heard in a confused yell.—" Come out, ye spalpeen—oh, the devil's luck to ye, and we got ye, anyhow." Hundreds of ragged, though strong and handsome fellows pressed forward, through the screaming crowd, to the coach doors, and threw them open, with an apparent determination of violence that could not but alarm an English traveller. Luckily, I was outside, or I should have imagined myself the object of the pursuit. When I crept from the roof, and forced my way into the inn, which I accomplished with some difficulty, I was soon informed of the cause of the uproar. There had been a murder committed some time before, from that exhaustless source of blood and violence, in this unhappy country, the collection of tithes. A policeman had deliberately shot one of the mob, which had assembled to watch the proceedings of the proctor's constables. He had been arraigned at the assizes at Cork, the day before, and acquitted. It was expected by the populace that he would return this day to Macroom, by the coach; and had he done so, it is not difficult to imagine the fate that would have awaited him. Peaceable as the crowd was, had the object of their assembling appeared, flushed with the victory of an acquittal, the market-place of Macroom would have been strewed with his limbs. When, however, the crowd was satisfied that the delinquent was not on the coach, they gradually dispersed, without any disposition to riot. I was assured that there was no apprehension on the part of the inhabitants of the town, notwithstanding the extraordinary assemblage of so many, and so apparently lawless a mob. In the madness of their revenge, the Irish seldom commit wanton mischief; and their most violent and lawless assemblages are always unaccompanied by the uncalled-for injuries which too often are the result of English crowds. They have a wild love of justice, which pervades even their acts of greatest intemperance.

I was not at first aware that in this town very tolerable private lodgings might have been procured, and, unluckily, I established my quarters at the inn—I say, unluckily; for, though I found some accommodation, it was not of an order which kept pace with the magnificence of the charges. The traveller must not expect to find at any of the inns, out of the principal towns, such inordinate luxuries as carpets; he may, however, reckon pretty confidently on finding a red-headed monster, shoeless, stockingless, and capless, acting the part of a waiter—one who will hold back her matted locks to give her eyes a chance with one hand, while she hands you, between her thumb and finger, whatever edible you may demand, perfectly good-tempered, and wondering what can possibly ail the stranger who is surrounded, as she conceives, by every earthly luxury.

In consequence of the frequent visits of regiments, especially during the war, there happened to have been provided for the officers some decent apartments. These, the sportsman who determines to take a week on this station, should secure; though he must take care to do here what he should do throughout Ireland—drive a *good bargain*; for so impressed are all the "parvi mercatores" of this country with a belief in the exhaustless wealth of the English, that no scruples restrain the violence of their inordinate expectations.

The appearance of poverty and desertion which the town presents is much heightened by the neglect of those whose means are not doubtful. It will be found the characteristic of almost every Irish town, nay, of almost every mansion, that time and mischief are suffered to do their worst; nothing is ever repaired. Even in well and substantially built houses, every second pane of glass has given way to a board nailed across the window, or a still more offensive paper patching. Bricks, or stones, or tiles, as they fall from the piles of buildings, which really would constitute a handsome range, if in repair, are suffered to remain where fortune may place them, till the wheels of the heavy carts crush them into the dust and mud which no municipal law controls. This latter is not offensive to the inhabitants; on the contrary, they seem to enjoy the softness of it, as all the female part of the population and the children are shoeless; and it is observable that they always choose the softest and deepest mass of mud, in which to crowd together for their mutual salutations or disquisitions. The smoke, which many years of turf-fire has supplied, has contributed greatly to the dingy desolation of the general appearance. Whitewash would set all right; but, though the lime-stone may be had for the fetching, the habits of the people appear inveterate, and the suggestion of the improvement it would make is met by a stare of happy independence.

These particulars are stated more in the way of description than complaint. I would give nothing for the society of that sportsman who could view the wild freedom of this country, and complain of the coarseness of his fare.

While thus attended by the red-headed girl, who understands not a word of English, and while the bacon and potatoes, unaccompanied, smoke on the board, let the remembrance of the wild rivers and mountains come to the sportsman, and furnish the rest. In traversing them, he will find no "Take Notice," in a walk of three hundred miles!

Mine host informed me that there was but one man in the town who knew anything of fishing; and at my request he was sent for, as I had resolved to begin operations forthwith.

By the time I had finished my humble repast, the native sportsman was announced. One glance was enough to show that Owen was a character—a mild, humble, and amiable one—of intelligence beyond his station, and in which much of native independence of spirit was blended. His form was singularly emaciated; and I at once learned that he lived in a secluded manner, with a bed-ridden mother, whom nothing could induce him to desert. He had never been known to submit to any kind of employment; though, during the cold months, it had been frequently a matter of surprise that he continued to support himself by the rod. Sometimes, indeed, in the depth of winter, he has been known to take salmon from the river Lee; and although his frame had little more of substantiality than the coarse rod which was his companion, he often walks from thirty to forty miles a day; and a happy day for him is that which brings to his companionship a fellow-sportsman.

Of Owen I inquired the locale. His history of the river Lee was much that which I have given it. He shed tears, after a glass or two of whiskey, over the failing salmon, in consequence of the increase of pike; and we settled to commence operations the next morning at an early hour. Our plan was to be provided with pike tackle, as well as for trout and salmon, and to take with us a boy who should carry the gun, and accompany us to the Lake Inchgeelah. I kept him with me the whole evening, while he produced for my inspection what he called his *colours*, which were bundles of feathers. These were his treasures— the mine, whence he drew all that he enjoyed—and nothing could exceed the dexterity with which he manufactured a singularly coarse, but, upon the whole, effective imitation of large flies.

After having listened to his instructions as to the colour, if the day was dark—the falls, in which we might expect to find fish—and the best way of meeting the river across the Toom Bridge (about three miles from the town)—I astonished him by my declaration that I held all his apparatus in the most supreme contempt: that if there were salmon and trout in the river, I would undertake to offer him any *bet* that I would exceed his skill, either measuring by number or weight, provided he adhered to his flies;—nay, that he should choose his ground, and I would follow him up the river.

His astonishment soon gave way to an incredulous smile. Yet the mildness of his character, and the natural genius for flattery (which requires not the aid of the blarney-stone to develop) inherent in Milesian constitutions—and which especially pervades the lower classes—restrained him from any contradiction. "To be sure and it is not for the likes of me to doubt your honour—your honour knows right well how to catch fish—and I'd be sorry and grieved to think I'd do more than your honour's honour—but, may be, I know the river where the fish lie; and perhaps, by chance, I'd bate your honour anyhow without intinding it at all at all—but your honour knows best."

I now told him I relied not on flies, and at once produced my trolling apparatus.

As this book is to be read by sportsmen, and as much of the amusement I derived in this tour is attributable to a kind of angling utterly unknown in Ireland, and I believe little understood in England, I shall once for all describe, as I did to my incredulous friend Owen, the means I adopt. The fullest explanation may perhaps be excused; because, without some patient trials, in which the angler may meet disappointment, the real superiority of bait angling may not be achieved. But the art once acquired, the whole genus of the salmon, even down to the sparling, is at the command of the sportsman. He defies even the weather, and meets all the difficulties of the longest drought by a more astute mode only of presenting the lure.

The rod should be about twenty feet, running tackle; and, at the end of the line, use eight or ten feet of fine gut—Hook No. 3 or 4. Load the gut with split shot, according to the power of the stream, always remembering that the bait must be carried down at the bottom of the stream—that bait is *the roe of the salmon*. It is prepared by Scotsmen, who take the salmon in November, for the purpose of securing the spawn. The receipt for preserving it is as follows:—

Take the full roe of a salmon, wash it carefully from all particles of blood, and then separate the grains: when this has been carefully done, pour over the whole a strong brine, made of common salt and saltpetre, equal parts, and let it remain six hours; then drain it thoroughly, and place the whole in a slow oven, till it assumes a toughness. Then pot the whole down, so as to exclude the air, and it is fit for use.

On the production of my store, Owen expressed his surprise at the clear scarlet of its colour; but he still doubted its efficacy in Irish rivers. Appointing, therefore, our meeting for five in the morning, my red-headed ancilla led the way to my half-glazed apartment.

CHAPTER IV

Advice to Sportsmen—Mode of Conveyance—An Irish Pony and his Food—Delight of the First Cast—Failure and Success—Irish Astonishment—An Irish Sign—Native Hospitality—A Sportsman's Dinner—Natural Magic—Lake Inchgeelah—Directions for Fishing in this Lake—Hints to Anglers and Sportsmen in general—Character of the Kerry Peasantry—An Invitation to Dinner—Irish Servants—An odd Establishment—An Irish Kitchen—Irish Hospitality—Wine and the Ladies—Whiskey and the Gentlemen—An Irish Dinner Party—The Sporting Major—Longbow-ism—An Irish Angler's Exploit—Sporting Extraordinary—A Dance—Prospective Sport with the Major.

At five o'clock my Mercury was with me. The excitement of the new country, and the wildness and irregularity of all I had seen, had so hung on my imagination, that I had slept little; I was ready, therefore, at his call; the pony and chaise, which I had bought at Cork, and ordered to be sent on to me at Macroom, had arrived, and was led to the door.

Ere we start, let me advise every sportsman to adopt this mode of conveyance. A mountain pony, with a light gig, will supply all the wants of post-horses, which, excepting in the beaten tracks, are hardly to be found. The mode, too, of feeding an Irish pony, namely, on potatoes, is convenient, as they may be had at all cottages; and the animal thrives greatly on them.

I found Owen had neither scrip nor staff. His long rod over his shoulder, and his gaff strapped on his back, a short pipe and a tobacco-pouch, were all the store he had prepared to face the blast of a March morning. The wind blew and the torrents descended; but what were wind and rain to us? they constitute the fisherman's fine weather, and amidst these mountains there was little other.

After a drive of three miles, we resigned the gig to a staring mountaineer, who was directed by my companion, in Irish, to

THE WIND BLEW—THE TORRENTS DESCENDED.

take it to Inchgeelah Lake, and there await our arrival. I shall not soon forget the feeling of delight with which I ran across the bog that intervened between the road and the dark and dashing river, to take my first cast in so wild a stream.

Owen had already commenced for salmon, while I elected to troll for pike. For this purpose I had procured a small samlet. Mile after mile did we trudge, sometimes stopped by bog, and

"With some difficulty we landed him."

compelled to journey round—no traces of former footsteps to direct our course, yet uncheered by a *rise* or a *run.* We at length arrived at a waterfall, where once, in happier times, had stood a mill. Here I changed my tackle, and adopted the roe; convinced that if there were trout in the stream, they assuredly would be found in a spot so congenial to their habits. Weary with my walk, and the fatigue of trolling, I threw down my rod with my line at length in the eddy, and was watching the success of Owen's casts with the fly. "Hurrah!" exclaimed he, "your honour's rod is clear gone entirely."

I had just time to catch the butt, which was slowly moving on the edge of the stream, and lifted it upwards. It was fast at the bottom—it cleared—and up sprang a fine sea-trout of four pounds weight, fresh run from the sea, by the silvery whiteness of his scales. With some difficulty we landed him; but who shall describe the aghast expression of my companion's countenance? It was clear he had imagined my infallible bait was some delusion of my own; nothing that I had said of its virtue had made the slightest impression on his mind. Regarding me, while he held the fish in his right hand, with a stare of astonishment and wonder, he at last burst forth—"Your honour's a fisherman anyway—your honour has got the power of bewitchment—the likes was niver seen in Ireland. Faith it's a fresh run; the devil a fly they'll touch to-day; hurrah, but your honour's a fisherman."

Recovered from his surprise, we pushed our way upwards towards the source of the river Lee and the Lake Inchgeelah. The route was in the highest degree picturesque, though the morning was cloudy, with occasional rain. Owen had succeeded in taking one salmon, and myself three sea-trout.

At length we arrived at what is called "the public," a small cottage, with a piece of turf dangling at the door, to indicate to the initiated that, if nothing else at least, good potheen might be had there. It was situated on the edge of the lake. The only neighbours were two policemen, whose station was also on the banks of this neglected and almost unknown expanse of waters.

The lake is about five miles in length, and varying from one to three in breadth. A few straggling cabins may be seen under the surrounding rocks, whose inhabitants were of the most destitute order. Into whatever cottage or cabin we entered, however, the proprietors were all civil, and anxious to oblige the stranger. The feeling of hospitality is indigenous. The turf fire was instantly made up; the kettle—the only article of cookery, and almost of furniture—was immediately suspended; the potatoes washed; and the wooden platter prepared.

Our mountain walk had made these preparations acceptable. The trout were soon split and scored, and laid across the now clear turf; and they furnished an excellent meal.

The conversation between Owen and the listeners was conducted in Irish, and, although I could detect that I was the chief subject of it, I was not quite aware that the superstitious feelings of my companion had literally induced him to represent that there must have been some magic in the mode of taking the sea-trout. The men examined my tackle, looked cautiously at me, and seemed to be impressed with some suspicions. The arrival, however, of the policeman, who, I had understood, was the only fisherman of the lake, and who spoke English, relieved me from all further embarrassment.

Inchgeelah Lake is romantic, and in the highest degree beautiful. It is the recipient of another range of lakes, situated about five miles from the spot I am now describing, but into which no pike can ascend. The upper lake, therefore, which is laid down as Lake Alua, is filled with trout, not large, but of singular beauty and flavour. The lower lakes present no other sport than may be had from trolling and night-lines.

So simple and poor are the wretched inhabitants of the banks, that they have not the means of adding to their deficient food by fishing. Not even a boat has yet graced the broad expanse of the lake.

I found that the policeman was furnished with a rod, which he now produced, and we sallied forth to adopt a mode of trolling that has been very little used in English water. As we were obliged to fish from the banks, it is no doubt the most effectual way; though, if this water had been furnished with a boat, trailing would constitute excellent sport. The mode to which I allude is trolling with a fly. It is thus made: on the largest sized pike-hook bind round coarse worsted of light and gaudy colours, and with the two eyes of peacock's feathers for wings, the whole bound on to strong whipcord, cast with the wind, and jag the fly along the surface.

In this way we were all successful, and had the pleasure of presenting our entertainers at the cottage with three or four very fine fish, resolving to carry the rest home. The sport, however, is not exciting. The pike is a dull fish, and, though he will sometimes run very freely, it may happen a dozen times that he will not stir, however tempting the lure.

This spot presents varied fishing: the river, for salmon and trout; the Lake Inchgeelah, for pike; and the upper lake, for fly-fishing, for trout of a smaller kind. If accommodation could be had at the "public"—which, indeed, might be managed, by sending thither some little furniture—a short time might be very delightfully spent in these wilds. It should not be forgotten, also, that the wild fowl are numerous in the autumn and winter—that the whole district is free as air to the sportsman—and that there is not the least apprehension justly to be entertained of any violence from the inhabitants. Their manners here, as throughout Kerry, will be found obliging and amiable; and let me observe, in common justice, that whatsoever representations it may please certain political bawlers to make, or cause to be made, against the general subordination of the peasantry, it should be remembered that the calumny is uttered against those who have no means of rebutting it. In fact, I believe a more peaceful and inoffensive race does not exist, than that inhabiting the county of Kerry.

D

On our arrival at Macroom, I found an invitation to dine with a gentleman in the neighbourhood, and immediately dispatched Owen with the fish, and a note, containing my acceptance of the invitation.

It would amuse an Englishman, who, for the first time, dines at the table of a genuine Irish family, to contemplate the immense profusion of the substantials, and the droll appearance the servants cut, fresh from the stable, in their master's old clothes. As one passes through the passage to the drawing-room, it is not unusual to see four or five shoeless and stockingless women, with their hair over their eyes and faces, flying before you, into the dirt holes, called, in this country, kitchens. These are helps for the occasion, and are reinforcements, generally drawn from the neighbouring cottages. One turns a spit, the other sits by the fire to blow the turf; one smokes a pipe over the ragouts, while a fourth looks on—it being an acknowledged principle, that it will require five times as many women servants in Ireland as in England to do a given quantity of work.

In general, a dinner at "the house," as any respectable domicile is termed, is a day of rejoicing and jubilee. Every cottager on the estate claims privilege to offer suit and service, and if he can assist no one, or his services are not accepted, he can ever avail himself of the old request, viz. to light his pipe—which he not only lights, but smokes in the kitchen—into which, if by any wrong turn you should unhappily chance to put your nose, so vile a compound of villanous smells would assail you as would effectually damage the ardour of your mastication.

It is fair to do justice to the Irish in their feasts. They mean to be hospitable, and deem excessive profusion of edible matter the greatest proof of that intention. Unwilling, however, that you should lose that idea by any desultory succession, the whole is crammed on the table at once, without any regard to order or consistency; of wines, nothing is known. It is true, wine is placed on the table, as a matter of form, to amuse the ladies, who, indeed, are the only persons who do not treat it with negligence. But the instant the loads are removed from the table, a tumbler and wine-glass, together with a small jug of hot water, are placed before each gentleman. In the middle of the table are two glass flagons, each containing about a gallon of whiskey, and every one proceeds to use, what are significantly termed (par excellence) "the matarials." Then commences the true Irish ebullition of feeling. No sooner are "the matarials" produced, than, as by a sudden inspiration, those who had previously been restrained and silent, at once conceive that they have patriotism and sense, and are determined to prove that position.

On my arrival at the house, I found the company to consist of the host, an hospitable and kind one—Major K——, who, I believe, in compliment to myself, had been invited, as he was a thorough fisherman—the priest of the parish—an Irish barrister—and a couple of those young gentlemen who may pass for anything; they were, however, I believe, in this instance, law students.

On our introduction, I learned soon from the major, that he had been, since the battle of Waterloo, resident as a fisherman at Killarney. It did not require much to discover, from himself, that his funds were restricted to the allowance of the government, which, with all his soul, he detested, or, that he had told stories of his exploits in the art of fishing, till he absolutely himself believed them. It was difficult to reconcile the perfect honesty of his character with the broad assertions he made; nor was there even apparent in his manner, while so making them, the least distrust of credence; he took it for granted that every man believed what he would indubitably have upheld, at the risk of life, had it been doubted. The priest was the only man who dared to ask if the major was *sure* of anything; and, to him, the reply was, "Do you question it? By my sowl, and the blood of the K's, it never was doubted before! There was that affair of the salmon: Lord V—— told me, that, if any other man had told the story, he wouldn't believe it. I sent my friend to him, Father, and he acknowledged that he believed every word of it." Then, turning to me, "You may do as you like, sir; you are an Englishman, and know little of Irish fishing. By the powers, you'll larn what it is to be a sportsman!"

"Hear the major," says the priest; "he'll tell the story."

"By the sowl of me, and I'll tell it anyhow."

"Tell it right, major."

"Is there a man would say that to me but your own good-looking self, now, Father?"

I begged to hear the story.

"You *must* believe it," said the priest.

"And who doesn't?" said the major, gulping down his third tumbler of punch, and slamming the glass on the table. Then, turning to me—"Sir, everybody knows the fact—I caught a hare and a salmon at one cast of the fly!"

"Oh, Benedicite!" says the priest.

"None of your holy bother, now, Father. I'm after relating to the gentleman this remarkable adventure. Give me the matarials."

The needful was soon prepared; and the major, directing his conversation exclusively to me, proceeded to say that, while fishing in the Lee, not far from Macroom, he saw a fine fish rise under the opposite bank. He immediately drew out his line, so as to enable him by a cast to reach the exact spot. He had previously put on two large flies, such as are commonly used for salmon in high water. He drew back the line which would extend thirty or forty yards behind him. On endeavouring to make the cast, he found he had, as fishermen call it, "hitched behind." At this moment the salmon rose again in the same spot, and, in his eagerness to cover him, he gave a strenuous jerk, with the intent of breaking one fly, and covering the salmon with the other. Splash into the river went something heavy, which immediately took to swimming towards the opposite bank, close to the spot where the salmon had risen. The action of the animal so effectually played the other fly before the salmon, that he forthwith seized it, and both were well hooked. The major continued to relate that hereupon commenced a hard struggle; sometimes the salmon was on the surface, and sometimes the other was drawn under water, till, by judicious management, both were safely landed, and proved to be a fine hare, hooked by the leg, and a salmon of twenty pounds weight!

"I made them both a present to our worthy host," added the major, "and it's myself that ate part of both."

"I'll bear witness to the eating, at any rate," said the priest.

"And it's I'll bear witness to the catching," said the major, "and who'll deny it?"

So earnest was the major, that I would offer no dissent; but, on the contrary, intimated my surprise at the singularity of the adventure, with the utmost confidence in the fact. This so pleased him that he begged to be allowed to make my punch, which he could do *in rale Irish proportions.*

The next story the major warmed into was of his catching a rat by a dexterous cast of the fly; and a pike, which at once seized the rat, was safely landed.

"Oh," cried the priest; "is it the rat you're after? now be aisy, major; you know we never had the rat for dinner."

"To be sure you didn't; but everybody knows the fact, and none but an unbelieving Jew or a priest would dare to cast discredit on the account."

"It's impossible to surpass the story of the rat and the pike, and I defy the major himself to go beyond it," said the priest, appealing to me. I admitted that I thought it was the extent to which such exploits could be carried by any concurrence of circumstances.

"Extent!" cried the major; "drink your punch. Here's to our host! Oh, it's in Ireland you'll see the wonderful things."

"And hear them, too," said the priest.

"Troth and you will, if you listen to the whining preaching of the Fathers of this day. Extent, indeed!"

It was evident the major was on his mettle, and he ever and anon seemed boiling with some concealed yet important mystery. The students grinned applause and acquiescence, while the barrister thought that it would, in ordinary cases, have required stronger evidence to convince the world in general, although for himself he could entertain no doubt.

Our host now invited us to replenish, and the conversation took a general turn. Politics, the wrongs of Ireland, the Catholic claims, and Protestant ascendency, in turn, were discussed; in all which the major was inobtrusive. I could not but observe that he gulped down draught after draught, hastily; and when matters had settled into a calm train, and the affairs of Ireland were undergoing a fearful review, smash went the glass of the major on the table, and immediately followed his brawny fist, which made the numerous tumblers ring a violent change.

"Extent! is it extent you mane? Look ye, sir—I am a Major in his Majesty's army, and am paid by a rascally government: and, sir, I have never lost my character for veracity. Extent!—by the honour of the commission I hold, I once rode a salmon astride out of the stream, and spurred him ashore!"

A burst of surprise and admiration, from those least acquainted with the major, followed this assertion.

"Rode a salmon ashore? Impossible!" says the priest.

"*Verum quia impossibile*, I presume you mean," said I; "the major will explain."

"Troth and I will, and the devil help the spalpeen that is not satisfied with it. I repeat again, I rode a salmon astride, and spurred him ashore.—Father, you know the shallows leading to the mill of Ballyvourneen."

"A good spot for a salmon," says the priest, "but bad for riding him."

"You shall hear—I had been to Ballyvourneen, and was

returning to Macroom, on horseback, in the evening. I had had a long ride. Where the road passes by the side of the river, and along the shallow which falls into the *good people's hole*,¹ whom should I see, hard at work with a salmon, but Phelim, the piper. Hold on there, says I—and, booted and spurred as I was, I dashed into the stream, and seized the rod from the piper, who never had a steady hand, and was timid. The salmon was in the hole, above which I stood in the shallows, and about midstream. The moment the fish moved, I knew his weight to be above forty pounds, for it's meself can tell to an ounce the weight of a fish at the first plunge. Away went the salmon, and away went the reel. I held on firmly and tightly till the line was nearly out; when, all at once, the fresh-run fish dashed up the stream. I reeled away as quick as lightning, lest I should lose my hold; and, as the stream was strong, I bent my knees in the water to get a firmer hold on my legs, and to give me the power of winding quick. Suddenly I felt myself lifted off my legs! Oh, Bubbaboo! says I—it was but an instant—Is an Irishman ever at a loss?—I caught hold of the line for a bridle, stuck my spurs into the side of the fish, which I now found closely stuck between my legs, and with one bound we were both in the high shallows, where I safely landed the monster, to the immortal honour of fishing and the excellent dinner of Lord V——, who swore if any other man had said he had caught him in the same way, he would not have believed him."

Whatever the surprise excited by the former stories, it was nothing to this. The priest thought the major must have been mistaken; I assented to the fact, because the major told it; the students laughed; but the lawyer was silent. The major had enough to do to assure all parties, over and over again, that the relation was true—one of the party had winked, and all forthwith acquiesced.

¹ Good people's hole—a spot supposed to be haunted by fairies; who, although the cause, as the Irish suppose, of all possible mischief, are thus designated in deprecation of their wrath.

Each gentleman having now done his duty with the punch, the piper was called in—and amid the joyous revels of the dance, the priest, with a good humour which greatly pleased me, was the first to volunteer the jig with a lady who happened (of course by the merest accident) to be the prettiest of the party.

It was late ere we rose to depart. My leave-taking was a matter of difficulty; the cordiality and warmth with which I was pressed to prolong, or to repeat my visit, being echoed from every part of the family. Having at last, however, succeeded in making my acknowledgments all round, and while hastening to the door, I was arrested by the grip of the major, who assured me he should with much pleasure join me at Killarney, and would show me some real fishing; adding, that he had still in store some surprising stories of the philosopher's art. "Extent, sir? I shall yet have the honour of surprising you."

CHAPTER V

Characteristic Scenery—Encampment of the Whitefeet Rebels—Romantic Escapes and Dangers of an Irish Gentleman—Irish Hospitality—The Lake of Inchgeelah—Delicious Treat—Difficult Road—Inn of the Desert—Splendid View—Irish Ingenuity—History of an Irish Fisherman—His Devoted Affection—Heroic Self-devotion—Death of his Betrothed—His Filial Affection—Character of the Irish Peasantry—Sporting renewed—A Double Bite—Start for Killarney—The River Flesk—Noble View—Coltsman Castle—Sporting Notices—Killarney—A Perfect Gentleman !—Ill-effects of English Generosity on the Poor of Killarney.

From Macroom to Ballyvourneen, a distance of fourteen miles, the road lies along a branch of the river Lee, and through scenery of the wildest character, consisting of sudden projections of rocks, with here and there a cultivated patch. Here the plough is unknown; all the husbandry is performed with the primitive spade, and even the labour of other animals would be unknown, but that the carriage of the turf from the bogs to the isolated huts gives occasional employment to wretched hacks, which speak, by their condition, the grinding poverty of their owners. The silence of the wilderness is alone broken by the occasional low of the straggling cattle; while, to the mind of the traveller, miles of uncultivated bog, here and there broken by masses of projecting rocks, present a proof that he is indeed in a land neglected and oppressed.

The road which pursues the course of the river Lee is protected to the right by a chain of mountains of precipitous character, cutting off all communication from that side of the country, except by such narrow passes as the goat may have established; upon the brow of these mountains, once the scene of human massacre, can now only be seen the hovering eagle.

On the height of this chain it was that the Whitefeet rebels —to the number of 20,000—poorly armed, and worse led, once encamped themselves. Harassed by the severest pursuit, cut off from supplies of every kind, in this ill-judged position they awaited the attack of the military, till, by hunger hundreds expiring, and surrounded on all hands, they made a rude and defenceless assault on the troops, to whose discipline and judgment these misguided creatures fell an easy prey. The bloody history of this insurrection is too well known to require remark; seventeen were hanged in the market-place of Macroom, amidst the silent but deep execration of the populace, whose revenge had been excited by the reckless disregard for property which the insurgents had evinced.

The track is now without a mark of the carnage by which its beauty was once defaced. The clear turbulent river rolls on in silent grandeur; the peaceful angler may now cast his line on its bright waters, and meet none but unoffending peasants!

I must not forget to do justice, as I pass, to the character of a gentleman whose seat is in this neighbourhood, and who is mixed up in the tragical events to which I have referred; I mean Mr. B——, of Kilbarry. It was by his courage, skill, and prudence, that the effects of the insurrection were averted. Amongst others, he was especially marked for destruction, and singularly romantic were the stratagems he used in gaining intelligence of the rioters' movements, and in evading their designs. His house was suddenly beset and as suddenly reduced to ashes. The rebels had been taught to believe that, in this act of destruction, they had accomplished their revenge by burying him in the ruins. So well were his plans laid, and so well were they acted on, that, having prepared the military and put himself at their head, many hundreds fell into the hands of the authorities. He now enjoys a pension from government as some small remuneration for the heavy losses his property sustained, and as a testimonial of the valuable services he on this occasion rendered. The character he has acquired for hospitality—a quality, indeed, valuable in these wilds—has aided the general esteem in which he is so deservedly held. All the guides to strangers who visit these mountains have full instructions to bring their charges to his house; nothing can more offend him than the neglect of the guides to obey this injunction. Owen was strenuous on this point, and I yielded to his solicitation: although I had the misfortune to find the excellent proprietor from home, there was no absence of friendly cheer on my presenting myself.

The lake above Inchgeelah is one that will repay the visiting. It has already been remarked that it is separated from the lower lake by a waterfall, up which the pike cannot ascend. It is crowded with trout of a small size, but very delicious quality. They will take any fly that is not too large, and, as I fished for them, I used seven flies, frequently bringing two, three, or four, to land at once. The largest did not exceed half a pound. Mr. B——, of whom I have spoken, has here erected what is termed a lodge, for the purpose of offering accommodation to the visitor; should it not be occupied by any previous applicant, there is no danger of a refusal when applied for.

Having filled my basket with trout, and the rain beginning to descend, I dispatched Owen for the pony which we had left at a hut on the road. We were soon on our road, and bad enough that is. Some of the acclivities we were obliged to assist our pony to surmount. At length, however, an isolated tower appeared in the valley—the once proud residence of nobles, whose names exist no more. It is now the dreary retreat of a few policemen, under whose protection is established an inn —truly an inn of the desert—every second pane, as usual, patched with paper, although obviously bearing indications of an expensive structure. Through the village of Ballyvourneen, if it may be so dignified, flows a branch of the river Lee, and on it is erected a mill. The situation is splendidly picturesque, formed by an abrupt valley flanked by declivitous masses of rock.

No sooner had we arrived, and the refreshment Owen and myself stood so much need of had been supplied, than I prepared to try the stream at the mill-tail. It was now evening; the cold rains had subsided, and, for the first time on these mountains, the sun broke forth in peculiar splendour, tipping all the rugged masses above us with gold. The face of the landscape at once altered by the sudden gleam: and, with that change, a change came o'er our sports. These were not damped by the success we met. I found the fly useless, and betook myself to the salmon-roe. In about one hour I had taken thirty trouts; not large, indeed, but of a very excellent quality. It was quite dark as I returned to the inn, resolving to devote a day to this stream.

The untiring ardour of a sportsman, who has a new country before him, is not difficult to account for; but the elasticity of spirits which kept up my attendant began now to excite my surprise. He had walked nearly thirty miles of a mountainous country—wet the whole day—yet ever cheerful, uncomplaining, and full of alacrity. My own sense of weariness directed my attention to his comforts. He modestly declined all but a little tobacco which fortunately the inn supplied.

There is a good-humoured ingenuity in Owen's mode of making a request, which I should do him injustice in not recording:—

"Well, Owen, I have determined to stay to-morrow, and try the stream above the mill."

"It's your honour will kill the trout, to-morrow, any way."

"But I shall start early—what hour?"

"Oh, your honour will never be too early; and we'll see Killarney in the evening."

"I hope we shall have better weather. The rains are endless."

"To be sure, the rain will come down to-morrow, but your honour's niver bothered by the rain. Oh, it will be fine weather, anyhow, for your honour—it will be fine weather for me—rain away—barring the price of tobacco."

"But you'll be wet again, Owen, and you will have to put on your wet clothes."

"That's barring the price of tobacco, you know."

Rain, wind, and damp clothes, were all one thing in the consideration of my patient and ever cheerful companion, if accompanied by tobacco. Of this I ordered a supply.

The desolation of the place, joined with the howling winds without, threw me at once on the society of this wild philosopher, who had rather adopted me as a master than I him for a servant. The first glass of punch opened his heart, and I found no difficulty in extracting his history. It was simple, and more touching from his own lips than I can pretend to render it. Perhaps it consists only of circumstances which are of daily occurrence, yet I fear that a being in every respect so kind, and generous, and devoted, is not frequently the inhabitant of any country.

I have already said Owen was the sole support of an aged mother, from whom no inducement could sever him. He was a tall and gaunt figure, though of slight make, and of a countenance sunken as with premature age. The eye, nevertheless, bespoke intellect and vivacity, and would sometimes lighten in an arch drollery, which gave great effect to his general conversation. He had been born and bred at Macroom, and though his knowledge extended little beyond the streams of the neighbouring valleys, his mind had cherished the most refined affections. He had never swerved from his original bias, the native freedom of the soul which animated him; and this which in others of better fortunes might have made a statesman of the highest character, or a conqueror of countries, had made him a fisherman. Wild was the sport—exciting and uncertain the effect of the labour—calling and admitting no man his master, he felt that he bounded over the well-known rocks, through which the rivers dashed, a free man!

He had been betrothed to the daughter of a farmer, whose home he had in his wanderings frequented. The idea of marrying with fortune even enters into the calculations of these cottagers; and a small array of furniture, with the site of a cottage and the promise of a lease, are considered a fair ground on which a youth may propose for his bride. These had not Owen; and the absence of them was enough to ensure his dismissal by the stern father of his light-haired girl, who, nevertheless, admired his character and determinedly favoured his suit. So rigid, however, was the guardianship of the father, that little or no opportunity was afforded of their communicating. At length, in the general distress, when the cholera visited these remote deserts, and, with a fatality unknown in other and more civilised districts, the father fell a victim to the raging contagion. A ban was put on his house; his little stock was seized for arrear of rent and tithe, and all refused to receive the destitute and afflicted daughter of a home where the deadly contagion had been known to rage. Owen immediately brought her to his own humble home; and his aged mother, who ever adored her son, offered every consolation within her little means to assuage the anguish of the afflicted girl.

Night and day did Owen traverse the mountain streams, sometimes ten hours a day; up to his middle in water, without food or comfort did he throw his unattractive fly, in hope of the success which would supply the means of subsistence for his dependent family. The mind of the poor girl, by her sudden calamities, and, perhaps, by long watching during her father's disease, had contracted a melancholy which nothing could alleviate. The devoted mother of Owen had watched by the bed of her son's betrothed with unceasing affection, while the lover spared no labour that would lead to the production of those little comforts which her declining health required. Strange that having by great success accumulated a sovereign, he set off for Dublin on foot, without any provision for his own expenses, but relying on the resources of the numerous streams over which he must traverse for the supply of his daily food and lodging (the latter I believe more frequently in the clefts of the rocks than elsewhere), and all for the purpose of consulting an eminent physician of whom he had heard!

Sad is the story of the invalid. The mother watched and prayed by her bedside for three lingering months, while fell consumption made its fearful and undeviating progress. She died as my humble friend re-entered his cottage with the prescription in his hand, and which he had that day borne for fifty Irish miles, with bright anticipation of its sanative effects. As he entered his lowly abode, the pallid lips of the innocent cause of his labours could but bless his name, and recommend to his unceasing care and affection his kind, enduring, and benevolent mother, who never for an hour had left the sufferer alone during his absence, but had even denied herself common necessaries (and those, alas, in that country, are contained only in potatoes and turf for fuel) to supply the young and patient creature with the little comforts her store could furnish.

She died, blessing the name of her betrothed; with one hand in that of the mother, and one embalmed in the tears of her lover, she breathed forth a spirit as pure, as grateful, as angelic, as ever inhabited the breast of the high-born daughters of wealth and refinement.

"At that moment," said my humble companion, "I vowed to cherish my mother; at that moment I called on the beloved being to hear my oath that nothing should separate her from me! No thought of other woman has entered my mind from that day to this. I love my mother, not only because she was ever a kind and good one, but because, in the day of my distress and anguish, when my whole soul was concentrated in another, she was my staff and my support.

She did for my angelic girl all that I had wished to do—my only hope and incentive in life is her preservation and comfort—to supply them I think no labour too much; and when, after a day's disappointment, I return home with an empty basket, I have the satisfaction of thinking that this is but a test and a trial of my affection to my beloved parent!"

These were not, indeed, Owen's words, but they were faithfully his sentiments. The brogue with which they were clothed rendered them more simple, but not the less affecting. In a ragged mountaineer did this noble affection betray itself—in the humble, laborious, and contented creature, who, for his own gratification, amidst storms, and wet, and cold, and fatigue, sought only a little tobacco, did I recognise as proud and as honest a heart as ever dignified the form of man!

My readers will forgive this episode—I took it as it passed me—I noted it amidst the search for amusement, and it gave a train to my thoughts in studying Irish character, which may, perhaps, be referred to the source by those who follow me.

Affection, filial affection, is the strongest trait in the Irish character. In the course of all my travels never did I see that sacred affection violated. In the number of their children do the Irish peasantry rejoice — in the hope of an early family do they marry young. They calculate on their children as their wealth, and look upon their offspring as the resources from whence, in age and in sickness, they must derive their subsistence and their happiness. As yet there are no poor-laws—Nature steps in and supplies the place of legislation by the warm gratitude of the child to the parent. In every cottage may be seen the decrepid and the infirm of the family peacefully passing the remainder of their days, their wants supplied by their children; and I believe nothing would appear to an Irish mountaineer more unnatural than the neglect of filial duties. In England, the father, tired of the burden of his children, seeks to be freed from the alliance; and the child, not unfrequently seeking amidst the world a better home, neglects that of his infancy, and forgets the claims of those to whom his being and early nurture are owing. Too frequently may be seen the parents supplied by the parish with those necessaries which would have been unnoticed in the luxurious household of the child.

Nor does this state of things seem to create surprise, or to excite reflection on an ingratitude so generally shared. In Ireland it is otherwise; the ban would be put on that child who should neglect to nurture and provide for the authors of his being; and, though other virtues be neglected, no quarter would be shown to him who should forget the duties of the child to the parent.

By four in the morning Owen was on the alert, and, with pipe in mouth, rod in hand, was ready for the sport. We fagged up the stream about a mile above the bridge, where we found a broad expanse of water, not dignified by the name of a lake, but designated the Inch.[1] Here I changed my roe for flies, and, after the second cast, found myself tolerably well engaged with a white trout. Not, however, quickly reeling up, I was suddenly astonished by a heavy weight, for which I was little prepared. I was not long in ignorance: a pike had taken a fancy to my trout. Of course I troubled him little. My fly-gut stood till I had convinced myself of the determined voracity of the creature, which would rather suffer himself to be restrained by the line than abandon his prey.

Owen had secured a tolerable salmon; and, as usual, the rains descended in almost heavy sheets of water rather than in separated particles. We agreed, therefore, to abandon our post at Ballyvourneen, and push on for Killarney.

To this end our arrangements were soon made. Leaving Owen to bring on the pony, I mounted the Cork and Killarney coach.

We soon reached the river Flesk, at the point where the

[1] A common name in all Erse or Gaelic districts, from *inis*, an island or water-side meadow.—ED.

Clydah pours in its waters, which form by their junction a broad and rapid stream, falling into the bosom of Killarney. On ascending one of the hills, the whole view at once burst on the sight. Lakes of immense extent, here and there dotted with islands, covered the expanse, and called forth the liveliest

A PIKE HAD TAKEN MY TROUT.

feelings of admiration. The wild beauties of Switzerland seemed here blended with a more sober variety of objects; while the anticipations of the sportsman were excited by the beauteous variety of water and mountain.

We now passed one of the prettiest modern objects in the neighbourhood of Killarney—a castle on an abrupt ridge of the Flesk, which, at the distance of the road, presents a very imposing appearance. It is named, from the builder and master, who has exhibited considerable taste in the choice of the site, Coltsman Castle.

Although the Flesk, which runs by the castle, is at certain seasons celebrated for the variety of its fish, it is by no means a river to which I would direct the angler's attention. In the summer, when the waters get low, no fish are to be found beyond the smallest species of trout; but, in the autumn, when the mountain floods begin to descend, the whole tribe from the lakes of Killarney push up to sandy and gravelly beds to lay their spawn. This is the time when the spear is in requisition, as the large trout and salmon may be found in the shallowest parts, digging holes with a determination and strength that would hardly be ascribed to them. They are easily taken, but are out of season; and, though I have frequently fished this stream through the autumn, I never took one fish which was not sickly and poor. It would appear that the extensive waters of the lakes are necessary to the renovation of trout, as the sea is to the salmon after spawning.

As we approached the miserable cluster of houses which constitute the town of Killarney, there was a manifest alteration in the appearance of the peasantry; and the baleful effects of an indiscriminate generosity (if it may be so dignified) in the visitors to this spot became everywhere conspicuous. There were two gentlemen on the coach, armed with every implement for the destruction of game and fish, but evidently as yet unseasoned to the climate. It was not difficult to collect that they were perfect gentlemen, their conduct throughout the journey from Cork having evinced irrefragable proofs of their claims. As the coach passed the ragged and shoeless creatures, one amused himself by throwing halfpence, and at length challenged a miserable-looking youth, who had pursued the coach, by the offer of half a crown if he would keep up with us a mile. The road was newly covered with broken flint, and the lad's anxiety to select the shortest way wholly overcame the caution which should have directed his steps. He had almost achieved the undertaking, when the loss of blood from his wounded feet, and want of power to continue the exertion, overcame all his efforts, and he sank on the road amid the violent laughter of the liberal patron who had excited his attempt.

There is altogether a new character observable among the poor, and they are the chief inhabitants of Killarney; there is idleness exemplified in its most intense degree; and the effects of it, among all classes of expectants, are almost sufficient to deter the visitor from any long stay at these beautiful lakes.

CHAPTER VI

Arrival at Killarney—Strange Costume—Street Annoyances and Beggars—Character of the Inhabitants of Killarney—Lord Kenmare and the Lakes—Inn Accommodation—Doherty, the Fly-maker—The Lions of the Lakes—The Major—Impudence and Imposition—Advantage of Private Lodgings—Price of Provisions—Impositions of Innkeepers—Hints to Anglers at Killarney—The Major's Narrative—Hoaxing—A Fighting Tailor—The Major's Revenge.

On our arrival at Finn's Hotel, we were surrounded by a host of human beings covered with rags, or having rags of all possible variety of colour and fashion hanging from their bodies rather than covering their bodies, the nether limbs of the more juvenile being absolutely naked. The dress of the boys, even those of twelve or fifteen years of age, was whimsical; and, as I find that it is a style which is everywhere adopted, I may as well describe it particularly; it consisted of some sort of jacket and a shirt, the latter extending about a foot below the waist, and hanging in strips, which, as the rough wind visited them, formed flags little calculated to accomplish the purpose of clothing.

Hundreds of men, women, and children flocked round the coach, and beggars of all descriptions impeded the entrance into the inn. All seemed bent on one determined purpose—that of robbing the unfortunate traveller; some by prayers for long life to him, others by offers of assistance to see the lakes, others by the display of the most trumpery specimens of shells, little boxes made of the arbutus tree which abounds on the islands of the lakes, by the offer of flies, etc.; the whole constituting such a din and clamour as make a hasty retreat into the inn a work of difficulty as well as necessity.

The crowds of idlers of all descriptions which constitute the residents of this town exhibit the character of the Irish in an unfavourable light, and may, by persons who extend their inquiries no farther than a visit to Killarney, be mistaken for the general one.

Here are congregated an immense mass of persons who are attracted by the hope of some good fortune, which they suppose is to arise from the numerous and wealthy visitors who arrive in search of the picturesque. Through the winter they have no settled employment; they rely upon the coming summer for their store, of which they never accomplish the accumulation; and though more money is, I doubt not, spent at Killarney than in any other town in Ireland of equal population, poverty is nowhere more extreme, or wretchedness more congregated. They are, nevertheless, a romantic and problematical race.

It is their object to appear as poor and destitute as possible. They fully expect you to open your purse the moment you look into their cabin, and have no notion but that every visitor's business is to give something to *them*. Too indolent to make provision for the future, and unassisted in their extremity by poor-laws, they are infected by a sort of constitutional disposition to begging, which enervates their own energies, destroys all feeling of manhood, and renders them a speculative and chance-calculating set, every one looking for some singular advantage which is to arise they know not how or when; perhaps by the providential advent of a stranger, or the all-promised influence of O'Connell. Meanwhile, however, it is not worth the trouble to set their house in order, or to do anything that is not absolutely necessary to their present existence. If you ask a wretched naked Killarney man to hold your horse for five minutes, he expects you will throw him at least a sovereign for the trouble, and looks with wonder at a few halfpence. Every man of this class looks in the smallest service for enormous gains; and he would rather wait in expectation of such a remuneration for a year than secure that which is within his reach by steady industry.

This disposition to begging and hope of accidental advantage has banished every feeling of independence. If any landlord should build comfortable cottages (as some have), the people would only inhabit them in their own way, viz. by making pigsties of them. They make no effort at cleanliness; and though the interior of their cabins, which are here of the most wretched description, is ever black with the smoke of the turf—and though they have lime at every corner, and in such abundance that it needs only the fetching—you would never induce one to apply it to his walls; if he did so, it would give an air of cleanliness and comfort to his habitation, much against his disposition and his interest; he would appear too happy to excite commiseration; his landlord would expect some rent, which is ordinarily paid by an appeal to the debtor's utter destitution; and begging (the besetting vice of the town) would be less profitable. The pride of independence and the endeavour to make appearance of well-doing, which are generally seen among the lowest orders of the English, are here wholly reversed, where a wretch deems himself rich in proportion to his poverty, and appeals ever to his squalid destitution, which he regards as the best means of getting a livelihood.

Although arrived at Killarney, so kindly has the main landlord dealt by the inhabitants and visitors that from no part of the town can the lakes be seen. The great charm which the view of those lovely waters is calculated to create is effectually extinguished by the high walls and inclosed domain of the Earl of Kenmare, the proprietor of nearly the whole of this side the lake. This he has walled in, wholly depriving the town of Killarney of any peep at the waters, which, I suppose, his lordship deems his own.

On my alighting at the inn, I found tolerable accommodation. I was surrounded at the door by a host of *fly*-mongers. Crowds of fishermen and boatmen beset the inn at the news of an arrival; and many with books of flies, which there could be no hesitation in pronouncing the greatest impositions on the unsuspecting stranger. Among these was a veteran in the fly-tackle manufacture, one Doherty, who has a hump-backed son, with some ingenuity. He showed me an immense collection of gaudy affairs, for which he demanded an enormous price. To get rid of him, I bought a few, manifestly to the chagrin and displeasure of Owen, who had just come up with the pony, and who did all that winks and nods could do to save my money. "Sure now, Misther Doherty, his honour knows right well you're a capital fly-maker and fisherman anyhow; but his honour knows the wathers, and it's meself that knows 'em too, Misther Doherty, so don't be bothering his honour just now."

"Och, is it yourself, Misther Owen, that wants to tache me? My flies are the only flies for the wathers here. His honour will want a boat, to be sure, and it's meself, too, will have the getting."

"Troth and it's never yerself, honey, that'll have the getting the boat."

"Boat, your honour, for the upper lakes to-morrow?"

Four or five free and easy gentlemen, under the disguise of sailors, now thrust themselves half a foot in the door. "There's the Eagle's Cliff, your honour; and there's the wonderful echo of Ross Castle, where, if you ask Paddy Blake how he is, it's himself will say pretty well, thank ye!"

Pestered with this *posse comitatus*, not to mention the additional annoyance of the windows and doors surrounded with beggars, from among whom escape were hopeless, in endeavouring to see the town, I was glad to excuse myself by ringing for the landlord, who did not think the intrusion of so many applicants for my patronage at all unseemly or uncommon. With some difficulty, therefore, I deferred my arrangements, and dispatched Owen to see if Major ——, my Macroom friend, had

"Among them was one Doherty"

arrived at home on the banks of the lake at Cloreen, where he had given me his address.

In about an hour the major returned, and insisted on my forthwith coming to his cottage, where he had some of the best whiskey in all Kerry. I found under the major's protection a manifest difference in the importunity of the beggars, bugle-men, and boatmen, who retired when they saw the major. "Faith," said he, "and ye may thank me for saving ye from the train of locusts which infest the place. Not a boat goes up the lakes (for they are all in the hands of the two innkeepers, and their lubberly, idle crew) for less than two pounds a day, what with aiting, and drinking, and bugling, and humbug. These fellows play into one another's hands, and get a dishonest livelihood, bad luck to 'em. I'll have the honour myself to show you the lakes, and, if we have a wind to-morrow, some tolerable sport."

As I purposed to stay at Killarney some time, I did at once what I strongly recommend all sojourners there at once to do. By the major's assistance I engaged very comfortable private apartments at eighteen shillings a week, including attendance, fire, and cooking. I then visited the market-house, which was well supplied with abundance of sea-fish and meat. The prices were as follows:—pork, 2d. per pound; beef, 3d. to $3\frac{1}{2}$d.; mutton, 4d.; a cod-fish, six pounds, 1s.; fowls, 10d. a pair; chickens, from 6d. to $6\frac{1}{2}$d.; potatoes, $4\frac{1}{2}$d. per stone.

With all the necessaries of life, therefore, at so cheap a ratio, it is rather surprising that the inn charges should be as large at Killarney as in London; and it shows how necessary it is that strangers, by their arrangements, should defeat such unfair imposts.

My next step was to secure a boat; this the major kindly undertook, and agreed with a man at Ross Island, at four shillings per week, for a small, but very convenient one for fishing.

I am particular in all these matters, because, without this information, English anglers and tourists will be deceived by the persuasions of persons, that the lakes can only be properly visited in one of the inn boats, at a charge, for crew and all, of about two pounds per day; an amount very ill suited to the real amusements of the sportsman. The fisherman, indeed, requires privacy; and fishing from a boat, with a crew of ten or twelve, would be useless.

These arrangements complete, I accompanied the major to his cottage, where no sooner had we arrived than the proof of friendship was produced—"the matarials"; and no sooner had he dispatched the first tumbler, and given all directions necessary to his two gardeners, and boatmen, and domestic servants (for two ragged good-tempered boys fulfilled all those offices) than I could perceive that a suppressed rage was forcing its way to ebullition. By his second tumbler, and when he had been joined by one of two of his friends whom he had sent for to meet me, he became communicative. His first injunction to me was, that I should be aware how I accepted the acquaintance of any Killarney visitors. A wound was still rankling in his bosom.

It would be difficult to follow the major through the disjointed variety of his exclamations, by which he made me understand the source of his chagrin, for a true knowledge of which I was indebted rather to the running commentary of his friend than to his own explanations. It appeared that two gentlemen had arrived at Killarney, armed with all the implements of piscatorial destruction which cockneyism could devise. Hearing that the major was the *genius loci*, they had presented their compliments to him, and requested the honour of sharing a bottle with him, an invitation the major could not answer to the rubicundity of his nose, if he had refused. After some time, the strangers informed the major that it was their intention to make a book—a vice very common amongst all visitors to Killarney; and hinted not very delicately that the inhabitants of Killarney had better pay respect to them, if they valued a good character with Europe and the world. Now the major had a great contempt for books and book-makers; and had, I believe, seen, during his residence at Killarney, as many of the latter as the former. Hereupon the major had begged to be informed of the nature of the intended work, and, finding it was to celebrate the wondrous beauty of the lakes, at once had proffered all his knowledge and assistance. These had been gratefully accepted.

We have said that the major mortally hated books — and especially that kind of book-making rather prevalent among the English—which professes to enlighten the world on matters which they, the book-makers, have gathered from the foolish impressions of an ignorant peasantry or prejudiced natives. The major was determined that the wonders of Killarney should not be forgotten amongst the gentlemen's notes, and forthwith proceeded to describe the wonders of the Deaf Lake, a small pool so called, at the top of one of the mountains that surround the town. He explained that the most extraordinary phenomenon existing in Ireland, and for which philosophy had been wholly unable to offer any explanation, was this—that though the lake was not more than three hundred yards wide, yet it was impossible to convey across it any sound. This, he said, had been frequently tried, and he offered to accompany one of his new friends to the morning's trial. So singular a phenomenon was worthy of note; but the major made a stipulation that one only should attend the trial.

After considerable labour, they the next morning had reached the pool; and the major, planting his friend on the one side, proceeded himself to the other. He then commenced a series of grimaces and contortions, indicative of the most boisterous efforts to convey some words to his listening companion, who adopted the most approved system of acoustics, by putting his hands to his ears and stretching as far as possible over the verge of the lake. Not the slightest sound reached him. The surprised listener now ran round to the major and protested that he could not hear one word, although it was manifest that the major had made every possible effort. They then changed places; and great, indeed, was the surprise of the stranger to find all his bellowings met only by the same efforts on the part of the major that he himself had previously used.

"Is it possible you did not hear me?"

"Not a word."

"Why, I shouted as loudly as possible."

"You seemed to do so. I could perceive you were opening your mouth and inflating your lungs, but no sound reached me."

"Did you not hear me request you to speak out, major?"

"Certainly not."

"Wonderful!"

On their return, the expressions of astonishment were repeated, and the time of descending the mountain was fully occupied in discussing the merits of so wonderful a case.

Here, had the joke rested, it had been more satisfactory; but the note-taking stranger published the unexplained mystery so ubiquitously, that he soon became aware of the imposition which had been practised on his credulity, and purposed most furiously to resent it.

In a day or two, our major received an intimation that an explanation or an apology would be necessary, and he heartily d——d himself and the note-making knight together—himself for volunteering a dangerous joke, and the other that he had so little Irish blood in his veins as to be unable to bear it. As an apology was out of the question, the old pistols were rubbed up. The affair, however, getting wind, both the parties were summoned before a magistrate, and then a singular discovery was made. To the magistrate's question as to his station in life, our note-maker first described himself as a gentleman.

"Of what class?"

"Of the London class."

"Have you any trade or profession?"

"Yes, a profession."

"What is that?"

"Am I bound to answer?"

"I conceive so."

With much hesitation, therefore, he confessed that he was an eminent tailor in Bond Street.

The indignation of the major now broke out. "What," said he, "have I been wasting my time and lowering my honour by associating with a tailor! Thunder and turf! he is the first snip that ever cut me before. To be called out by a snip!"

Whereupon he appealed to the magistrates, and expressed his hope that the tailor might be instantly transported, at least, for having offered so incurable an indignity to an officer in his Majesty's service.

The magistrate, seeing that the affair could go no farther, dismissed the case; but the major's indignation could not be stayed; he deemed it his duty to give full explanations of his blamelessness in the affair. Indeed, so cast down had the major been by the dishonour of having been called to account by the tailor, that he had scarcely been able to face his friends until that day, when an unhoped-for revenge was by accident thrown in his way. The tailors had been shooting on the lake. By ill luck the boat was capsized just as the major and his little crew were passing them. The major's magnanimity prevailed—he saved them—but could not resist the admonition which the circumstance suggested.

"Oh, Bubaboo!" cried the major, having brought both into his boat. "By the powers, you should be after staying at home and minding your own hot goose, and not be bothering here to get nothing but a cold duck."

The tailors were no more seen; but the major still boiled with abhorrence of Killarney note-making visitors.

CHAPTER VII

First Day on the Lake—Ross Castle—Splendid View—Accidental Sport—A Disappointment—The Evil of Sight-gazing—Scarcity of Salmon in the Lakes—Island of Innisfallen—An Impromptu Breakfast—Beauties of the Island—The Monastery—Coasting—Famous Sport—The Eagle's Nest—Extraordinary Echoes—The Pass—The Lower Lake—Residence of Mr. Hyde, Rector of Killarney—Trouting—Directions for Bait—How to astonish the Natives—Wonderful success of Salmon-roe—Lord Kenmare's Cottage—An Angler's Dinner—Turk Lake—Its Monster Trout—Angling Exploit of Lady Headley—The Major in his Glory—Enormous Trout—More Hints to Sportsmen at Killarney.

It was a cool, cloudy, yet, to the sportsman, a beautiful morning, as I entered my little boat, which Owen had already brought to the landing-place of Ross Island, with a view of trying the first or lower lake, sufficient of itself, indeed, to supply a continued change of fishing-ground for some weeks.

Ross Castle, which is the only place allowed for embarkation, is an ancient ruin of some beauty. It consists of a lofty square tower with embattlements, on the very verge of the lower lake. From the castle itself the view is splendid, and will repay the trouble of mounting; it forms a perfect panorama of Mangerton, Turk, and Glena mountains, and the lakes which are named from them.

There was an aspect of gloom over the lake, which, in the opinion of Owen, augured favourably for a salmon. We first mounted, therefore, two salmon flies of a temperate order, and started for what is called the salmon course. That is, the deep ridges by the sides of the several islands which everywhere spot the lakes of Killarney. It is to be noted that for salmon fishing these courses must be strictly observed, while trout will only be found on the flats in the neighbourhood of the shores.

The wind being off Ross Castle, we at once suffered the boat to drift, and began our cast. As we continued to throw with the wind, and before the boat, the lower lake in all its majesty opened by very gentle degrees, and expanded itself in boundless beauty. As we drove onward, the noble Toomies and Glena arose, abruptly and boldly, from the very bosom of the waters. Overcome by so singularly beautiful a scene, I had thrown down my rod, and had almost unconsciously taken the pencil, the boat still drifting down the course. O'Donoghue's Prison, a perpendicular rock, thirty feet from the surface, now presented itself; having passed which, the modest, arbutus-clothed island, Innisfallen, came in view. It is a spot covered with verdure, and in charming contrast with the barren promontories which everywhere else presented themselves. As I was engaged in contemplating the agreeable variety it presented, I was startled by Owen's sudden exclamation: "Oh, bad luck to it, but your honour's rod is gone: a salmon, huzza!"

I had just seized the reel as it was passing the edge of the boat, and found that I had indeed a heavy fish to contend with. He had taken the fly while trailing (as it is here called) behind the boat, the breeze just giving sufficient way to keep the fly on the surface. Now came the tug of war. The danger of being wrecked was imminent, for rocks everywhere surrounded us, while the power of the fish gave evident proof that he was fresh from the sea. All difficulties, however, appeared in a few minutes to have been overcome, and my prize was at the surface, hardly capable of another effort. While just on the point of drawing him gently to the boat, that Owen might gaff him, the mouth gave way, and the fish remained at two or three yards distance, motionless on the water; before, however, we could approach him, he recovered his power, and slowly moved downward.

Our disappointment was extreme; Owen threw the hat from

his head, and tore his hair. "If your honour had been minding the fly, perhaps——" Owen hardly dared to proceed, but it was manifest he thought I had ill-managed the fish. I was in disgrace, it was clear. "But," said Owen, "your honour played him well."

Fortune seldom forgives a bungler, and we had no further chance of a salmon, having now completed the whole course. We, therefore, put on our trout flies, and drifted towards Innisfallen. In this kind of fishing we were immediately successful; and, indeed, scarcely a cast was made as we approached the land without a rise. It was not long, therefore, before we had secured two dozen trout, though not any of very large size —generally from a quarter to half a pound each.

The great decrease of salmon in the lakes of Killarney is attributable to the river fishery established all up the Laune, of which we shall afterwards speak, by nets. The run from the sea to the lakes does not exceed twelve miles; the river is drawn at every spot calculated for the halt of the fish, nightly; and few, therefore, now escape to the lakes. Indeed, the salmon fishery of the lakes may be considered almost extinct, though sufficient is still taken by nets on the shallows to supply the town at 4d. per pound.

We now landed on Innisfallen, which was spread with a beautiful carpet of verdure. Here and there are occasional openings, which, through the luxuriance of the foliage, give views of the lake. The lofty trees, in almost every variety, form arbours of considerable extent; and amongst them the arbutus, which appears to have been indigenous. Smith, in his history of Kerry, seems to think that it was first planted by the monks on this island, an opinion which its existence on all the other islands seems to contradict.[1]

We now descried the major's boat rowing hard towards the island, and we made a signal that we recognised him. He was soon with us, accompanied by his two men-of-all-work, and a

---

[1] The arbutus is indigenous to this district, and to no other part of the British Isles.—ED.

bugler. "By the powers, and you were stirring early this cool morning; that's a proof of the sportsman; what luck?"

We exhibited our trout, and related our discomfiture; he expressed his surprise at our having met a salmon so early in the season, for which he said he had now ceased to fish on the lakes, at least till the autumn should return. But from his boat was produced a fine lake trout of five pounds, which he had taken by trailing. The lads were active, and in a few minutes an excellent turf fire was blazing; three sticks, gipsy fashion, were stuck up, the tea-kettle was boiling, the cloth laid on the velvet green, and the trout suspended for roasting. The major had not forgotten a good dried salmon, which, broiled with some of the smaller trout, furnished forth a noble breakfast.

We employed some time in rambling over the island, which has been so long and so generally celebrated for every species of romantic invention. I find that Archdall speaks of the monastery, the remains of which give grandeur to the otherwise beautiful spot. He says that, in 1180, "this abbey being ever esteemed a paradise and a secure sanctuary, the treasure and most valuable effects of the whole country were deposited in the hands of her clergy, notwithstanding which this abbey was plundered by Maoldwin, son of Daniel O'Donoghue; many of the clergy were slain, and even in their cemetery, by the M'Carthys."

It is said that a collection of bones were discovered beneath the threshold of the oratory, and supposed to have been the bones of the clergy thus slain. I think, however, the practice of making the islands of these lakes burying-grounds, which will be noticed of Lake Waterville, will give a better account of them.

Having sufficiently admired the beauties of Innisfallen, we now proceeded to coast the other islands, and the day's sport began in earnest. The major's boat having drawn off about a hundred yards, we both drifted towards a cluster of rocks.

There were two rods going from each boat; and, as the sun occasionally broke forth and was again clouded, we found as much as we could do in taking trout. At mid-day the major hailed us, and, on comparing notes, we found our number to be 67, his 108—all fish of the same character, and about the same size. We, therefore, set forth, wearying of the monotony of trouting, towards the pass of the upper lake, the major being the leader.

At the Eagle's Nest, which is a splendid promontory overhanging the pass between the lakes, an explosion took place that had been nearly fatal to my equilibrium, as I was standing in the boat, and carelessly throwing my fly as Owen rowed.

"Ha, ha!" said the major; "d'ye hear the answers?"

These were the echoes from the different mountains, which returned many times the sound of the major's duck-gun, which he had just discharged, and as distinctly as the original explosion, till it died into a kind of thunder. The succeeding silence, broken only by the dashing of the waterfalls which supply the lakes, was singularly impressive, and we paused on the oars to enjoy the change. After a few minutes the major's bugle sent forth a shrill blast, which was repeated in a varying key from mountain to mountain; the scream of the rock birds formed a chorus, and the mountains seemed to vivify.

We now came to the pass of the Old Weir Bridge. The lakes were not high, and the small river which separates them was hardly deep enough to allow our boats to be rowed up. We, therefore, lightened burdens, while one lad brought the boats through.

The sight of the upper lake was more surprising, though not of such extended beauty as the lower. The shores are abruptly rocky, and there are few places that will admit of a landing. The islands, which are numerous, present less beauty than those of the lower lake. On a green base, however, between the lofty ranges of mountains, may be observed one dot of white, surrounded by plantations of variegated hues.

It is the residence of Mr. Hyde, a clergyman, and rector of Killarney, and forms the only feature which recalls one from the belief that we are in an uninhabited wild.

At the major's instance we now changed our tackle, and for flies substituted small trout of two or three inches long, which the major had provided, and which will be readily found in all the little brooks falling into the lakes. These we put on in the following manner: pass one large hook, the curve of which should be a full inch, through the mouth and body of the bait, and bring the hook out through the tail, so that part of the body may be on the curve, in order to make the bait spin well. Then, with a needle, sew up the mouth of the bait, and fasten it tightly to the hook to prevent its slipping. This done, attach two good swivels to the line, and let out thirty yards as the boat is gently rowed. One rod from each side the boat will keep all clear.

Having thus provided ourselves, we proceeded to row round the lake, which is of about two or three miles in length, and, in places, of about one broad; nor had we traversed far, before an halloo from the major indicated his success. He had taken a sea trout of four or five pounds. While he was holding up the fish for our admiration, a sudden check was given to one of my own rods, and a clattering of the reel called me into action. This was a good beginning; for, in a few minutes, I was in possession of a lake trout of about six pounds. I did not, however, succeed so well afterwards; for, though there were several runs, the inconvenient manner in which the hook is necessarily placed defeated its object. By this mode of fishing it more frequently happens that the hook takes effect outside the mouth, as the running fish always seizes its prey in the middle.

Having now arrived at the top of the lake, we entered a fine rapid river. It was my turn to instruct the major; my tackle soon changed—I produced the salmon-roe.

Owen began to smile in anticipation of the surprise by

which the major and his crew would be overwhelmed, as I trudged up the rocky banks. This is a river which feeds the upper lake, and is apparently its principal spring. It falls from the mountains through a long chain of cataracts and alternate bog valleys, which, though difficult and sometimes dangerous to get through, will amply repay the enterprising bait-fisher who shall visit it. At Killarney the fly or trailing only are in use, neither of which is suited to the fishing of a river of this description. Yet it is in this river, being the head of the lakes, that the fish are commonly found of the best order and size. A fly would be useless on the surface of the boiling whirlpools below the cataracts, and trailing impossible.

Having loaded my line with a heavy bullet, I stopped at the first fall, and commenced the fatal mode of angling. Fatal—as I believe it to be the only certain mode of taking trout, salmon, and all of that order, without reference to weather or season.

The major was incredulous, and smiled. Having examined my tackle and the bait, he pronounced it more curious than effective, and was certain, whatever effect it might produce elsewhere, it could avail nothing in Ireland.

"By the powers, but that's an odd kind of fishing," said the major, whose countenance had undergone a complete change as he saw me deliberately land a fine trout of two pounds, and immediately drop my line into the same place. Trout after trout appeared in continued succession, till the major declared he would burn his flies, for the true secret of fishing remained yet to be learned.

"The divil a fish any soul but yourself can extract from this execrable river," exclaimed the major, "though we all well knew that the finest fish are to be found up this stream in the spring. Netting is out of the question—flies useless—groping impossible—so that we have been always constrained to regard this bog as holy ground, which would never repay the angler for traversing."

Here was the day's best sport, but, as I felt that it was at the expense of the major's pleasure, after having secured a dozen fine fish from one fall, I put up my tackle, resolved when alone to revisit this river, and abandon the fly-fishing on the lake. Some few days after I did so; and putting up at a little cabin on the Kenmare road, six miles from Killarney, and dignified by the name of the half-way house, I had incredible success on the banks of the stream. The only drawback was the wretched accommodation at night, it being nothing more than a pallet and what covering my own clothes afforded, used blanket-wise; while the whole culinary catalogue of the hut was comprised in one pot to boil potatoes. If, however, any succeeding angler should, warned by my example, take with him all the necessaries, he will find the poor people willing to afford him all they have—their labour and attention; while the sacred river—for so I must term it—will prove an inexhaustible fund of amusement.

On our return homeward we again landed at the cottage belonging to Lord Kenmare, which contains a room for the accommodation of visitors, and affords a decent *salle à manger* for those who bring the mangibles with them. Although persons live at the cottage, and, under the hope of very considerable and disproportionate remuneration, afford you an opportunity of cooking, yet they are permitted to sell nothing. If, instead of this kind of rental, his lordship had procured a proper license to allow some decent person to sell for the relief of visitors on the lake, who are frequently overtaken by unexpectedly boisterous weather, and who have not provided themselves, the accommodation had been more complete. Here, however, the foresight of the major was not at fault. A collection of all his little household would afford was quickly spread before us, and, I believe, the air of the lakes had well qualified us to do all his preparations justice. We made trial of the large lake trout, which, though of a deeper red than the salmon, was not equal in flavour to the inviting appearance. It was dry, and required the assistance of condiments, with which, of course, we were not provided. The smaller trout, however, are delicious. They should be scored crosswise, and put on a gridiron; no further preparation is requisite to render them a most agreeable dish.

Our repast finished, we returned through the pass; and the major, having reloaded his gun, repeated the experiment of the echoes; but they were by no means so clear or distinct, as by this time the wind had arisen. To hear them under every advantage, the day should be still; the reverberations are then perfect.

Having regained the lower lake, we found that it had lost all its solitary grandeur. Numerous boats floated on its surface; parties, accompanied by flags and bands of music (if so execrable an association of performers can be so called), were everywhere seen and heard, while we made the best of our way to Turk Lake.

This, after an hour's hard row, we reached. Turk Lake is separated from the grand, or lower lake, by a range of islands. There are two passages into it; that by the side of Denis island, on the Glena side, is the most convenient, and certainly the most agreeable route.

On entering the lake the ear is immediately arrested by the sullen roar of a distant cascade, which falls through a chasm which separates Turk from Mangerton mountain, and forms one continued sheet of foam from the fall to the basin below, and thence, through a bridge, joins the lake. Although this lake is generally esteemed the best for the sportsman, and does sometimes yield trout of a better character than either the upper or lower lake, the height of the mountains, which on all sides surround it, renders it generally so calm that few opportunities exist of effectually throwing the fly on its waters.

After some attempts, which were attended by no success, I proposed to proceed to the fall, and again try the bait under the cataract. Here I was again successful; and, after having secured several fine specimens of the dark lake trout, the major

"Here, indeed, the Major was great."

seized my hand in an ecstasy of delight, and protested that I was the only English angler who he had ever believed understood anything of the art. He insisted on my passing one day more with him on the lake at the top of Mangerton, to which, the next morning, we proceeded.

The lake to which I allude is Lake Gutane, four miles from Killarney. We arrived there in my pony gig, and found a boat in waiting. The fly was not attempted, as, in this lake, trout of fifty and sixty pounds are to be found, which can only be taken by trailing. Here Lady Headley succeeded in landing a trout of twenty-seven pounds weight. Although that size is considered ordinary, it was spoken of as an exploit worthy of being recorded; performed, as it was, by a lady.

For two hours we were wholly unsuccessful, until a breeze, or rather a gale of wind, began to create some anxiety as to our power of keeping the windward side of the lake. With the boat running rapidly before the wind, smash went the rod in the middle. Owen secured the butt, and we now found ourselves in a most dangerous position. To abandon the fish, which was obviously a monster, was impossible; indeed, had certain destruction been before Owen, he would never have yielded his hold. Meanwhile, the boat was drifting rapidly towards the rocks, and I was myself obliged to seize the oars; and employing all the strength of which I was master, hailed, in terms of distress, the major, who, in the other boat, made the best of the way to our assistance. Here, indeed, the major was great. He jumped from his own boat to ours, directing the lads to take us in tow, and brought the trout to the best bearing he could with the broken tackle. An hour at least was employed before we could safely anticipate success. The fish was sullen, and would frequently betake himself to the bottom, whence, until he pleased, it was impossible to dislodge him. Luckily, however, he ran towards the middle of the lake, and we were safe from the rocks which threatened danger to ourselves and release to him.

"Forty pounds, on the honour of a British officer!" exclaimed the major.

I ventured to express my disbelief.

"Forty pounds to an ounce; feel him."

The major placed the rod for a moment in my hands. The effect was that of being fast to a log of wood, which occasionally rose and descended—nothing more. After the major had gradually reeled up a great portion of his line, before he or any of us expected it, the creature gave a bound from the surface, three or four yards high, and exhibited, indeed, one of the monsters of the Loch Gutane. The major's dexterity was now really worthy of admiration. The rod was down in a moment, so that his antagonist took nothing by his leap. That was his last effort; he soon appeared on the surface, occasionally shewing the whiteness of his stomach, and was cautiously and safely gaffed by Owen.

The length was two feet one inch and a quarter, which, however, was very disproportionate to his weight; he appeared to have grown only in thickness and breadth; and, on our weighing him in the evening, at the major's cottage, he proved to be just nineteen pounds and some ounces.

The major protested he never was out before—that my tackle had deceived him—and that he despised the capture from the unnecessary trouble it had given.

Several times during my stay at Killarney I fished this lake with no better success than two or three trouts of from two to five pounds: and, although I do not doubt that there are still to be found fish of from forty to fifty pounds, yet the distance is too great to enable the sportsman to fish for those of the larger size at the proper time, viz. at daybreak in the morning, or late in the evening. The road down the mountain is dangerous, and though I intended for this purpose to have passed one night on the banks of the lake for the purpose alluded to, so many new and interesting scenes of action presented themselves, that I did not realise my intention. It would be quite worth a night's trial; and I am assured that the enterprising sportsman who would fish during the night with a very light-coloured trout, well swivelled, would be rewarded by a prize worthy his perseverance. The lake is very little known, and seldom attempted, from its dreary position among the most frightful mountains which even this wild scenery presents.

CHAPTER VIII

The Rivers—Residences of James and John O'Connell—Lord Kenmare—The Gap of Dunloe—Major Mahony—Beaufort Bridge—Residence of Mr. Mullins, Member for Kerry—The River Laune—Excellent Sport—Izaak Walton—The Major incredulous—Sporting extraordinary—A Cure for Everything—Killarney Scandal—Lord Headley—The Irish Agents—A Stag-Hunt in the Lake—Extraordinary Scene of Irish Jollity—Timber-Hunting in the Bogs—Extinct Animals—Unpopularity of Lord Kenmare—Reasons for it—Beauties and Merits of Killarney as a Watering Place.

HAVING now tried all the lakes, I took leave of the major's kind surveillance, and, accompanied by Owen, proceeded to try the rivers; the most beautiful of which is that which carries the united waters of the lakes into the Castlemaine Bay, and thence into Dingle Bay and the Atlantic. This river, which is in the lower part continually disturbed by netting for salmon, is little fished by the angler; the lakes presenting a much broader expanse, and a much more convenient bosom for the fall of the fly.

There is a good road by the side of the lake, by which are passed the residences of James O'Connell and John O'Connell, brothers of the immortal Daniel, and gentlemen of independent possessions; retired in their mode of living, and, I believe, highly respected and beloved by all parties, even here, where the perverse conduct of Lord Kenmare, himself a Catholic and a professed reformer, has occasioned a dissension among those who are professedly liberal in their politics.

The fall of the stream from the lake is at first hardly

perceptible, but increases as it advances to a noble river; it is bounded by varied and bold banks, covered with trees, and, to the fly-fisher, almost inaccessible. It here receives several tributaries, and, if the lakes of Killarney were absent, would alone form a fishing station of no ordinary promise. Passing along its banks, we arrive at the opening, celebrated as the Gap of Dunloe, at the foot of which is situated the residence of Major Mahony. It is a wild and sudden severance of the mountains which confine the lake, through which there is a mountain pass, and now a road of considerable picturesque beauty. The entrance to the Gap is very narrow, and the mountains on either side are perpendicular. The pass is directed by the side of a small black lake—black from the reflection of the high and perpendicular mountains which overshadow it—and narrows so fearfully, yet so wildly, that many have failed in achieving the ascent from the horror which is calculated to overwhelm timid and nervous persons.

These magnificent scenes, which make the passes of Borrowdale and the Devil's Bridge mere nature's toys, the angler will leave unexplored, and pursue his journey to Beaufort Bridge, a handsome structure, leading to the lodge and park of the Honourable Mr. Mullins, member for Kerry.

Into the park the angler may enter, without let or hindrance: the porter of the lodge will civilly open the gate for his admission, and, though the grounds for nearly a mile on the banks are beautifully and tastefully laid out, he will find himself free as air to pursue his sport. In all probability he will receive an invitation to avail himself of the accommodation of the house, which stands at no great distance from the river.

From March to May there is no better sport for the angler, content to seek what is here called the brown trout, than may be found in the river Laune. Its extent is about twelve miles, seven of which are well calculated for the salmon-roe; and here, on Owen's arrival with the pony, and such refreshments as I had ordered him to bring, I had, from the bridge falls alone, extracted upwards of eighty of good size and in excellent season. Owen had now given up all surprise at the use of the bait, and confessed he was no fisherman. He, therefore, occupied his time in laying the cloth, which he had brought, on the green lawn, before the house of Mr. Mullins, and close to the verge of the river. A neighbouring cottage added to our treat the luxuries of hot potatoes and boiled trout; and, as we sat down to our repast, I threw my line into the river and lodged my rod on a tree. Not a moment had I to enjoy Owen's ample arrangements; no sooner had I selected my fare than a tug at the rod required my attention; and, indeed, so magical was the *bait*, that it appeared (which I believe to be the fact) to have congregated the fish. My success on this river was so great, that I fear to weary my reader by recounting it; but it must be remembered that this mode of fishing was wholly new, and that the bank, from which my rod was suspended, was covered with trees, and consequently impervious to the fly-fisher.

The visit to the river Laune was pregnant with amusement, constituted of that calm and reflective enjoyment, which is the true source of the fascinating art;—covered with the now abundant foliage from the sun's rays—our meal spread on the turf—the inspiring spring-note of the numerous birds; and, above all, the exciting success of the day brought to my fullest recognition the peaceful delights of our father and friend Izaak, who, albeit unused to this mode of securing trout, enjoyed all the pleasures of the more moderate victory over the roach, chub, and dace. One of his maxims I have never omitted to act on—one which I can confidently recommend as the grand panacea for all the annoyances of the world—one that will outlive the rest—" study to be quiet."

On our return to Killarney, I found myself possessed of upwards of eighty fine trout, varying from one quarter to two pounds, and began to consider how I should dispose of so monstrous a store. I at length resolved to dispatch the whole to the major, who, knowing better than myself how they would be

THE RIVER LAUNE.

properly distributed, would, I was assured, apply them to the use of the really deserving poor. It is a fault among anglers that sufficient care is not taken in the disposal of their produce. It is his duty to seek proper objects on whom to bestow the fruit of his success, and this determination reconciles his amusement with the object of usefulness.

In a short time the major was with me; and I lost no time, in my really comfortable lodgings, in ordering a supply of the "matarials." He pressed my hand with an ardour which, I was sure, denoted that I had risen in his respect, and I saw I was fixed for an evening.

"What size is your English net?" said the major.

"Net?—I never used one."

"Be aisy; let Owen produce it; d'ye mean to assert here to me—an officer holding her Majesty's commission under a rascally government—to me, who have fished these lakes and streams ever since the year 17—, that that load of fish came out of the Laune by the help only of a rod?—impossible!"

"Never mind, major; it is true."

"Then you will depopulate Ireland with your magic bait; and the sooner I give you your billet and route, the better it will be for the fishermen who remain behind. But you must not leave to-morrow. At six I have ordered you to be chanticleered —to view the stag-hunt—it will be a glorious day."

I readily ceded all my previous arrangements to this occasion, and gave my promise to attend the major at his appointment for the next day.

As "the matarials" attenuated, I found the major relax into his old disposition to communicate the wonders of sporting, and, indeed, of all other things; and the evening closed with a description of the effect of some grand medicine, which, being of the quack order, possessed, of course, the most contradictory virtues, and was equally applicable to every species of disorder or accident.

"Cure? by the powers, and nothing can equal the grand

preservative! it cures all diseases and mends all mischiefs. If you won't believe me, hear what happened to myself, which, without the aid of this extraordinary medicine, you would have never heard. I was drying powder for grouse-shooting, and had, for that purpose, spread it on a large sheet of paper, before the fire; while stirring it, some unlucky spark fell on the stuff, and blew us all up together. Away went one of my arms here, another there; my head into the ceiling, and my tail out of the doorway. I was a lamentable sight to look upon, as I could not be seen at all, but by three or four different looks. 'The cordial,' exclaimed I; the cordial was brought—poured into my mouth; the first draught brought back my legs, the next my arms, to their proper places; the third attached the trunk to the rest; and I was whole and sound as ever!"

I had also the several facts, that, at one stag-hunt, the animal had dived from one island and come up at another, two miles distant; and also that a boatman, who had seized one by the horns as the hunted deer was swimming, had securely mounted his back, and fairly traversed the lake, throwing a fly and catching trout at the same time.

Although these stories seem monstrous, they all undoubtedly had some foundation; and the good-humour and kindliness of heart, which were manifested in the major's every act, had begotten for him an indulgence in his amplification, on which no one who knew him would be desirous of trenching.

The morning arrived, and with it came the major and his *posse comitatus*, to escort me to the lake, to witness, and, if need were, to assist in the stag-hunt. The weather was boisterous, and even dangerous, for I shall be well understood by any nautical reader when I describe the seas of the lakes in a gale as singularly short and rapid. Nothing but keeping the boat's head to wind will brave the difficulty; and, on embarking, even the major expressed some apprehension. Seeing, however, others start, we set forth; the major at the helm, encouraging his little crew, among whom Owen was now associated, much to his disapproval. I would not understand his winks; and, amid the roaring of the winds, and the shouts of the assembled parties, our little launch was pulled out. The rendezvous was at Innisfallen; and, I believe, every boat that the lake afforded was crowded by visitors and others, who were seeking to congregate on the island, forming a motley group not very easy to describe. Numerous parties were already on the island; some dancing to the pipers, who had severally selected some flat spot for their adherents, while many, too great or too affected to join in the general hilarity, contented themselves with a dignified parade.

The major and myself joined the dance till the cry was heard that the stag was started. A hundred bugles from all directions of the lake now summoned each party to their boats, which crowded the shores of the island, and ludicrous were the scenes of apprehension, screaming, and splashing, as the lake, now wild with storm, dashed its angry spray over the dignified segregators. Many boats put back to the lee of the island; but the major, relying on the skill of his little crew and his own steady hand at the helm, set forth, and we arrived at the opposite shore just as the hounds were descending to the strand. Splash went the affrighted animal into the lake, amid the shouts of the hundred boatmen who were immediately at utmost stretch to follow him.

Each crew was now put to the test of strength, and I must record the fact, that the major was not last; the shores were crowded with spectators—the mountains reverberated the sounds in continued echoes—the clamping of a thousand oars—the resounding bugles from the boats—the cries of cargoes upset in the mêlée—the alarm of the drowning, and the shouts of the foremost, raised all together a din that must fail in description. The chase, however, was not of long continuance. The sea was too high to allow the tired animal a chance, and he was secured by two boats in a state of exhaustion that took from the captor all the credit of difficulty or danger. The stag was then reconducted to his native wood, and turned loose for a future day.

Although I give this short account of the stag-hunt at

Killarney, I must, in justice, observe, that it afforded me individually no pleasure. The whole arrangements were artificial, and therefore, to the true sportsman, uninteresting. It is a piece of absurd pageantry; the only amusing part of which is the assemblage, after all is over, at the island of Innisfallen, where every true and loyal Killarney-man thinks it his duty to dance and get drunk, if he should have the misfortune to be sober for the rest of the year. The evening, however, unlike other Irish festivals, passed peacefully; and, with the exception of a few broken heads and one or two drowned, on returning to the mainland, the stag-hunt at Killarney was fraught with no particular consequence.

The deer which are preserved in the woods in the neighbourhood, and which furnish the hunt, are of the red species, and were originally brought from France.[1] Although they are still found in a wild state in Scotland, I believe Devonshire and Cornwall are the only counties in which they are now found in England. With the wolves they appear to have been destroyed in Ireland; once, doubtless, productive of those of a much larger and more splendid character of deer, now extinct.

The bogs of Ireland were once woods—the proof of which exists in the fact, that, in all parts, trunks of trees of immense size are found; and even now the traveller will not unfrequently find the natives boring, by long iron rods, to search for timber. Having discovered the existence of some hard substance, which they immediately recognise as timber, they proceed by continued boring to ascertain its length, and the depth from the surface, and by these discoveries decide whether the exhumation would be worth the labour. The timber so discovered is hard as iron, and perfectly black, and it is not extravagant to believe may have been thousands of years imbedded in the bog, its preservation being accounted for by the total exclusion of the atmospheric air. The Rev. Mr. Isaacson, in passing one of these numerous

---

[1] This is an error. There is no reason to doubt that the red deer of Killarney are of an indigenous stock.—ED.

tracts where persons were thus employed, discovered the head and horns of an immense animal; the former considerably larger than a bullock's, and the horns standing nearly seven feet high, and of a weight which could hardly be lifted by one person. The proportionate dimensions of such a creature must have been enormous; but, with the destruction of the woods, by some convulsion of nature which philosophers have not explained, also fell this noble race of deer.[1]

Wolves, however, still escaped; for we find a presentment made to the grand jury for their destruction in the county of Cork, so late as 1710; the inhabitants then complaining of their devastation.

---

[1] The horns and head of the elk were presented by Mr. Isaacson to the late Duke of Beaufort, in whose possession they now are.

CHAPTER IX

Kenmare—Blackwater—Liberality of the Rev. D. M——.—Irish Cunning and Roguery—O'Rourke, the Salmon-Poacher—Story of O'Rourke and the Magistrate—Gaffing at the Falls—The Poacher in Exile—The Flood—Singular Habits of the Salmon—Ascent of the Hills—A Sudden Storm, and its Consequences—Perils and Escapes—Fatal Catastrophe at Clydah—The whole of the Cattle and Inhabitants destroyed by a Flood.

From Killarney to Kenmare, 14 miles.

The most unfrequented, yet by far the most magnificent scenery lies between Killarney and Kenmare. The latter is a small town, containing a good inn; seldom, however, boasting any other guests than the poorer attendants of the markets, and the occasional visits of the tourist. Although, on arrival at the town, little beyond a wild and barbarous country meets the eye, the road will amply repay the journey. One miserable cot alone, dignified by the name of a half-way house, breaks in upon the general impression which steals over the mind, that the traveller is passing through an uninhabited country. The succession of mountains, displaying all the varied grandeur which forms so distinguishing a characteristic of Kerry, is here incessant, till, having traversed the now well-planned road fourteen miles, the sea bursts upon the view as suddenly as beautifully.

My purpose of visiting the Blackwater, a river celebrated for its fishing, though by English travellers little known, prevented my staying at Kenmare. This river presents to the tourist and the angler at least a fortnight's varying amusement; and, in the liberality and kindness of the Rev. D. M——, whose property it is, full reliance may be placed. His establishment is the oasis of the desert, while all around presents nothing but wild neglect and desolation: not an acre of land for miles under cultivation.

The strictness with which this river has been preserved has rendered nearly all the scattered inhabitants adepts in the art of fly-fishing; and even his domestic servants have been afflicted with the general desire to assist in gaffing, spearing, and hunting the salmon, although it has been always held a serious crime.

While I partook of an early breakfast, among others, who, like myself, were allured to the county by the high reputation it bears for sport of every kind, our host made frequent inquiries for one O'Rourke. At last O'Rourke appeared. There was a conscious knavery in his countenance, an archness in the eye, which betrayed the motive of our host's inquiries.

"Are there any salmon in the river, O'Rourke?"

O'Rourke smiled, scarcely knowing whether he ought or ought not to answer the question. At length an imperious repetition of the inquiry brought a confused reply: "To be sure your honour knows right well; how should I know, your honour? sure it isn't for the likes of me to be looking for salmon, or peering about the river any way."

"I ask you, sir, if there are any salmon in the river?"

"There are seven, your honour, in the first lodge, and eighteen in the upper pool."

"Then you do know?"

"Plase your honour, I don't pretind to know more than the rest, but the fish will show themselves, your honour, and one can't help seeing them, your honour."

"That will do. Be ready with the gaff."

"To be sure and I shall, your honour."

The light flashed from his eye, as, with a hasty step, he retreated from the room evidently overjoyed.

"That," said our host, "is the best salmon-fisher and the greatest knave on my estate. Notwithstanding the terror of dismissal, and the utter starvation which would be consequent on it, such is his propensity to poach salmon, that no consideration of this kind can restrain him. Salmon-catching is, indeed, a constitutional disease with him, and I am compelled to give special orders to my keepers to be ever on the look-out against all poachers, and especially against O'Rourke. Although he is now nothing more than a labourer on my estate, he was once in a higher employment; and such was the pleasure my father took in his company, especially when fishing, that he might have taken any liberty save that only of catching salmon. The cause of his degradation, however, was the irrepressible love of salmonry, which overbore all other considerations. It was his office to carry my father across the stream, which, as you may have observed, is, in many parts, exceedingly shallow and broad; yet, during the floods, to which we are sometimes subject, we have found bridges of little avail. It was the old gentleman's custom to visit his summer-house on the opposite side, and O'Rourke's duty to carry him across the stream, as the gout had at that time rendered him wholly helpless. About a year before his death, O'Rourke was performing his office with due care, and had already reached the middle of the stream with his gouty burden, when, as though struck with sudden madness, and uttering an Irish scream indicative of joy, he precipitated the old gentleman headlong into the stream, and threw himself into a hole which was close to the spot. Fortunately, my father recovered the sitting posture, and, perhaps, as fortunately, had presence of mind to keep it, although the stream was rapidly flowing as high as his arms. His screams brought assistance from the neighbouring cottage, whereupon O'Rourke jumped up with a monstrous salmon in his hands, which he held up by the gills. The curses of the old gentleman brought him to his senses; he awoke to the terror of his situation, which he knew would, during the paroxysm of his master, be fraught with danger. Throwing down, therefore, the salmon on the bank, he took to his heels, and was never heard of for at least a month.

"On regaining his home, the first business of the enraged magistrate was to grant his general warrant for the apprehension of O'Rourke; and, had he been then found, I do not doubt but that sentence of instant execution would have been passed against him. No warrant, however, availed; he was not to be found.

"It was not till some time had elapsed that a sportsman, who well knew the worth of O'Rourke as a companion, dining with the still offended magistrate, and having listened to the details of this enormity as accounting for O'Rourke's absence, presented a petition for the culprit's pardon. This, with great difficulty, was at length obtained, and proclamation being made forthwith, the delinquent came out of his retreat, which had been no other than the immense mass of rocks which form the last fall of the river. Here had he endured a month's imprisonment, living on shell-fish, obtained from the shore, which was within a few yards of the spot, and perhaps mainly assisted by the better fare which the river supplied. Nothing, however, could wholly reconcile my father to him, and, though restored to his employment on the estate, yet has O'Rourke never held up his head since he plunged the magistrate in the river to catch a salmon with his hands."

Armed with the gaff, O'Rourke, myself, and *fidus Achates* Owen, now set off for the river. When arrived there, I was somewhat amused at O'Rourke's account of the mode of life he had adopted while in retreat. The bridge, which is sixty feet above the rocks, where the last fall mingles the river with the sea, is of the wildest and most picturesque construction. After having shown us the precise hole where he boiled his potatoes at night, and the upper part of the hollow where, on dried seaweeds, he had made his bed, with the nimbleness of a monkey, though at that time at least sixty years of age, he jumped from one ledge of rocks to another, till he had gained the point of one which overhung the descending torrent, and there, with gaff in hand, awaited his opportunity. Strange as it may appear, this spot, if it could be maintained during the increasing flood after rains, would present continual opportunities of gaffing the salmon and sea-trout as they endeavour to jump the fall.

"Ah, your honour, we'll have a glorious flood to-day."

This prognostication was formed on an experienced observation of the habits of the salmon.

The river Blackwater is subject to sudden floods—torrents falling down from the immense range of mountains, each containing its lake. These lakes become sometimes overcharged, and it is not unusual to find a simultaneous burst over the precipitous falls of the stream, so that from a ripple to a flood is the change of a moment. Indeed, some parts of the river are so shallow, that a child may, at every two or three hundred yards, ford it. On the approach of a flood, of which the most experienced inhabitants of these glens can, perhaps, form no prescience, the habits and instincts of the salmon and trout from the sea are singularly evinced.

The fall from the bridge, to which we have just referred, forms a dark basin, protected on each side by perpendicular rocks. Such, however, is the transparency of the salt water, that, from the side of the bridge, although so much elevated from the level of the water, it is not uncommon to see crowds of salmon sulkily awaiting the increased stream to make their first leap. Whenever, even in the most settled state of the weather, and while the river is nearly empty, excepting only the occasional lodges, these fish are observed to congregate under the bridge, be sure of an impending torrent.

Convinced that, with this intimation from O'Rourke, and the dull and dense atmosphere above us, there would be little chance of sport, we proceeded up the river, leaving O'Rourke at his post, with the gaff, to supply the salmon for dinner.

As we ascended the hills by the side of the river, the stream exhausted, the pools motionless and transparent, the mists awfully capping the abrupt and prodigious heights, by which, on all sides, we were surrounded, weary with our walk towards the first lake, which is one of the sources of the stream (a journey undertaken more with the view of marking the ground for future operations, than with any hope of present sport), I dispatched Owen to the solitary house of the hills. It was the habitation of one, who, in this unhappy land, is termed and esteemed a mountain farmer; and within five miles is no other cot. While I uselessly threw a fly on the undisturbed surface, awaiting his return, and ruminating on the solitary grandeur of the scene, a sudden crash of thunder startled me; and, looking towards the heavy ranges of mountain which towered above me, I beheld black and threatening masses, that, in any other country than these regions, would not be described as clouds, but as substantial volumes, portending some grand catastrophe.

I stood on the verge of the stream, on a jutting rock, and turned quickly on these demonstrations from above to reel up my line and prepare for my retreat. There was an air of terror among the cattle, which were here and there scattered about the ledges of the river; and, to my astonishment, the rapidly increasing stream had already encompassed me; a new arm had been formed behind, while the rising torrent threatened me before.

There was a scream of birds, whose wildness seemed to belong to the sea; and I could distinguish human voices between the intervals of thunder. At length I beheld Owen and the farmer, on the opposite side of the river, directing me to some mode of escape which I could not comprehend, and using gesticulations of the utmost anxiety.

I now became seriously alarmed. Crash succeeded crash; the rain fell as in heavy volumes, hardly separated into drops; and I resolved to ford the stream which had grown behind me, not conceiving that so short a period could have so wonderfully increased its depth. The first step convinced me of my error. I slipped from the rock, on which I thought there was safe standing, and was instantly immersed in eight or ten feet of a rapid stream.

The first sensation which I recognised was a blow of some severity on my shoulder. I had met in my quick passage an obstacle, to which the preservation of my life was owing;—it was a sharp ledge of rocks, which formed the barrier to the stream. By one of those prodigious efforts with which in the moment of danger we are endowed, I threw myself out of the course on the bank, and now perceived that the current had already saved me three or four hundred yards of my journey homeward.

Panting and shaken by the roar of thunder above, and the dashing riot of the torrent below, I had but time to remove the blinding water from my eyes ere a fresh danger presented itself in the form of huge masses of rock, which continuously fell into the river, unable longer to endure the sudden shock. A bog was before me, over which I knew it to be impossible to pass; and I resolved to shelter myself, as well as circumstances would allow, by a projecting mass which still braved the current, until some advice or assistance should be offered by Owen, who, I knew, was on the look-out. Then it was, and for the first time in my life, I beheld and felt the power of the mountain storm. The enormous masses of clouds simultaneously burst over my head, and, for the few minutes they were discharging their unequal weight of water, I was still drowning; the torrent being hardly greater below than above me, and all seemed by one sudden convulsion to have become a raging sea.

To ward off the power of the descending cataract, I had covered my head with my hands, and, on my knees awaiting my fate, my arm was suddenly seized and I fell backwards, as I supposed, on some demon of the stream: it was the drowning wretch, who, to save me, had tempted the torrent's danger, and now lay extended on the rock. I raised him in my arms; he

"I RAISED HIM IN MY ARMS."

Facing page 38.

recovered quickly from his exhaustion, and entreated me to swim the lesser stream, as, in a few minutes, one more flood from the mountains would inevitably entomb us both.

Desperation was in the effort: I made it and succeeded, while my faithful mountaineer kept me fast by the waist; and I, being the taller of the two, was enabled to afford him the assistance he needed.

The bog was well known to him. Under his guidance it was soon traversed, and we arrived at the farm-house with no further hurt than some severe bruises and excessive cold.

The effects of these sudden storms were more deplorably manifested on the river Clydah, a stream which falls into the Flesk, and thence into the lower lake of Killarney. It is a shallow and rocky stream, sometimes falling down cliffs and rocks of immense height. Small as it usually is, it was once guilty of terrible destruction.

In the year 1832, the month of June was singularly dry. The 15th of that month put forth the appearance of a brilliant day; the sun shone out in unalloyed splendour, and diffused heat and life around. On the banks of the Clydah might be observed the rustic dwellings of numerous humble families, and in the midst of them the mansion of a gentleman who had devoted himself to the exercise of that hospitality which is almost the distinguishing characteristic of the Irish; at least, of those who are unpolluted by the extravagance of a residence in England. On the morning of the day above mentioned, he was surrounded by his family; the cottagers were enjoying the loveliness of the day; the cattle everywhere grazing on the abundant verdure which covered the slopes towards the river. Suddenly the sun became obscured—the roar of distant thunder shook the dwelling—fear started into every countenance—and, before any had time to communicate with another, a terrific cataract rushed from the mountains, sweeping all before it—bridges, cattle, houses, and their unlucky inhabitants, all hurled to an instant destruction. Such was the fury of the flood, that rocks of fifty tons weight were thrown from the bed of the river into the adjoining fields—the habitations of the poor retained no vestige of their existence—bridges, built on granite, at once disappeared, and the power of the flood reigned supreme. In one hour all was again still. The river assumed its usual form, trickling among the rocks, and here and there forming a slight bay. The sun shone forth with his accustomed splendour; but the inhabitants, whose smiling dwellings had before given a charm to the scene, were no more heard! Every human creature, whose habitation was on the banks of the Clydah, suddenly perished, without warning and without apparent cause.

CHAPTER X

A Mountaineer — Harvest-Hunters — Kerry Agents — Influence of the Catholic Clergy — Causes of that Influence — Safe Travelling in Ireland — Temper of the Irish Peasantry — Means for Improving their Condition — Abundance of Wild Fowl — The Secret — Return to Killarney — Kellorglin — Lake Carraght — Wales's Inn — Fishery on the Carraght River — Lob-Trout — Fishing in Lake Carraght — Disappointment — Seal-Shooting — Castlemaine Bay — Birthplace of Daniel O'Connell — Arrival at Cahirciveen.

THE mountains about Kenmare are of the most wild and stupendous order, and I am in doubt whether the finest of the Swiss scenery in any degree surpasses this. With mine host, whose humble roof had sheltered myself and Owen, I remained the whole day, the waters not having subsided. He was a tenant of Lord ——, whom he had never seen or heard of in the country, further than that he is the proprietor of the soil. This man's condition may be taken as the general one of the mountain serfs. His family consisted of three daughters, an aged mother, a wife, and two infant sons. Being literally without all other provisions, I joined in their meals, which consisted of potatoes alone, poured out on a table with a ledge. The family stood around, and all partook of the humble fare with a kind of contentment and cheerfulness which would, I apprehend, be exhibited by no other persons in the world. The refuse of the meal was carefully collected and applied to the feeding of some fowls, which the daughters kept for the purpose of supplying clothing by their sale. For this purpose alone does any of the family visit a town; and on such occasions they have to traverse an almost trackless country, shoeless. There was *no pig*—the sign of prosperity in an Irish cabin; nor, on inquiry, did I find that any of the cotters could afford to sustain this useful animal.

Notwithstanding the utter destitution of these poor creatures, the man was by no means deficient in intelligence; and, from his inquiries as to what was doing in parliament, and what measures Mr. O'Connell proposed to bring forward in aid of the Irish, I learned that he had the means of acquiring information on these subjects, which were seldom in the power, even in England, of persons so situated. The numerous families we meet with in England, who come over to the harvest, are of this order. He paid £3:10s. for his cottage and plot. Labour was at fourpence per day, when it could be had, and that was seldom, as his own ground required his care at the time labour was in demand.

The plot having been planted, the whole family set off for Cork; this they accomplish by carrying with them as many potatoes as each can bear, and the stock of fowls, which are disposed of at the first town. They find no difficulty in traversing Ireland. Every cabin is open to them, and the sympathy and kindness of the lowest order of Irish poor for each other are worthy of admiration. The duties of charity to their fellow-beings are strongly inculcated by the priests, and it is on this class alone that their instructions appear to have full effect. The houseless and destitute wanderer will seldom want a meal of potatoes, or, at least, a contribution towards one; wherever he applies, his bag is burdened by the addition of a few potatoes, till the whole amounts to a good meal. By this mode of charity, the destitute are sustained from town to town. Their passage-money, by a butter-boat from Cork, is paid from the small proceeds arising from the sale of the fowls; they take, as their sea-store, all the remains of the potatoes first boiled, and generally arrive in Bristol utterly destitute. On the road, one of a party gets employment, and the earnings of one are amply sufficient for the sustenance of the whole. They sleep in hovels, generally by the permission of the farmers through whose grounds they pass on their way to the interior of England; and, I believe, it is but justice to say, that they have on no occasion been found guilty of depredation.

The harvest having commenced, they generally get from two to three shillings a day, all of which they keep with the greatest care, sustaining, sometimes, sixteen hours' labour for successive days, without better sustenance than potatoes and milk afford.[1]

On preparing for return, one of the party carefully sews up the whole of the earnings in some part of his dress least likely to be examined, and they proceed homewards, still exhibiting all the outward destitution which accompanied their arrival. Applications for assistance are regularly made, and generally received at each parish through which they pass homeward; and so careful are they of what small sums are given them in this way, that out of them they frequently make an additional store. Their journey homeward is prosecuted in the same way, assisted by the kind contributions of the poorest, for they never apply to the rich; and, on their arrival, the amount is carefully shared amongst them, and their rents duly paid. By this time their potatoes are fit for digging; and, if the produce be good, the family is sustained by them alone, in the way I have described, for a considerable portion of the year—while the few days' labour at fourpence, or, at best, sixpence per day, serves to eke out the rags which can hardly be said to cover them.

"Is this the way you usually live?" I asked at the end of our second meal.

[1] The use of reaping machines has almost put an end to Irish labour in English and Scottish harvests. Farmers who used to require twenty harvesters can now dispense with more than three or four.—ED.

"Faith is it; sometimes worse when the crops are poor."

"And you live peaceably and cheerfully in this way?"

"Peaceably enough, your honour."

"But you are content?"

"Your honour sees we are content. Content till the Liberator, all honour to him, shall restore our rights—give us labour and its value—not that we shouldn't be content and peaceable without this. Your honour sees the helpless old woman, and the good girls there—better children never breathed. My heart has been sometimes near to breaking when the crop has failed, and they have been obliged to walk every day to the shore, six miles off, to bring each a load of sea-weed as manure, at twopence per load. Many a time have I seen them fainting under their burden; but it was that or death: they are good children."

The poor fellow could hardly refrain from tears, while the daughters, conscious that he was speaking of them, left the hut.

"But why have you not sought the town in the neighbourhood; there would surely be respectable employment for them?"

"That might be, but I wouldn't part with my children, and your honour knows little of the numbers that are already starving in the towns: where would they get kindness or assistance in sickness and distress? In your honour's country there are poor-laws—hospitals; and your people are not left to die; but here are none. I couldn't part with my children, though, God knows, there is little enough for us here, and our English journeys have not been so profitable as formerly: the farmers refuse to employ us since some change about the English poor; and we are a small arrear in rent, which the agent threatens to distrain for. However, the fowls go next week, and we shall make up that. But we are content—we must be content."

"Does the agent take no interest in your welfare?"

"None."

"Does he never call?"

"If the rent is in arrear. The country is bleak, your

honour: there is but one person who traverses these mountains, or feels for the inhabitants in a time of scarcity or of distress."

"And who is he?"

"The priest."

"Does he visit you often?"

"Whenever we require him."

"What remuneration can he receive from you?"

"Remuneration!"

"What do you give for the attendance required of him in sickness?"

"Our thanks, our respect, and our love are all he receives from us; but he has these, and he should have our hearts' blood, if it were wanting to prove that he has them."

This devotion to the priesthood, throughout the south of Ireland, has been the subject of the grossest misrepresentations. Anathemas against their influence and the abuse of it have been uttered in both houses of parliament, at all public meetings, and almost in all societies. To the superstition of the Romish Church is that influence wholly ascribed—the power given by confession, and the utter darkness and ignorance in which its communicants are held, are referred to as sufficiently explaining the source of the blind obedience which is paid to the Irish Catholic clergy.

Religion has nothing whatever to do with it. The influence they enjoy, and everywhere I took occasion to seek information, arises from those causes which—over the minds of an oppressed and starving population, a population not deficient in intelligence and warmth of feeling—would succeed, under any religion, in achieving the same results.

Nothing can be more unjust than the violent attacks made on this generally useful body; and it is to be lamented that those attacks are made in places where they have no opportunity of defence, where the audience is one-sided, and where they themselves are unrepresented. Full of prejudice against their supposed misdeeds, I sought everywhere an introduction to the priests. I found them, I may with truth say, universally well informed; many of them persons of the highest acquirements, yet humble and content with the smallest remuneration—they have no personal wants. They have no families to distract and divide their attention, or to inspire the wish to possess and amass wealth. The donations by which they are supported are voluntary; the performance of their duties, severe as they sometimes are, exemplary. They have, individually, and as a body, but one grand object—the furtherance of the interests of their religion, and the acquirement of the love and respect of their people. That those objects are achieved by the unceasing attention they pay to all, in sickness and distress; at the hour of midnight, called from their beds to traverse a trackless mountain to administer comfort to the sick and dying, where not even the meanest accommodation exists; even under such circumstances the Catholic priest will be found watching by the departing, and comforting the mourners. He is, in such districts as these, the father and the friend. With this what can the form of religion have to do? The complaining Protestant incumbent, who receives for no service, because none is ever called for, the ample income which is drawn from the produce of a soil already overcharged, from the poor earnings of the poorest people in the world, joins in the outcry, so universally set up in England, against the priestly influence—the priestly dictation. Have the Protestant clergy ever used the same means? When did a Protestant clergyman start from his bed at midnight, at the call of a wretched cottager? When did he journey behind his guide over miles of mountains, to administer comfort and the forms of religion to beings in destitution, who have nothing to offer in return but their gratitude. But this is nightly the labour of the priest; in this, and the exercise of the kindly offices to his destitute flock, consists his power; and to the use of that power, in a way deserving, if the truth were known, the highest commendation, is the internal peace of Ireland mainly owing.

While I am on this subject, let me endeavour to remove an impression which militates much and unfairly against the interests of Ireland. The districts on which I now write are little known, because little visited; and, among inquirers on the subject, I have found a distrust of the inhabitants—a suggestion of danger. There is none. Every Englishman may be assured that in no country in the world is he more safe. My route throughout Ireland was out of the ordinary track—the sportsman will always choose the most unfrequented paths—but, during a residence of two summers, spent chiefly in places little known to the English, I never experienced a loss of any kind. The crimes of the Irish poor, destitute as they are, are not those of theft. But were property lost, an application to the priest would immediately be the means of its restoration; a general exhortation at the mass would have that effect, while of personal violence there is no instance. No stranger, I believe, was ever yet molested among them. On the contrary, every cottage would be open for his accommodation; and whatever it contained would be at the service of the traveller.

But let us not be deceived by the notion that the Irish peasantry are or will be content in the state of destitution to which they have been gradually brought; let us not imagine that they are unconscious of the deprivations they suffer, or of the inequality of their lot, in comparison with other nations. They will be found generally intelligent, and even clever—they endure their fate in silence, it may be, but in hope—they look, through their priesthood, to the power of one man—a power, which, originating in the instructions of the priesthood, has been established by a daring perseverance never before exercised in their behalf—a power, which, as long as the oppressions of the people last, will not only endure but increase.

It was said by Cobbett that the cultivation of the potato was a misfortune—I believe it.[1] It is the lowest sustenance to which the human frame can descend—below it, there is nothing

[1] This was written ten years before the great potato famine.—ED.

but death. To this, the absent landlord, the grasping middleman, and the oppressive exaction of tithes, have reduced all the rural districts of Ireland—one step farther, and destitution and despair will be fraught with their natural results. Why should they starve? Why should any people starve? It is against the common law of nature, which is, above all, the law of society. If regard for the law, and obedience to its mandates, bring death—nature cries out, break it, and live. It is a cry not to be resisted—it is a cry that will be obeyed.

Contending interests and factions repress the melioration of the condition of the Irish peasantry. It is not poor-laws, for the peasantry are exemplary in their kindness to their relations—it is not hospitals or subscriptions—it is the residence of their landlords, and employment for a now redundant population. It is the reclamation of lands, to meet the demands of an increasing people—it is the establishment of manufactures on the broad and splendid streams, which everywhere irrigate the country—to give a market for produce, and wages to the labourer. The first of them would produce all the latter—the first would reinstate the poor, and, perhaps, bring the lord of the soil to some slight knowledge of the state of those thousands who starve under his dominion.

The surprise and gratitude which beamed in the countenance of mine host and his wife, as I placed a small sum in the hand of the infant while taking leave, showed how far I had exceeded their expectations, and how little accustomed they were to kindness of any sort. There was an indisposition to receive it, and a protestation that they were too happy to have had the honour of sheltering me; all which being overcome by my request that they would refer to it no more, the man requested to be allowed to accompany us over the mountain pass. I visited again the banks of the river — it had fallen to its ordinary volume—and all the flats were covered with sea-fowl, attracted, no doubt, by the shoals of small white trout, with which the river, after the storm, abounded. Among the rest, the cormorants were numerous, pieces of rock, which jutted from the river, being here and there covered in one dense mass. My gun was now in requisition—so unaccustomed were these animals to any annoyance from man, perhaps even to his sight, that I found no difficulty in approaching a flock, thus settled, and sending the contents of both barrels amongst them. The death of many of their number scarcely disturbed them—they flew upwards, and, in a few moments, again assembled on the same spot. The screams of every class of sea-bird, which followed the report of my gun, conveyed the idea of our being amongst an interminable flock. As we passed down the rocks, following the course of the river, new coveys met us at every turn. It was hard work to load—my powder was becoming exhausted—and I regretted I had not a better supply, as one of the flat pools of the stream exhibited a dark mass of ducks, widgeon, and teal.

"Your honour's our friend?" said my host.

"Certainly."

"It's pity your honour has no powder, and another gun—a heavier gûn would send better—your honour will be secret?"

"You may trust me, safely."

"I will fetch your honour a gun—an old one, but a true one—and powder."

"Where have you these things?"

"Not a man on these mountains but knows where both are to be found. Your honour will own the gun, if any inquiry. God knows when we shall want it." The confidential whisper in which this was conveyed disclosed much of the state of general content in which the Irish mountaineers are held. It would be dangerous to break the peace of such a people.

From Kenmare I returned to Killarney; and, having taken leave of the major, who promised again to join me so soon as I should arrive at Galway, I dispatched Owen with the pony, and followed the course of the town to Kellorglin. This is a singularly interesting walk of twelve miles, though the lower part of the river becomes tame and flat as it approaches the sea. The late rains had greatly swollen the river, which was now clearing, and I was anxious not to lose the golden moment. Trout were abundant; many of good size, notwithstanding the continual netting of this river; and, as I crossed one stream, a tributary to the Laune, about six miles from Killarney, I found the fall, under the bridge, crowded with those fresh run from the sea. A fly was useless—a good worm, well scoured, would have been effectual at this moment—and the best substitute for the resistless bait I offered. I took upwards of forty common trout and sea-trout, from a quarter to a pound and a half, under this fall alone. I met with many anglers—rude ones indeed—they were fly-fishermen, and had met no success. The fish they had taken were all small; and, from observation on all the rivers I have fished, I ever find the smaller size most greedily rise at a fly, while the heavy fish are generally to be found in falls, where the fly could never attract. The bait is, therefore, the only mode of fishing these fastnesses; and, even then, it must be offered with some skill. Much will depend on the weight attached to the line, as trout invariably take the salmon-roe at the bottom. If, therefore, the fall be deep and turbulent, I append a heavy bullet, three feet from the hook; that the former, lodging on the ground, plays the bait in the eddy with such effect as to attract fish even from a hundred yards distance. There is much in this plan. I now approached the sea; the river was still, and subject to the tide. I therefore put up my tackle, and pushed on towards the little town of Kellorglin. All the civilisation of Killarney had vanished; I was now approaching the wildest part of Kerry, where no intercourse with England existed, and where the Irish language was in its native purity. Most of the peasantry, however, understood something of English, and had little difficulty in directing my route.

At Kellorglin will be found a very humble, but not an uncomfortable inn; and, above all, I recommend the angler to spend one evening here, for a very essential purpose, that of procuring flies of a gaudy feather, exactly suited to the fresh-run salmon, among which he may anticipate abundant sport. There is a very ingenious artist at Kellorglin, the only fly-fisher of the place. I sent for him; and, supplying him with hooks and gut, he made for me a dozen salmon-flies, not easily to be surpassed in the delicacy of their construction, and certainly not at all in the attraction they present. He was well rewarded, by a glass of punch and a shilling, for his evening's work.

The Lake Carraght, which is situated about six miles from Kellorglin, is a splendid, though utterly neglected lake; and, in visiting it, the sportsman must lay his account with the loss of all the usual comforts. He should provide himself with necessaries at Kellorglin; and, among other preparations, he must ask leave of the renter of the river to fish the stream up to the lake. This permission, although granted by a person who pays a heavy sum annually for the river-fishing, I believe to Lord Headley, is never denied. On my application, I was informed that the river was quite open to me, and that the renter would have great pleasure in meeting me on the banks, near the weir, in the morning.

The only house on the road towards Cahirciveen, which presents any accommodation, is at Wales's, the bailiff of Lord Headley, which is about seven miles from Kellorglin, and very invitingly situated between two rivers, each about half a mile from the house. One is the Carraght river, the other a mountain stream, of considerable volume; and there is this extraordinary peculiarity attached to them—up the Carraght is found nothing but salmon; I believe there is scarcely an instance of the white trout making up that river; the other is crowded with white trout, and not a salmon disturbs them. Both these rivers fall into the sea, within a mile of each other, behind Wales's house; yet, as by a marine arrangement, the fish never invade each other's dominions.

Wales himself carries on a fishery of considerable extent, at the mouth of the latter river, where, at one draught of the net, it is not uncommon, at the end of May, or the beginning of June, to take from six to seven hundred white trout, some of from three to four pounds in weight. Nor does this appear at all to decrease the supply, so entirely are they unmolested in the river. On my arrival at the little inn, I found that the host was an Englishman, many years, however, resident in Ireland, so many, indeed, that he appeared wholly to have forgotten the relative value of things, and to have adopted, to the fullest extent, the delusion so general among Irish innkeepers, that all the English are afflicted with *l'embarras de richesses*. No doubt a very reasonable agreement might be made with him, as at all other stations; but I, having made none, the more strenuously advise all who follow me to establish a clear understanding of that nature. His house is well situated as a station; and, should the weather be rainy (which in these mountainous districts may generally be expected), exhaustless sport would be found. Here, having established my headquarters, I sallied forth to keep my appointment. I found the proprietor at the weir, accompanied by my ingenious friend, the fly-maker, who had brought the whole of his feathers, for the purpose of suiting the day. From the weir to the sea, it should be known that there is but one lodge for salmon; and, though the distance is a mile, not one will be found at any other spot below the weir. The lodge is a flat, about a hundred yards from the weir; and, though I had fished carefully, from the road upwards, without a rise, no sooner had my fly fallen fairly on that spot, than a fish, of six or seven pounds, rose to meet it. He broke off. It is very difficult to hold the young salmon, especially in streams. Their mouths are tender, and if the hook should not take effect in the bony part of the jaw, they break off at the first struggle. My new friend and myself now began in earnest, and, out of twenty which were hooked in the course of two hours, on the same spot, we were successful in landing only three. One of these I took to Wales's, and, having invited him and the fly-maker to join me, a substantially good dinner was put before us, and ample justice done to it.

It is a mistake to cook salmon quite fresh. The flakes are hard—the oily matter which, by keeping, insinuates itself into the flesh and renders it tender, is curdy. Although fresh salmon is generally sought, and as generally esteemed, a day's hanging is a manifest improvement.

I now visited the river on the other side; and, changing my fly-tackle for the roe, invited my company to view a new style of fishing. They were perfectly incredulous till they saw my success, which, indeed, was almost incredibly great; the late heavy rains having brought the white trout into the river in such abundance, that it was impossible to find a spot, below the bridge, and towards the sea, which possessed not its silvery tenant.

In this river I met a species of trout new to me; it is common, however, in Ireland, and in some of the rivers in Scotland; and appears to be a bastard between the common and the sea, or white trout.[1] It is called a lob. It is found only in brackish water, in such parts of rivers which are frequented by the fish from the sea, as are subject to the tide. On the retirement of the tide, these fish are most ravenous, and may be taken with almost any bait, but especially with the salmon-roe. They are found of three and sometimes four pounds, are exceedingly muscular and violent, but by no means good for the table. I was assured that these fish are so destructive of the spawn of the sea-trout and salmon, that a premium would be given by the proprietors of rivers for their destruction. Certainly, their eagerness for the roe was unprecedented, taking it even from the surface, before it was well in the water. They are less timid than other fish of their species, and would afford sport even in the finest weather, when neither the salmon nor white trout could be moved.

[1] It is now held by the best authorities that this fish is merely the common river-trout (*Salmo fario*) which has acquired an estuarine habit.—ED.

This day deserved to have been marked with a white stone. It was a day of splendid amusement—the success such as would have gratified a wholesale fishmonger—but, alas! the produce here was of no value; after all my labour, and after the exhibition of my pride, in depositing eighteen fine trout at the inn, mine host, with a coolness that almost made him mine enemy, requested the pleasure of my company at his salting-house; where, from one draught at the low water, at the mouth of the same river, that very evening, I beheld a heap of not less than two hundred fish, chiefly of larger size than any I could boast. The chagrin and mortification I experienced were heightened by the smile of all parties, as they took their leave, and bade me good sport.

The Carraght lake, however, was untried, and I dispatched Owen, on the pony, to endeavour to procure a boat, so that it should be ready in the morning, at a certain spot, nearest to the road, or rather pathway, which led to it. A dreary path it is, by the side of the rocky stream, which sometimes falls down heavy precipices, at others, spreads over a vast space; not a tree or shrub to vary the monotony of the vast masses of black stone, which seem to have directed its course. After an hour's difficult riding, early the next morning we arrived at Lake Carraght. There were traditions of trout, of sixty, and even eighty pounds, taken from this water. I was fired with the accounts I heard everywhere, and resolved to try my fortune for the highest prizes alone. Having, therefore, put on our trailing tackle, and young samlets for bait, we set off, keeping, as Owen recommended, the deep courses. Four times round the lake did we industriously row, without an indication of an inhabitant; and it was late ere, wearied and disappointed, we sought the hovel, where the pony had been left, to return to our inn. We could not condescend to attack the white trout in a spot where every retiring tide gave hundreds to the net.

That evening Owen and myself held a council of war. It had been disgraceful to have abandoned so fine a lake. It was clear we had not adopted the right means of fishing it, and I was determined to make a bolder attempt. I was aware that, in many large lakes, the best trout are only to be taken by a ground bait; and this I determined to try. I therefore directed Owen to take some salmon-roe, load it heavily, and endeavour to secure from the river some eels, which, it must be remarked, throughout this part of Ireland are regarded as noxious vermin, not only unfitted for food, but even for sight, so horror-stricken do all the Kerry people appear in their presence. Meanwhile I arranged a stout cord, one hundred and fifty yards long, with a hook of good size at every second yard. This I wound round a deal board of exactly the width of the hooks, so that they were not entangled in the process. Owen was successful in eel-catching, and brought a basket full, with which, the next morning, we started.

On arrival at the lake, my first care was to select two stones, of sufficient weight, for each end of the line. Alternately on the hooks were put a small trout (which are easily caught by the hand, under the stones, in the tributary rivulets) and an eel, cut in two. The line was then sunk, at length, with a large cork, as a buoy, in the middle of the lake. Having done this, we commenced our trailing with better tackle—I say better, for I attributed our want of success, the previous day, to the unskilful arrangement of the bait, which was not properly swivelled. Now, however, I had corrected that error, so that the fish twirled in a most inviting manner; and, being resolved to employ our time like real sportsmen, I directed Owen to row, while I attended the two rods, one from each side the boat, and also threw a line, with four flies of different sizes and colours. This was fishing a lake in earnest; and, I believe, never was success greater. The first fruits were from the flies, and I landed a small salmon; next from the trailing line, both of which were run together; and, in the agitation of the moment, had nearly proved fatal to myself and my companion, as he threw down the oars, forgetting where he was, to seize the rod, which was quietly disembarking itself at the summons of one of the lake monsters.

The anxiety of both, as the fish ran foul, can hardly be described. I blamed Owen whenever his game crossed my line, and he thought it was just possible that I might keep mine clear of his. After some bickerings, blamings, and, I fear, intemperance on my part, Owen landed his fish. It was a lake trout of twelve pounds, which we had both determined to have been thirty—short, thick, black, and ugly—with a mouth almost as large as that of a pike. What my candidate for the honour of the atmospheric region may have been, I cannot tell; he threw himself once out of the water, disengaged himself from the hook, and left nothing but my mutilated bait.

This disappointment, however, did not check our exultation at the safe arrival of Owen's fish. We both burst into a fit of laughter at the appearance of the ugly creature, while Owen assured himself and me that there were trout still to be caught in that lake of seventy pounds, and that we had only received this as an instalment.

We now proceeded to take up the dead line; and, flushed with our recent achievement, I will not attempt to describe how anxiously we drew up this buoy rope. On raising the stone towards the boat, a struggling power, which I could hardly resist, indicated the presence of some of the lake monsters. Yard after yard was hauled in—I paused—Owen swore it was one of the celebrated trout. I thought so till the line reached the surface and betrayed a dark-coloured and ferocious-looking eel, of seven pounds. The butts of our rods were now in requisition; and, after a flagellation that would have been ill sustained by any other creature, he was landed; next hook, still a struggle; an eel again—again and again. As I proceeded, however, a dash was made that showed the presence of a more vivacious creature. I held on the line in the utmost anxiety—I brought it to the surface—it was, indeed, one of the lake monsters, of which we had been so laboriously in pursuit—but I had no power to govern him—for a while darting ahead—then towards the stern—now leaping from the water, and falling with an appalling splash—at length, he made one dart under the boat—one of the hooks caught—the line broke, and our hope was

FREED FROM RESTRAINT, WE SAW HIM ONCE MORE.

annihilated. Freed from restraint, we saw him once more dash from the surface, and then disappear for ever.

Who shall paint our mortification. Owen's countenance, always lengthy, was greatly elongated. I stood in surprise for a moment, drew in the remainder of the line in an affected resignation, but spoke no word. I motioned Owen to row towards the shore, quietly packed up my tackle, and we proceeded on our road homeward. I dared not trust myself to speak—all our arrangements were made in silence—nor was it till we had half accomplished our journey to the inn, that Owen ventured to hint *that it was a large fish.*

" What fish ? "

" The trout your honour lost."

" I lost ? "

" No; that the line lost. By St. Patrick, he was a rale one."

" It is impossible to say."

" Sixty, at least, your honour. I knew him by the breadth of his tail; his tail was broader than both my hands."

" You think so."

" I saw him a dozen times."

" Owen, say no more about him; he was a large trout. If we told the story, we should hardly gain credit, and neither of us any satisfaction from reciting our ill-luck—let us forget it—but that trout was the largest of the lake."

On arrival at our inn, we found our host busily employed in boiling down seals for their oil. This led me to inquire, and I soon learned that they abounded along the Castlemaine bay. I therefore ordered the gig early, and made preparations for an attack. The road from Wales's to Cahirciveen is now excellent, and perhaps one of the most picturesque in Ireland; sometimes elevated on eminences, above the beautiful green bay, from which, on a calm day, can be seen the fish scudding over the white patches of sand. Not a hut interrupts the wildness of this lovely region, which I passed through on a singularly fine morning. Whenever the shore, which it frequently does, approached the road, I left Owen in charge of the gig, and beat out my own track among the rocks. Although I could frequently see the seals, mounted on little jutting eminences, before I could creep towards them, within the distance of two or three hundred yards, they splashed into the sea. At length, when the curve of the bay suddenly presented me no less than ten or twelve, of all sizes, I rushed towards the sea to intercept them. They had the benefit of both barrels among them; but, failing to strike the head of any, nothing but the rising blood on the wave showed that my load had taken effect.

Although unsuccessful with the seals, I was not so with the cormorants, puffins, and teal. The abundance of these birds supplied continual sport, although it is to be lamented that the useless birds predominate greatly. The teal were shy and few.

We now passed the bridge, which leads over the river, forming the little harbour of Cahirciveen. Here I resumed the bait-tackle, and found tolerable sport, among a small-sized white trout, which were now abundant in all the rivers of this district. As we approached Cahirciveen, the black and desolate mountains of Iveragh broke through the clearing atmosphere; while the sun, now flashing on the broad Atlantic, presented a scene of wild splendour. I now deemed that I had, indeed, reached those regions into which no civilisation had yet penetrated,—immense tracts of uncultivated bog, abruptly broken by a sudden mountain, behind which another of greater elevation rears its head, itself again and again succeeded by masses, if possible, still more black and awful in their combinations.

Little as this road is traversed, considerable sums have been expended on it; and, assuredly, its boundaries present sites for marine residences of an extraordinary beauty. The view over the Castlemaine bay, of the Atlantic, and, in the distance, the fairy island of Valencia, possesses a rare combination.

If I were to fix on a spot where I would hope to pass the rest of life's fitful dream, in quiet retirement, it would be impossible to select one of more accumulated advantages.

On the right, between the road and the arm of the sea, which receives the Cahirciveen river, is Cashen—now, alas! a ruin—used only for the occasional shelter of cattle. It is prettily situated, and was once the residence of the chief proprietor of much of the surrounding country. It was the hospitable mansion of the father of that extraordinary man, who is now inextricably associated with all the destinies of Ireland. It was the residence of the father of O'Connell.

I could not pass this spot without a closer examination; the now unglazed window of that room in which the "best abused man in the world" first drew breath was pointed out; and I paused, to carry with me a faithful reminiscence of so interesting a spot. My sketch occupied some time; and, on its completion, I walked towards the ruin. I disturbed my *fidus Achates*; Owen was on his knees, uttering a prayer for the welfare and success of his country's indomitable friend. As what he uttered was in Irish, I had some difficulty in arriving at the substance of his orisons. "Your honour will forgive an Irishman. Long life to him who liberated Ireland!"

"What benefit has the liberation bestowed on Ireland, Owen?"

"Is it your honour asks that question in earnest?"

"In earnest."

"Sure it is not for the likes of me to tell your honour what the O'Connell has done for his country—the world knows it. Faith, it's to him we owe that your honour's parliament ever cared about us at all. It's to him we owe that your honour visits our country and inquires about us; and it's to him we owe that we are represented at all in the master country, which conquered us, and kept us under martial law for many a day. Oh, it's meself that remembers the time when a candle shouldn't be lighted, but a troop of soldiers would hunt in upon us and abuse us. Oh, we were slaves then, any way."

"But how has O'Connell remedied all this?"

"Long life to him, and he has remedied all he can. We may have a light, if we please, now; and we may walk about, without being stopped by the soldiers; and it'll not be long before we get law and justice, and Catholic magistrates, that will believe the truth from a Catholic. Oh! the devil fly away with all Protestant magistrates that find all Catholics guilty!"

"And do you believe the Protestant magistrates so decide?"

"Faith, and your honour may say that. Sure all the world knows it. If we had among us a spalpeen who would swear anything but the truth, he had only to turn Orangeman and

From a painting by R. Allen.

THE BIRTHPLACE OF O'CONNELL.

Protestant; he couldn't swear too stoutly or too much. O'Connell has smashed the Orangemen, and an honest man may now have law, and sometimes justice."

That this was a feeling too generally disseminated, whether justly or not, was evident; that there had existed grounds for such impressions, may be readily inferred. It must not be imagined that the services of O'Connell are not understood by the Irish. Frequently have I been astonished by observations from the poorest class, which have betrayed more judgment than even the refined London press has sometimes exhibited, in discussing the groundwork of his popularity and influence. The frequent announcements of the decline of that influence, from some ill-explained or party squabble, can create nothing but a smile in the traveller who has made himself acquainted with the firm reliance placed in him. The reproaches of mendicity, which seem to constitute the standing thesis of abuse, "pass by him like the idle wind." He is no beggar; he had, long before he received one farthing from his countrymen, in the way of contribution, added to the independence bequeathed him, a fortune, and a fame that was better than fortune; an income, that, with half the personal labour he now undergoes, would have ensured a more certain, and, perhaps, not more contracted income than he now receives from his countrymen. If he receives, like a beggar, he has the redeeming quality of spending like a prince. He is not rich, nor can ever be so; his hospitality and devotion to his country's interests forbid it.

We now passed the handsome mansion of Charles O'Connell (late member for Kerry, and son-in-law of the O'Connell), and a handsome erection, that seemed to stand forth as an example of the use to which the noble streams, which everywhere irrigate this part of the country, might be applied. It was a mill, built and carried on by a relation of O'Connell's. A few minutes more brought us into Cahirciveen. It is a pretty town, for Ireland; and the appearance of comfort which pervades it at once evinced the power of resident proprietorship. In 1815, the entire village consisted of fifteen houses, and those of a mean order. Now will be found two streets, some handsome shops and buildings, a good inn, and vessels, of one hundred tons, at the quay, and between 1500 and 2000 inhabitants; perhaps the most peaceful, increasing, and prosperous spot that Ireland can boast. Such is Cahirciveen; in the wilds of Iveragh, without the local advantages of direct roads to any large market, but with the paramount benefit of a considerate and popular landlord.

CHAPTER XI

Cahirciveen — Comfortable Inn — John O'Connell — Portrait of the Liberator—Mountain Hunting—A Sportsman's Breakfast—The Mass—State of Crime in Kerry—Party Feuds—The Lawlors and Cooleens—A Smasher—The River Inny—Waterville Lake—Courtesy of Mr. Butler—Live Lamb for Dinner—Produce of the Weirs—A Deathbed Scene.

From Killarney, 40 miles; from Tralee, 36 miles; from Dublin, 183 miles; from Waterville Lake, 6 miles; from the River Inny, 3½ miles.

THE town of Cahirciveen is of very recent origin—it bears all the marks of rapid improvement—the houses recently erected, and of a handsome structure. Its situation is singularly beautiful, being sheltered by the island of Valencia, and having a navigable river of two miles. It is protected from the great northern storms by the range of mountains composing the district Iveragh, and affords a site, particularly adapted to embrace the commerce (such as it is) of the whole southern coast of Ireland. Here is a comfortable inn, kept by no less a person than John O'Connell, Esq., one of the many cousins of the renowned member; although I say kept by him, I must have it distinctly understood that he interferes *not* in that or any other portion of the business which is carried on under his name. He is, at once, a wine and whiskey merchant, storehouse-keeper, and general dealer. At his store may be found almost any matter of convenience, and even of luxury. His house, which he has himself erected at considerable expense, furnishes rather the hospitable mansion of the friend, than the venal accommodation of the innkeeper. This is, by no means, an uncommon combination of trades and character amongst some of the Irish districts; and, after having afforded you all the accommodation which you could reasonably expect or desire, you are left rather to form your own estimate of the expense, than be made subject to any charge; indeed, so unreasonably moderate were the expectations of the host, that it became necessary to add voluntarily to the carte, in order to constitute a fair remuneration; nor will the traveller find, in putting up at this inn, if I may so term it, any want of education or intelligence in his landlord; whom, however, he must not scruple to meet on terms of equality, which will not be long ripening into those of friendship. Here the traveller will find what is not common in Ireland—excellent beds, and a snugly-furnished room. Over the mantelpiece, the first object which struck my attention was a large print of Daniel O'Connell, Esq., framed, but not glazed. Daniel appeared in his travelling-cap, for an indulgence in which the *Times* newspaper did not forget to assail him with all the epithets of puppyism; there was, however, a somewhat *outré* addition to his face, as it appeared over mine host's fireplace, and indications of war, not, as it should seem, very congenial with his interests, had been liberally added; I mean a pair of large mustachios, obviously appended by the hand of an unskilful artist; and, lest the characteristic of his country should be wanting, an enormous pipe was stuck into his mouth. Aware of the high veneration that is, throughout these districts, accorded to the great original, my curiosity was excited to discover how this contemptuous mark of disrespect had arisen: it appeared that, a few days before my arrival, some officers had been quartered in the peaceful town of Cahirciveen, and, as a matter of necessity, had taken up their residence at O'Connell's, there being no similar accommodation at least within twenty miles. After having partaken of the best the house could afford,

"The cry of the lad warns them to watch in all directions."

perhaps not having been too chary of the excellent whiskey, which was always there to be found, these *soi-disant* gentlemen had amused themselves by offering, perhaps, the only insult in their power, to what they considered the democratic landlord; and, after their retirement to bed, the indignation of their otherwise hospitable host had been displayed by turning them all into the street; in this, it appears, he had met at first some resistance, but, before so athletic and powerful a form, little in the way of personal objection could be opposed, and those who had wantonly offered this unprovoked insult were glad to make the humblest apology which meanness could suggest, before they were readmitted. The insult, however, was not to be wholly pardoned, even by apology, and the next day freed the house of the aristocratic warriors.

Perhaps there is no one who enjoys greater general esteem among his friends than Mr. John O'Connell, and he may rank among his most intimate the chief of his name. I was shown several dogs, and, on the second day after my arrival, found my excellent host prepared to give me a day up the mountains. Starting at four in the morning, in about two hours we reached a summit of one of the gigantic and almost trackless mountains of Iveragh, and overhanging the broad expanse of Lake Waterville, of which I shall hereafter speak. The view at the opening of day was magnificent; the silence unbroken but by the cries of the numerous wild-fowl that hovered over the surface of the water. The process of hunting in these precipitous districts, where the hares abound, is thus conducted. A small terrier is dispatched under the charge of a lad, accustomed to the dangerous crags which afford shelter to the victim: the hunters and the greyhounds remain stationary till the cry of the lad warns them to watch in all directions; as soon as the hare appears, the dogs are loosened, and the scramble then is among the sportsmen to the highest crag to obtain the best point of sight. So fatigued, indeed, would one unaccustomed to this sport be, that I was compelled to entreat my leader to desist, after three excellent runs, killing two hares; but, alas! we found we had four Irish miles to walk before we could gain even the humblest roof.

This is the sport of Daniel O'Connell, who, as soon as released from the anxieties of political turmoil, with the utmost gladness escapes to his retreat at Derrynane (about six miles from Lake Waterville). Day after day will he be first to rouse the slumberers—his fellow huntsmen: it will not be uninteresting to give an account of the last day's sport of this kind, which he enjoyed in the year 1838.

At four, he was found at the window of John O'Connell, rough in his dress, and wholly Irish in his manner and brogue. "Hurrah, boy; the day will be over, any way, before you're up." John, recognising his cousin's voice, was in a few minutes by his side, accompanied by three pairs of greyhounds, in which Daniel took the utmost pride; off to the mountains trudged the Liberator, beating, in his strides, even his brawny and athletic companion; they stepped over the ledges of rocks, which overhang immense ravines, with the lightness of a boy, and, by his shouting and hilarity, manifested a lightness of heart which would hardly be reconcilable with one whose mind must have been charged with so many heavy considerations. Equal even to the fatigues which in his boyhood these mountains had so abundantly created, and entering into the sport with every demonstration of delight, it was not till long after his companion had surrendered that he proposed adjourning for refreshment. Having accomplished the journey to the house of Mr. B——, who resides at the head of Waterville lake, the two sportsmen sat down to breakfast. I shall be minute in describing the statesman's. First, a large bowl of new milk, which instantly disappeared; then a liberal allowance of cold salmon, soaked in vinegar—a very common dish—of this he ate very heartily; after which he finished a bottle of port wine, took leave of his entertainers, and set off to walk six miles to his home.

I am not aware that any commixture could be more iniquitous, nor that any would have agreed better with the stomach of the Liberator.

Dura ilia messorum !

How much of all that has been achieved in battle, in the senate, at the bar, has been owing to a strong digestion. How many thousands have sunk under the bare difficulty of facing, without trembling, the apprehended evil! How often the weakness of the nervous energies alone depresses powers capable of the highest objects! It is not unreasonable to refer the phlegmatic contempt of reproach, the indomitable perseverance through every difficulty, the moderation under success, and the calm determination under adversity, so manifestly the distinguishing characteristics of Daniel O'Connell, to a strength of digestion, seldom the concomitant of the great mental acquirements which are conceded to him by all parties.

On Sunday I attended, first, the established church, which is a neat little edifice; a rectory of about £600 or £700 a year, but, as usual, the rector is an absentee—residing, I believe, in France, while the duties were performed by a curate. Our congregation consisted of about seven persons, among whom were the official Protestants, I mean the policemen. Yet, the service was performed in an exemplary manner; and I had the pleasure of receiving from the clergyman an early visit. The mass, however, presented a congregation of upwards of two thousand persons, collected from all parts of the mountains; hundreds walking shoeless many miles to attend the solemnity. I afterwards became acquainted with the priest, and found in him a mild and amiable man, with none of the pugnacious and anathematising spirit which is so generally represented as the characteristic of the Catholic clergy. On the contrary, he had obtained the veneration and love of his numerous and scattered communicants, by the same means that have been so successful elsewhere—by the spotlessness of his private character, and his devotion to the religious consolation of the poorest as well as richest of his flock. It would be difficult to find him absent at the time of distress; he knew all his communicants, and they knew him. He did not, however, visit them in a carriage, or refuse a midnight attendance on the most destitute of his mountain dependants.

Nothing, up to this part of my journey, could be more subordinate, obliging, and kind, than the conduct of the peasantry; and I looked in vain for any of those exhibitions of violence which fill our newspapers. In answer to all the inquiries I made, I found no one who could recount any atrocities which could have justified Mr. Inglis, in his book on Ireland, in the expression of his wonder at the gross amount of a Kerry sessions. The numbers, as he places them, indeed *look large*, if the offences be not nicely discriminated: they were, in his time, for one quarter, 199! and "of these," as he says, "174 cases implying the undue exercise of physical force." Yet, on examination of his own account, there were but ten for larceny, all the other cases being riotous assembly, Hibernicé, a row, and the cracking of divers heads at a "pattern." *Ten* only, in his own list, are set forth as even *charged with crime;* but "these cases implied the undue exercise," etc.: that is a very awful announcement, and well calculated to promote the views of a rabidly Tory newspaper, and prevent the benefits arising from English visitors who would, if the beauty of this and most of the stations in Kerry were well known, and the truth relating to them ascertained, crowd to Ireland instead of the Continent.

The Irish peasantry are very much addicted to the "undue exercise of physical force" among each other. At a "pattern" (patron saint's day), which is a fair, where vast numbers assemble for all purposes — hiring and being hired — of meeting old friends and separated relatives—of purchasing or selling—the whiskey does its mischief. Stick-combats are the consequence; and a broken head or two are healed by shaking hands with the head-breaker, and being better friends than ever. There is, indeed, a kind of feud which must be spoken of more seriously; I mean the assembly of clans for the purpose of trying their strength against each other; although much of this has been, by the exhortation of the priesthood, abolished, yet a feeling of rivalry and jealousy has been handed down to the clans, which it seems almost impossible to subdue. The Rathkenny riots did much to impress the peasantry with the dreadful consequences of these feuds, and I have heard of no subsequent outbreak. That, indeed, was a terrible affair. The Lawlors and the Cooleens were parties, between whom had been nurtured a feud of centuries' standing. Neither party knew the offence of the other, but a boast that a Lawlor was a better man than a Cooleen was sufficient to awaken implacable ire. In 1834, the two parties met at Rathkenny; a regularly ordered combat ensued, till, at length, the Lawlors gave way, and made towards the river in retreat, to which they were pursued by the conquerors. To avoid the stones and blows of the pursuers, too many crushed into the boats, which were overset, and forty persons, chiefly young men, were drowned. It is but just to the Cooleens to say, that, at the occurrence of this distressing misfortune, none could be more active than themselves in giving assistance to the drowning rivals, and but for their assistance many more must have perished.

Although this catastrophe gave occasion for sweeping condemnation of the Irish, when calmly considered, it will be, by the unprejudiced, regarded rather as a misfortune than a crime. The conquerors had never contemplated the effect which ensued; the circumstance had occurred in the hereditary rivalry, which excited an annual trial of strength and skill. But even these exhibitions have given way to the better instruction the people have received.

While, however, I speak generally in favour of the peaceable and subordinate dispositions of the Kerry peasantry, I cannot omit to notice one crime that did come under my own observation. Whatever atrocity is contained in it will be well extracted, and put forth by some noble marquis or Tory hireling.

An old man, whose bald head was streaming with blood, was introduced to the magistrate. In the custody of the constable was, also, a strong, good-humoured-looking fellow, who seemed anxious to tell his tale. The injured party, however, was directed to state his case, which he did, by assuring the magistrate that he was peaceably going to his home, at Currane, and had met the prisoner. He had "given the time of day to him," and walked on; the sun being very hot, he had taken off his hat for *coolness*, when, to his surprise, without the least warning, and without having offered the least provocation, he received a blow on his head from a stick, which felled him to the ground. The magistrate indignantly demanded what excuse the prisoner could have for so unprovoked an assault upon an old man. The prisoner considered for some time; at length, he burst out into the following defence:—

"It's true, your honour, as the ould man says; he passed me on the road, and, just at that moment, took off his hat, and showed the most beautiful shining head; the sun lit upon it, as it bobbed up and down in the ould man's gait. By the powers, all the blood came to my fingers at such a head; oh! what an elegant head intirely for a crack, sis I; and, before I could consider, your honour, I had fetched him the smasher, and sure your honour's self could hardly have done less, may be, if your honour had been unluckily thrown into so powerful a timptation."

It is needless to say that the powerful temptation did not operate as a justification, and the smasher of impulse was consigned to a fortnight's durance.

The river Inny, which lies between Cahir and Waterville Lake, will be found worth exploring by the angler. In August, I am told, it is literally crowded with sea-trout; and, indeed, I found abundant sport at an earlier period. It is a drawback, however, that not even the humblest inn can be found in its neighbourhood, and it must either be visited from Waterville or Cahir, at both which stations the sport is superior. The Inny, therefore, is little known; and I question if one angler in a year visits it. It may be said to be a maiden river; and, though dreary, the walk along the banks of the lower part, and the rocky crags of the mountainous passes, through which it runs, will be found replete with all the wild scenery which here abounds.

Three miles farther on, and the summit of a hill at once discloses the broad expanse—the deep, sullen, and dark waters of Waterville Lake. From this summit its whole extent may be viewed, which stretches five miles in length, and is divided only by a small river, if it can be so called, of five or six hundred yards long, from the bay of Ballinskelligs, which adds its cerulean beauties to the gorgeous beauties of the scene. At first, the stranger is impressed with an idea that the lake itself is nothing more than an arm of the sea; the fall is ten or twelve feet only from it to the bay, but sufficient to protect it from the influence of the tide, and affording, for the whole tribe of the genus salmo, an easy transition from the salt to the fresh water. A small cluster of cottages, which forms the newly-arisen village of Waterville, and situated at the very edge of the fall, covers from the view the mansion of Mr. Butler, whose property the short but productive river is, and whose house is almost attached to the profitable fishery.

Having secured my lodging, which consisted of a single room, the only one vacant in the village, and which was, indeed, the lodging of the priest of this district, who was then absent on one of his rural peregrinations, I dispatched a note to Mr. Butler, requesting permission to fish the river. To this I received a courteous and immediate reply, containing full leave to do so; and having sent also for Segueson, the only fisherman of the place, Mr. Butler's boat was put at my disposal for the lake. The next thing was a selection of flies. If supplied with the materials, I found Segueson an excellent hand; he knew the exact colours above and below the fall; and having learned the particulars that, at the head of the lake, there were two rivers, both celebrated for trout, that the lake itself was redundant in sea-trout and the heavy brown lakers, as they are called, I proceeded to arrange my swivels, and prepare for the morrow's attack. My commissariat was not so easily arranged; there was nothing to be bought; the nearest market for bread was Cahirciveen—as for all the other *necessary luxuries*. I dispatched, therefore, the running messenger, who should not be forgotten; he is the Waterville postman, and, without a shoe, has, I believe, for years, run twenty miles a day without an intermission. My inquiries for the butcher's supply, for I had really lived on trout and salmon till I was tired, was met by a stare of surprise. I learned, however, that, by giving due notice, lamb might be had from the mountains. At this prospect I cheered, and requested the requisite notice might be given. On the following morning, my *ancilla* announced its arrival, and I was luxuriating by anticipation on the splendid dinner it was to afford.

"Would your honour wish to see the man?"

"By all means; let him bring in the lamb also."

After waiting a few minutes, open flew the door, and in bounced a lovely little creature, which, for a moment, stared me in the face, and then ran to hide under the table.

"Why, the lamb is alive!"

"I drove him and carried him seven miles down the mountain for your honour, as word was sent up last night."

"Why, what am I to do with a whole lamb?—What is the price?" It was a very fine one.

"Why, it's dear any way, your honour—three shillings is the price, but, as I have had a good step to bring him, perhaps your honour would not be backward in giving three and sixpence."

Three and sixpence was paid, to the delight of the mountaineer, who had doubtless exceeded the market-price by a shilling; and the little trembler was soothed into confidence—not converted into a meal. He became my attached companion during my stay, sharing every meal with an acquired air of right, for, if he were not first attended to, he adopted the offensive style—butted at my legs, and pulled off the scanty table-cloth. On my departure from the country, I made a present of him to a gentleman, who assured me that he would never part with him, and that he should have full liberty in his fields for life. I heard afterwards that he had fulfilled his promise, in giving the little fellow ample liberty, but that the object of his kindness had soon lost all his engaging and impudent tricks, and had become quite sheepish.

I walked down to the weirs, the produce of which amounts, as I am informed, to £700 or £800 per annum. In four traps it is not uncommon to take from 500 to 600 fish, nightly, in the full salmon season; and, perhaps, a more astonishing sight could not be presented than the shoals of these creatures, one over the other, constituting, in their confined cells, almost a solid mass; the boiling stream, which rushes through the bars of their prison-house, keeps them not only alive, but perfectly well, till the arrival of the higglers, who take them alive up the mountains, and to the towns, many miles distant. None, I believe, reach England. The land-carriage is too great, and they have no means here of pickling or preserving, otherwise than by common salt. But, when the length of the river, from the weirs to the sea, is considered—not greater than 400 yards—that immense sport will be found for the angler, in that short run, will easily be believed.

It had rained the whole day; and, towards the evening, I mounted the salmon-roe, determined to try its effect on fish just up from the sea. The water was a little discoloured, and highly favourable to my experiment. A more glutting evening I never spent. The moment the bait was in the water, it was seized; and I believe that I should have had no difficulty, had my industry kept pace with my success, in loading a donkey with white trout of all sizes. I was obliged to change my situation for salmon, four of which I caught on the same evening. I will not attempt to depict the surprise of Segueson, at whom Owen directed continual gibes, as the fish made their appearance on shore; the former had never seen or even heard of the salmon-roe, nor could divine what charmed compost it was. He protested that, on such an evening, the most skilful fly-angler would not have secured a fish. But here, also, the same disappointment arose; the fish were of no value, as the poorest cottagers, whose food is the potato, and generally that alone, care little for fish, which abounds under their very doors.

On returning to my lodging, my attention was arrested by an arrival, indeed extraordinary in these parts; it was absolutely a post-chaise, and contained two gentlemen, who had fully expected to have found some magnificent hotel. As it was, there was neither food nor stable for horses, nor accommodation for themselves, beyond that which a cabin and two beds, or a wet mud-floor, could supply. Like true anglers, however, they had not been deterred from the prosecution of their sport by such small hindrances; wisely judging that, where *the fish are*, the fishermen commonly *are not*. As soon as I thought the arrangements were complete, I assumed the superior, because the first arrived tenant, and invited the strangers to partake of the preparations made in my own little camp, perfectly convinced that they must otherwise have remained destitute till the morning: they very gladly accepted my invitation. They were Irish gentlemen; one, I believe, an eminent surgeon of Cork; a fact which he had in confidence communicated to me, as it was by no means his wish that he should be professionally called on. This, however, did happen; for, as my attendant, a little fat Irish girl, brought in "the matarials," she was in tears. On inquiry, I found that "the spirit of Patrick Macguire was passing," and that all the village had assembled to view the solemn sight. There was no getting at the nature of his illness, or the object of the assembling of so many persons. I looked at my companion and solicited his inquiry. "I was afraid of this," said he, "but I must go." Sending, therefore, for his little package, in which he always kept a few common drugs, we sallied forth to the cabin.

What a scene was there! In a mud hut, with a small hole, covered with paper, for a window, had congregated, at least, fifty persons of all ages, relatives and friends. The widow, by anticipation, was, with her face covered with her apron, rocking herself on a chair by the fire; the crippled grandam occupied the other side, seated on an inverted tub; while knots of busy talkers crowded round the straw couch of the dying man. No one offered to assist him; his spirit was passing, and it was all hopeless to interfere.

The first act of my friend was to clear the hut; this was not done without my assistance. I was obliged to explain that the gentleman was a medical man, whom I had brought; that air was the first requisite for the sick man. Incredulity seemed to mark the countenances of all, as they sullenly left the cabin. We then broke the windows open, and proceeded to examine the man, *whose spirit was passing*. It was now ascertained by my friend that he was in the last stage of a kind of cholera; no remedies had been applied, nor sustenance, but of the usual kind, offered. The poor fellow was dying of exhaustion, not of disease. No sooner had a little brandy, and a few drops of laudanum been given him, than he rallied greatly. Boiled milk, in very small quantities, was ordered to be given hourly, and my humane companion promised to see him again that night. On our return with that object, we found the hut crowded as before, at which both I and the surgeon expressed serious anger; but we failed in making the people understand that there was any possible chance of existence for one *whose spirit was passing*.

Their astonishment and gratitude, however, at discovering that poor Patrick Macguire was not only living the following day, but rapidly recovering, were fatal to my friend's amusement. The fame of this salvation of a dying man travelled with wonderful swiftness through the mountains, and, in the evening of that day, the door of his cabin was beset with the halt, infirm, and diseased. It was useless to protest against such an attack ; each case was introduced by such humility and earnestness that resistance was in vain, and the mud cot became the dispensary of a district of seven miles, during the remainder of the visit of the professional angler. He assured me that he had never, from any previous experience, thought it possible that such dreadful effects could follow from want of the due application of the simplest remedies, as numerous instances disclosed in this district. The disease most prevalent, and, to the sufferers, generally fatal, was rheumatism ; the patient required only to be removed from the wet mud floors, well clothed, kept warm and dry, to be restored to the use of those limbs which had wasted to nothing from want of action ; paralysis, arising from the watery diet on which they fed ; young cripples, whose distorted limbs had never been set after a fracture, all combined to show how necessary the extension of the provision the government has made, with regard to medical attendance on the poor, has become.

If I were a surgeon or physician, and contemplated retirement from the remunerative exertion of my profession, and were desirous of spending my latter days as usefully as possible to my fellow-creatures, and as happily to myself, I would not stick up a cockney dwelling in the neighbourhood of some large town ; I would drop on the romantic mountains of Iveragh, where the charitable exercise of my art would unite with the beauties of Nature to create a happiness, which none but those who can estimate life's value, by the power it gives of assisting our fellow-creatures, can enjoy.

CHAPTER XII

Enormous Eagle—Fishing in Waterville Lake—Morning-Breakfast—Island Burial-Ground—Funeral—A New Friend—The White Strand—Anecdote of the Duke of Wellington—Round Tower—Mullet-fishing—An Extempore Fishing Yacht—The Knight of Kerry—Colony of Fishermen—Fishing Arrangements—A Night's Fishing—An Unexpected Prize—Paddy Shea—The Perfection of Sport—A Great Haul—Cormorant Soup—Threatening Weather—Irish Superstition—A Storm—Courage of the Irish Fishermen—Dangers and Escapes—A Dance—An Event—Dangers of the Irish Coast—Frightful Scene of Shipwreck—A Suspicious Visit—Irish Smugglers.

AFTER the heavy rains of the preceding day, what angler but would arise to greet the morning sun, gorgeous as he appears, shedding his brilliant flashes on the regenerated pastures, which present a green carpet over all the scene, save only where huge and parti-coloured masses arise in independent grandeur, the impervious abodes of the wild sea-fowl, the eagle, and the fox.

Owen was at my window by four. The lines were all ready, having been well baited with small trout, which he had taken by hand in the streams. The swivels were on; Segueson had made the flies; our day's provisions were prepared, and, with as much delight as the anticipation of a glorious day could inspire, we rowed up the flat river which leads into the lake. The boundary is marked by some scattered rocks, which divide the stream from a long plain of bog; just as we arrived at this spot, a caution was given by Segueson; he seized the gun; our oars had scarcely ceased a moment, when a wild scream, and the discharge of both barrels, startled me. "Hurrah!" exclaimed Segueson; "down at last. St. Patrick, and he's an ould offender; row on, row on, take care of your legs." In a moment we were on shore, and I was in the midst of a danger I had little apprehended. A wounded eagle, of the largest size, lay screaming on the ground; there was life enough left to render him dangerous, as he crawled, or rather jumped towards us, flapping his enormous wings, and with revenge and mischief in the furious expression of his eye. The savage nature of this animal was never so powerfully exemplified. One snap with the beak had been enough to sever an arm from one's body;[1] by stones, the butt-end of the gun, and oars, he was at length dispatched.

He had been long and unfavourably known on this lake. Thousands of chicken, fowls, and salmon, had been buoyed in the air to serve his annual family, whose habitation no one dared approach. Segueson declared that there was a tradition of his having carried off children, and that his age was undoubtedly above a hundred years. However that might have been, it certainly was the largest of the largest kind of eagle, and, when erect, must have carried his head between three and four feet from the ground. I regretted that no one understood the art of stuffing; and, after several trials myself, I was satisfied to retain his feet in token of the victory; which I afterwards had, mounted in silver, converted into the handles of bell-ropes. The body of the noble marauder was consigned to the dogs of Mr. Butler. I fear they found him tough. We now advanced to the middle of the lake, and, under Segueson's direction, cast our baited long line, put out the swivels, and proceeded to throw our flies; Owen being pilot, and gently rowing the boat, so as to give full play to the swivels.

The flies were quickly successful, at every cast small white trout or those of the lake were landed—but no indication of any of the lake monsters. Twice had we made the likely course

[1] It is a pity that the author has marred this part of his story with such a gross exaggeration.—ED.

and no run. The sun had now become powerful, and a proposition was made that we should visit the beautiful island, which is one of the most remarkable ornaments of the lake. Within twenty yards of the landing-spot, both swivels were simultaneously run. I seized one rod, Owen the other; the length of line which was out gave us little power; the two fish darted across each other, and were in great danger of entangling and breaking the lines. Mine, at twenty yards distance, gave a leap, at least three yards from the surface; and, before I could provide against the shock of his fall, he had thrown his whole weight into the water, and departed with swivels, hooks, and a great portion of my line. I now assisted Owen, who had a less mercurial subject to deal with, and, after some time, landed a fine lake trout of eleven pounds. This formed a valuable addition to our contemplated meal; he was crimped and hung by the tail, while Segueson made the fire by the side of the ruined chapel, whose roofless walls contained myriads of human skulls.

Here I will describe a morning repast. First, a large iron pot, slung by three sticks over a good clear turf-fire; well washed, but not skinned potatoes; a fowl, split and well seasoned, and a crimped trout of eleven pounds—hot, even unto burning; plenty of lake water, clear as crystal; and finally, an infusion of the best Cork whiskey. All this, on a lovely island in the middle of the lake, a delicious warmth, a glowing sun, and appetite from exercise and free ocean air, which gently ripples the surface of the waters, who shall demand "what are the pleasures of the sportsman?"

Amidst the enjoyment of all this, I was aroused by a long and lugubrious cry, which seemed to issue from the opposite mountains to be reverberated by those of the lake's boundaries. Segueson crossed himself, took off his hat, said a few words in Irish, and replaced it; Owen did the same, and there was a silent mystery in the act which excited my curiosity. I found that this island was the burial-ground of the district for many miles round; that it had been so time immemorial; but that this peculiarity in the time of burial was preserved. No corpse was ever brought to the spot, excepting while the sun shone; and it was not uncommon for the relatives of the deceased to delay the last offices for weeks, that the custom might be complied with. I am not disposed to complain of the Irish howl; there is a demonstration in it which is well suited with the liveliness of feeling, which is a strong characteristic of the Irish; the cold formula of an English funeral would ill suit them.

The body was now embarked, and two other boats were filled with followers, who all continued the loud lamentation, which produced an awful effect in these wild regions. On arrival at the island, Segueson and Owen immediately covered their faces and fell on their knees. I also reverently removed my hat as the body was borne along; the widow, with dishevelled hair, and beating her bosom with her hands, then throwing herself on the coffin, till, at almost every step, exhausted by the violence of her cries, and the apparent madness of her grief, she fell to the ground—was raised by the others around her, again to join in the lament, again to inflict blows on her bared and bursting bosom.

The body was, in the deepest silence, committed to the grave; the young priest gave a short exhortation, and the people returned to the boat, supporting the now fainting widow. It was a scene that made a strong impression on me. The numerous assemblage which had attended the remains of the departed, showed a general feeling of attachment towards each other, for which in vain we look in more civilised countries; the kindness and sympathy which were by all shown towards the hapless widow, showed also that in her distress she would not be without friends to assist and protect her.

I was not wrong in this view. The young priest, whose unassuming yet pleasing manner much interested me, assured me that a subscription would be entered into by all the attendants on the funeral and others, to provide some mode of life for her; and that, though the deceased was a cotter only, by the help of her children she would be enabled to continue to meet her rent. That though there were no poor-laws to relieve the destitute, the private charities among the middle order were very extensive; in these, however, the greater proprietors of the soil seldom join.

After the departure of the mourners, I took a survey of this island. It had once been undoubtedly of greater extent; and, perhaps, the residence of some order of monks. The continual dashing of the waves of the lake against the side jutting towards the west, had materially diminished its size, and had probably rendered residence on it dangerous. Nothing remained of the buildings which must have at one time been extensive, but the tower and roofless walls of the chapel. It contained, as I have said, myriads of human skulls, heaped together against the walls; the numbers, indeed, were such, that it would have been impossible that they should have been accumulated from the ordinary burials which have, during the last half century, taken place on it; and it is reasonable to believe that this country, now wild and desolate as it is, was once much more numerously inhabited.

On leaving the island, we made for the head of the lake, and, in our progress, secured two very fine lake trout, of six and seven pounds each. The waters are supplied by two rivers, of distinct character; the one being of a mountainous, rapid, and rocky description; the other, a dull, sluggish stream, issuing from a long valley of bogs. Both are excellent for angling; the former for white trout and salmon, the latter for the brown or lake trout, which may, by the salmon-roe, be taken in almost any numbers.

At the head of the lake stands a farm-house; one of the most delightful spots, for sport of every kind, that can be imagined. It is a good house, and was originally erected, I do not doubt, for a better purpose than it is now put to. But here accommodation might be had; it would depend on the good spirits of the sportsman to make it a happy retirement.

On our return to Waterville, the whole village had assembled to see the eagle; countless stories were related of his depredations, and the cottagers spoke of his destruction as though some midnight robber had been removed from among them. Indeed, none of them dared at any time to let their fowls out of their dwellings until they had themselves arisen; and, generally, I found that the reason of their keeping them in their own houses was the dread of the eagles and the foxes, of which the impudence was irrepressible, coming almost to the very doors to pounce on their prey.

My friend, the surgeon, and his companion, had been on the river all day. The sun had been too bright for any great success, but they had, nevertheless, landed three salmon. They joined in my little dinner; so that, even in the wilds of Iveragh, I did not find myself without a companion. In the evening I tried the roe, from the bridge, with considerable success; but the salmon I there took were in bad season, having come down from the river after spawning. The flesh of one was quite white, and I regretted I had killed him.

As I stood on the bridge, I was accosted by a gentleman, in the English accent, to which my ear had been so little of late accustomed, that I almost fancied he must have been an old friend—he was not so—but a new one. He had the undress of an officer; and the gold band, round his blue cap, denoted that he belonged to the navy. He invited me to visit him, at White Strand; it was, he said, a lonely place enough; he was the commander of the coast-guard station there; but, as I should pass Derrynane, on my way, he solicited me to give him notice of my arrival, the day before, that he might have the deep-sea lines ready. I was much pleased with his hospitable invite, and determined to accept his offer.

In my way to fulfil this engagement, I passed Derrynane. So much has been said of the residence of the great proprietor, that I am disposed to dismiss it with a word. It is a straggling building, on the verge of the sea; its furniture is plain, but there is a hearty welcome to every sojourner. During his autumnal residence at the abbey, it is almost an open house; and not unfrequently are congregated within its walls much of the talent and worth that Ireland can boast.

On my arrival at White Strand, I found the lieutenant (for such he was) ready to receive me. I was welcomed by a very lady-like person, his wife, who had obviously made considerable preparations for my reception. After a very good mountain dinner, my host and myself put to sea, where we had nothing to do but to take up the long sea-lines, which his men had previously laid down, in about fifteen fathoms. The haul was tremendous; the whole of these shores, which are flat and sandy, peculiarly adapted for the best sea-fish, are, I believe, untroubled by a single fisherman. One would suppose, from the ease and quickness with which we took small cod, whiting, haddock, gurnet, and occasionally turbot, that the whole bottom was covered with them. Sea-fowl, of all descriptions, abounded; and, as the lieutenant furnished me with a gun, we made a tolerable selection of teal and ducks for the next day's dinner.

My host was a gentleman of refined manners, of the middle age, and had seen much active service. But he had eight children, now requiring education. This necessity weighed heavily on his spirits, as the small income which the government added to his half-pay, for the performance of the heavy duties of the coast-guard, would not allow him to send his sons to any distant school, and there was no human being of intelligence, above that of a cotter, within many miles. He had been stationed at the White Strand for nine years, cut off from all society, and all intercourse with persons of his own grade. He had ventured, on the resumption of power by the Duke of Wellington, to address a prayer to his Grace, not for any advancement of rank, but for a change of situation, where he might obtain education for his rising family. In preferring this very humble petition, he had referred to a circumstance which might possibly have recalled him to his Grace's remembrance. He had been the young officer who had safely landed his Grace's horses and baggage, on his first arrival in Spain, to take the command; on which occasion, he had been so fortunate as to have been honoured by Sir Arthur Wellesley's commendation.

He had received an answer, written by the duke's own hand —and it was almost with tears that he showed me the document —it was a cold and unfeeling refusal to interfere for the removal of the applicant; and that refusal was accompanied by the stoical and profoundly virtuous declaration, that *he* (the duke) *should never consider any personal service to himself as a proper ground for bestowing any public office, or of interfering in the arrangement of public duties.* Nothing can be more self-denying and magnanimous than such a resolution, in the First Lord of the Treasury, though something a little more polished might have been added to the style, in refusing the reasonable request of a meritorious officer. We are bound, however, to believe that his Grace's declaration is founded in perfect truth; and that it was services done to the state, and the state alone, that had gained so handsome a pension for Mrs. Arbuthnot.

While I was in this neighbourhood, I visited one of the round towers. The only opinion I can give, from a careful examination of the remains, is, that they were certainly not of a warlike character. It is remarkable that there are no remains of any entrance. The thickness of the walls, without any windows, would indicate the purpose of burial; which, perhaps, was the original object. The only inlet to the building was an opening of modern and rude construction, obviously not forming any relation to the original design.

That these round towers of Ireland may have been an improved form of the pyramid, is, perhaps, more easily shown than the wild theories of the writers on this subject can be established.

On our return from the White Strand to Waterville, a new kind of sport had presented itself. The mullet, which at this season of the year congregate around the entrance of the river, had formed a black mass at the embouchement of the lake. It was impossible to use a net, the shore being covered with rocks. Neither bait nor fly had the least attraction for them; and, although they might be seen in the sun as shoals of myriads, and as closely packed together as was consistent with their power of motion, no means had yet been devised of securing this excellent fish. Their annual visits, therefore, were always paid with impunity. I was angry at this, and spent some hours in endeavouring to allure them with flies, worms, bait, all to no purpose. On inquiry, I found that Segueson had taken some by salmon-flies; not in the usual way, but by accident. He had hooked them in the side, gills, and tail. An idea struck me that such a system might be available; and, stringing together about twenty stout pike hooks, I awaited the bubbling which indicated the presence of the shoal. I threw over them with a long rod, and jagged the line after it had sunk amidst them. This plan was comparatively simple, and I had the pleasure of adding to my fish-dinner, in which my friend, the surgeon, was generally joined, the exquisite mullet.

My quarters at Cahirciveen were, after a few days' stay at Waterville, resumed. I had heard, and was resolved to be convinced, that the iron-bound coast of Kerry was celebrated for sea-fishing. I had no difficulty at Cahir in setting up a good fishing yacht, which consisted of a newly-built sand boat, which, at a very moderate rental, was easily procured. With the assistance of the carpenter, we soon turned it into a very convenient vessel of about twelve tons.

There are no fishermen at Cahir; although the coast on the outer side of Waterville is abundant in every kind of fish, yet no regular market exists. The farmers, therefore, at particular seasons, make common cause in attacking the herrings and mackerel; few attempt any other method, notwithstanding the supply of fish in a Catholic country would be deemed so essential.

To remedy this want, during his stay in the country, the Knight of Kerry, whose property the isle of Valencia is, had invited a small colony of fishermen, consisting of four men from

Dingle. The terms he gave them were apparently advantageous; they were supplied with houses and small plots of land, a small hooker and tackle. The Knight, I believe, was to be supplied with one-third of the produce as his share, and the residue was to be equally divided among the men.

The plan had not succeeded, for I found that the poor fellows had gone through a very dreary winter, with little or no sale for their fish; and, on my arrival at the island, which is not more than three or four miles from Cahir, they were on the point of abandoning their engagement, and returning to Dingle.

It will be a satisfactory guide to my successors to set forth the terms I entered into for the services of this crew. Four were by no means too many for the heavy rigging in use among fishermen here. The boats have two masts without stays, and two very large sprit-sails, simple enough in construction, but by no means easy of management in a rolling sea, such as we were liable outside the island to encounter. In calms, also, it was absolutely necessary to have considerable strength in the boat; so that I at once engaged the whole crew. The captain's wages were, per week, seven shillings; the others received six shillings each. To this I subsequently made an addition, by supplying the potato store myself. Small as these wages were, in the course of a month the sum each had accumulated amounted to a small fortune. Having made all arrangements, among which the most important were the long lines and deep-sea tackle—a good cooking apparatus—we set sail down the Cahir river, the evening being beautifully serene. We arrived about six at the island of Valencia, where I found a very snug little inn, the hostess being an Englishwoman; and the welcome the English gentleman received was indeed cordial. Having supplied all little omissions here, we set forth for a night's fishing.

There are two outlets round the island, which will admit ships of considerable burden. Both, however, are of a dangerous character, unless under very skilful pilotage; the southern outlet passes by, on either side, immense and towering ranges of

NIGHT SPORT. *Facing page 137.*

perpendicular rocks of awful height. The sea has worn immense caverns under their bases; and, even in the calmest weather, the roaring of the Atlantic, as each succession of waves retires from the immovable mass, is singularly terrific. On the extreme point of Valencia there are the remains of Cromwell's fort; a position commanding the whole island, and effectually prohibitiug all hostile entrance into the harbour. Once having passed this fort, there is no landing-place for twenty miles round the coast, either way. A depth of twenty fathoms is found within a yard of the rocks which compose the coast.

With a gentle breeze and a favouring current, we reached the fishing-ground just as the evening was closing, first threw out our long lines, and brought to an anchor. We had hit the exact moment; no sooner were our lines at the bottom, than whiting, of a very large size, and such as are never seen in England, were drawn up. These were immediately put on the large hooks, and set out. Four lines, baited with mussels, were continually going, till darkness stopped our further sport. We now trimmed the fire; put on our enormous kettle of potatoes; erected a very comfortable tent, by the help of the sails and yards; and, with the addition of boiled whiting and good whiskey, enjoyed a capital supper.

While, however, we were busily employed in discussing these comforts, sundry vehement tugs at the boat's side indicated the neighbourhood of some of the tyrants of the deep. The first I was impatient to haul with my own hands.

"Arrah! Paddy Shea; is it yourself that'll be afther litting his honour lose his hands! catch hould and haul."

I found this assistance timely, as I had just come to a stand; the fish having, as the sailors call it, bored downwards. After another impetus, however, supplied by the assistance of Paddy Shea, an enormous creature of the skate kind was secured. He was as large as an ordinary table, and weighed very nearly one hundredweight.

The only mode by which we could, on our arrival at Cahir,

carry him up the town, was by thrusting one of the spars through his body, and thus suspending him between two men. Conger-eels were a terrible annoyance; but the occasional landing a ling, which is here held in high esteem, and which is indeed an excellent fish, again inspirited my little crew.

Paddy Shea, I soon discovered, was in high repute as a dancer, while my captain was somewhat celebrated as a singer. There was no lack of amusement between the frequent calls made on us by our lines. At length, however, one hand being constituted the watch, all were ordered to turn in. Our beds were by no means uncomfortable. The foresail, well folded, served every purpose of a couch; our time was short, as, with the grey of morning, we were to make our first haul at the long lines. We had now a good stock of ordinary fish, and I was impatient to see the result of the long line in the deep water.

Certainly the perfection of sport is the opportunity of fishing new ground. When I call the coast around the isle of Valencia new ground, it must be understood to convey this meaning—that it has never been attempted with a net, trail, or any other means than the deep-sea line, and even that has been very sparingly used.

The delight I felt at the first violent movement perceptible on the long line will be easily understood; and, as the white body approached the surface, the conjecture as to the kind of prey was highly amusing. The first was a fine cod; next, conger-eel; third, a large ling, skate, haddock; then only a row of heads, the bodies having fallen victims to the ruthless community by which, in their thraldom, they had been surrounded. Flat fish, and here and there a tolerable turbot, served to supply us with so splendid a cargo of fish as to render all further pursuit useless.

On our return homeward, millions of cormorants, forming black masses on the projecting rocks, attracted our attention. So little had these been disturbed, none of the fishermen who frequented the coasts around being possessed of fire-arms, that there was no difficulty whatever in approaching within gun-shot. With the first volley, however, all dived; the second barrel was ready for those who appeared first on the surface, many popping up their heads within three yards of the boat. The hand and eye must be quick, for the instant they perceive their mistake they as suddenly disappear. The sport, however, is very exhilarating, as it is endless; while, under a steady foresail and good breeze, the ground is continually changed. Puffins, teal, cormorants, gannets, and gulls, would, with a good breeze and a good shot, soon load a boat.

On returning to Cahir, we found we were possessed of about three hundredweight of fish of all descriptions. The weather had now become too warm for salting. I sent, therefore, a few to the inn; and gave public notice to all the poor of Cahir, who chose to come for their share, that they should be supplied. In this division, the produce really of value to the destitute and helpless, I took much pleasure; and I felt that the life of a sportsman is not necessarily a useless one; for, although the coast is so abundant in the produce, there are none possessed of the means or skill to furnish the Friday's meal. Of the birds, with the exception of the teal, which are not so numerous as the rest, I can say little in praise.

The cormorants make, I am told, a good soup, not unlike that derived from the hare; and, although the priests have decided that the puffin is not a bird, but a fish, and there is in consequence a general dispensation that it may be eaten on a Friday, I availed myself but once of the privilege. I was perfectly satisfied that, without the dispensation, I should have little sinned in that way. The plover, however, abundance of which are here found, roast well.

As yet, all my experience on these seas had been accompanied by singularly fine weather; but, on our third or fourth day, when about twenty miles from the Skelligs, we perceived a heavy roll of the sea coming in from the Atlantic; a hazy dulness gradually covered the horizon, and mixed its clear blue with the darker cloud; the breeze, which had hitherto carried us, now died to a perfect calm; nature seemed at once to fall into a sudden repose; not even the cry of the wild bird disturbed the distant echoes of the caverns, whose hollow recesses sent forth the accumulated wave, as if indignant at the intrusive volumes.

The darkness of day is solemn, and the spirits unconsciously flag. Not a fish was moving, aware of the coming change; the sea-monsters ceased from their prey; and nothing now was seen upon the increasing masses, which appeared causelessly to blend one with another, but an occasional shoal of porpoises making towards the land.

The crew looked at each other, and spoke in Irish, in a low and mysterious tone: at length, my captain ventured to hint that, as the sails were useless, and the weight of the masts increased the rolling of the boat, we might as well have all in, and take to our oars. Our compass was duly consulted, that we might not lose in the coming mist our exact position; there was little or no current, and, should we lose sight of land, the entrance to Valencia might be easily hit. It was on Friday; the effect of superstition was becoming manifest, and it was not difficult to perceive that my little crew, accustomed as they were to the sudden gales which come in upon this coast from the broad Atlantic, looked as much for approaching danger in the day as the elements.

Two hours were laboriously spent in pulling towards land; but the sea had, as we approached it, increased to a mountainous roll, while a few large drops of rain, and a suffocating heat, betokened the arrival of the storm. A scudding breeze tipped the surface of the swell; a distant crash was heard, which reverberated around the shores. The oars fell from the hands of my little crew, and each was momentarily on his knees, uttering a prayer in Irish, and crossing himself in great apparent agitation.

This done, for I would not interrupt their devotions, I began to remonstrate with them on the terror they seemed to exhibit.

I found myself utterly mistaken; there was no fear of danger; and as each rose from the performance of what he deemed an humble acknowledgment of the divine power, I could perceive a resolution and determination which reassured me in the coming difficulties.

The wind had now begun steadily to increase; scudding squalls passed rapidly; while, at intervals, the heavens opened with liquid fire. The masts were to be stepped; and here it was the coarse and rude style of rigging presented its difficulties. The weight of the sprits, which was enormous, aided by the sudden lurching of the boat as she fell into the trough, rendered the setting the foresail a matter of danger; but we were rapidly drifting towards the island, and no time was to be lost in getting the boat close to the wind. This at length accomplished, she became more steady, but the gale rapidly increased; and, as she mounted the now breaking summits of the heavy and long seas, it became apparent that we should not fetch the upper entrance of the island.

A consultation was now held, as to the propriety of getting up the mainsail, and at once putting her on the sea tack. The objections were, that we might lose our reckoning, and miss the entrance, while nothing but destruction awaited our falling below the island. The mainsail was at length got up; and now, indeed, we began to feel the value of good ballast. She stood up admirably—wet, indeed—but stiffly; and, though we found ourselves, by my unluckily letting her fall off a point just as she was rising, once or twice buried in the crest of a sea, we had no apprehension but that she would, in one tack, stand up for the harbour.

We kept well out to sea—gunwales under—just shivering the sails as the gusts increased, and still she kept to the wind. Another terrific crash of thunder, which appeared close over our heads, again prostrated my men. I began to be angry, as I, being at the helm, needed their assistance at the sheets.

It was at this moment that a squall came off the headland,

catching the sea at about a quarter of a mile from our little struggling vessel. The surface seemed uprooted; the foam danced over the ocean in a white mass; and, ere I could summon the attention of the men, the boat was on her beam ends. Luckily, on the first touch of the squall, I had put the helm a-lee; she ran up into the wind suddenly; and this, perhaps, was the cause of her righting. But I had run her too sharply up; the squall caught the foresail aback, smashed the mast, and, in an instant, our vessel presented a wreck.

The coolness and determination of my men was imperturbable, though I confess my own courage had long since flagged.

We had no difficulty, except from the tremendous rolling, in shipping the mainmast forwards, and again bringing our bark to the wind; but, no sooner had we done so, than a new and unforeseen danger sprang up; our compass, in the fall of the foremast, had been demolished, and I immediately fixed my eye upon an opening stream of light, which had emanated from the direction in which the island stood.

The gale now increased to a hurricane. Our spare sail was drawn round the leeward side, to form a bulwark, as nothing but keeping her well to windward could effect our safety. Every minute we were covered with a breaking sea; and one with a crest, that denoted the extent to which the gale had arrived, broke in upon the forecastle, and literally smothered Paddy Shea. The good-humour of the fellow, as he rubbed the water from his eyes, almost caused, in our state of danger, that kind of uncontrollable laughter from which even the condemned cannot on occasion refrain.

The danger of missing Cromwell's fort, at the southern end of the island, was pregnant with a frightful alternative—that of running before the wind, round the island, and entering by Bray Head. Fortunately, we were not reduced to this, for the wind came more free round Doulus Head; and, to our satisfaction, when we made the point, we found ourselves midway. The entrance became now the last danger; the sea, rolling in from the southern Atlantic, had assumed by this time a terrific height, and as each wave was rejected by the bold shores of either side, the mid-channel, through which our course lay, formed a mass of raging confusion, through which we ultimately dashed, with one or two seas completely over us.

"Hurrah!" exclaimed Paddy Shea—"we'll want no more washing for a week." "Hurrah!" exclaimed the rest—"It's the boat that'll do it, anyhow."

All confidence and honour seemed now, by general consent, to be placed in the boat. Our short passage round the island, to the quay, was readily accomplished, amid the utmost hilarity, which the cold, wet, hunger, and even the deprivation of the consolatory pipe, could not repress.

Thou who wouldst enjoy the pleasure of such an arrival, must undergo the disagreeable part of such a trip; and the cost is rather extravagant. We met every accommodation and comfort at the little inn, where we had, for an apparently indefinite time, established our quarters. Our absence had, it seems, occasioned considerable apprehension, and several boats from the island had gone round the Bray Head passage to look for us. They were returning just as we arrived; and, at the suggestion of Paddy Shea, we were to have the piper, "any way." He was sent for; the inhabitants of the island soon assembled, for a dance is an attraction not to be resisted.

As the storm raged, the piper played the louder; and, just as I had accomplished the difficulty of the jig, a half-drowned, shoeless, hatless islander burst into the room. He uttered something in Irish—the piper dropt his instrument, and each betook himself to his covering. It was some time before I could get any explanation. "It was no matter to my honour—my honour was to go to rest, any way."

Insisting, however, on hearing what was the cause of this sudden excitement, I learned that there was a large ship beating against the perpendicular rocks of the island, where every soul must inevitably perish.

It is to be lamented that so little is known of the Irish coast. From their ignorance of the appearance or situation of the few lights which are barely sprinkled along it, captains of foreign vessels continually mistake the Blasket lights for the entrance of the Shannon, and thus run up a blind bay—which Dingle bay is—without a harbour, and with very little possible protection from the weather.

This had been doubtlessly the case in the present instance. Having accompanied the rest to the heights which overhung the spot where the devoted vessel was dashing her sides against the huge masses of granite, a scene of the most harrowing character presented itself. A mastless ship was lifted up by a wave, twenty or thirty yards, and dashed against the rocks. Three of the doomed crew spread forth their hands to us as we hailed them from the cliffs in hopeless supplication.

"A rope! a rope!" was reiterated on all hands. On letting it down to the deck, one caught hold; but, before he could be raised one half the necessary distance, he fell from his grasp, and was buried in the raging sea.

We were mute spectators of the scene below. The cries of the two remaining crew were heartrending. One of those had been injured; for, as the vessel heeled, and apparently was settling downwards, the other took him in his arms and placed him in a momentary safety. This done, both wrung their hands, and looked towards us in their extremity. Once more did the vessel rise with the swell—one dash against the stern mass which formed their doom, and the whole fabric, with its burden, disappeared. The bursting waves rolled on, and the noble vessel, with all that she contained, passed away as a phantom.

This was the *Henry Brougham*—a noble vessel—and many a hut which now cheers the coast of Cahir and Valencia has been erected with the timbers of which she was composed.

The relation may seem trite—the reality was terrific. Little, indeed, is known of the horrors of this iron-bound coast; and, were it not for the occasional aid presented by the coast-guard, hundreds of stately vessels would here meet their fate, unpitied and unseen.

After having done all that our limited means would allow, to secure aid to any possible survivors of the wreck, we returned to the inn, greatly depressed by the awful scenes of which we had been witness. Here we found another arrival; a boat from Kinsale had pushed her way mastless through the lower passage round the island. The crew had by mere personal labour accomplished this extraordinary feat, having rowed sixteen hours, as they declared, without rest or food.

I could easily believe the latter to have been the fact. Those who are acquainted with Irish seamen cannot but have observed the patient endurance of hunger and labour which they manifest, without the least complaint. The fishermen on the Dingle side of the bay are accustomed throughout the year to endure the cold and wet necessarily attendant upon their dangerous occupation, with no further comforts than boiled potatoes and very slight covering afford; yet, without the least murmur, they are not unfrequently subjected to the deprivation of the potatoes, where the sea is high and smothers their little fire.

It is perfectly wonderful, that, with such miserable tackle as that with which their boats are rigged, more losses should not occur. I believe, however, I am correct in saying, that, in three years, not one boat's crew had been lost.

I visited the newly-arrived crew, and was shocked at the poor covering which had been opposed to the inclemency of the storm. Legs naked—nothing but a mass of rags, suspended from the middle, formed their dress. Neither hats, caps, nor shirts, encumbered their physical energies. But they were perfectly happy. Wet as they were, the panacea for all evils, the pipe, afforded the consolation which the possession of all other comfort would not have supplied.

They were not communicative, and seemed rather to fence

off all inquiries as to their mode of fishing, and the success they had met. It appears they had been overtaken before they had commenced their labours, and the first squall had carried both their masts by the board. Determined, however, to ascertain what the coast eastward produced, I applied my inquiries to one who seemed more disposed to frame answers than the rest. There was a look of suspicion directed to his comrades, as he replied to my interrogations, and a cleverness in the answers, that induced me to regard him with a stricter eye. I was confident I had seen him before. He acknowledged that it was so, and disclosed his under jacket, which I immediately recognised as the slight uniform which had been presented to him in Spain, in lieu of his ten pounds.

He informed me that he had starved through the country, till chance had brought him to Kinsale, where he had joined a fishing-boat, under hope of share. This was his first trip—and it had ended, he said, as all his other ventures had, in total discomfiture. He informed me that, notwithstanding the storm, they purposed to put to sea that night; a resolution I strongly opposed, as unlikely to meet with anything but destruction.

He took me aside. "Sir," said he, "I know I can trust you—you were kind to me in the packet—I have not forgotten it. Do not oppose our putting out to-night. We know the coast, and the wind is abating. This is, to us, glorious weather—the only weather, in fact, in which we dare face the sea. We have already done our business here, and hope to accomplish another wreck before morning on the coast of Dingle."

"Your fishing will be useless on such a night."

"Useful as it ever was to us. The coast-guard are still quietly asleep in their cottages, never dreaming of boats or landing on such a night and in such a hurricane—a whiff of good tobacco is, after all, the best thing in the world—and it is hard the poor should not be allowed the only comfort they ask, in their destitute and miserable condition. They will have it however, after this storm."

I now comprehended the whole affair. It was only in gales of wind such a crew dared venture to sea; or, having done so, would dare to land; to them and the stormy petrel the tempest brought joy. They were smugglers of the poor man's luxury—*tobacco*; they had that night run part of their cargo; and I was not long in discovering that even my own crew were their aiders and abettors. I did not blame them—and, as Owen would say, "small blame to myself for that same."

CHAPTER XIII

Visit to Waterville—New Mode of Angling—Mistake about the Potato Diet of the Irish—Cobbett right as to its Mischievous Effects—Drive to Tralee—Miserable State of the Peasantry—Prevalence of Scrofula and Consumption—Fine Mountain Scenery—Castlemaine—The River—The White Trout—The Lob Trout—Fine Shooting Station for Sea-Fowl and Grouse—Sporting Exciseman—Folly and Rapacity of Irish Landlords—The Surgeon's Tale—The Murderers—A Mysterious Character—Irish Court of Justice—The Trial—The Defence—The Cross-Examination—The Verdict—The Mystery explained—Three Pleasant Weeks—O'Connell as a Landlord—His Occupation at Derrynane—His Devotion to the Peasantry—The Dancing-Master in Ireland—Advantages of Ireland over the Continent—Cheapness and Security of the Living—Farewell to Cahirciveen—Departure for Dingle—Wild-Fowl Shooting—Fishing at Dingle—Hospitality of the Resident Gentry—Trout-fishing and Grouse-shooting—Causes and Remedy of Irish Discontent—An Irish Wake—The Irish Howl—A Victim of the "Good People"—A Fairy Tale.

As I felt that I had been personally obliged by my friend, the surgeon, at Waterville, I drove over to pass two days with him, previously to his quitting the country; and ordered my little yacht round to Ballinskelligs Bay, for the purpose of joining me there, and trying the sea-fishing of that celebrated spot. The time of the surgeon's visit had run out, and my purpose was to show him at parting as much amusement as the varied sports of the delightful Waterville would allow.

All our lake lines were in requisition, and it most fortunately turned out one of the best days we had experienced on the lake.

I found, however, that it was by no means a day of uncommon success with him; having followed my plan of night-lines and trailing, he had, with little labour, supplied all his poor patients with that which, indeed, many of them more immediately needed than physic—I mean nourishment. He had hit upon a new mode of angling, which had turned out very amusingly during the hot weather and fine sunny days, when exertion was by no means desirable. He had been fitting up three or four very long rods from the woods, which everywhere cover the sides of the lake. To these he had attached lines loaded with lead; and, baiting with the earthworm of the largest kind, had planted himself on some of the rocks at the back of the little island on the lake. Throwing himself on the grass, which covers the tops of the ledges, he had amused himself with a favourite book, while, as Izaak says, his "angles fished for him, and were put out to interest." He succeeded in killing very fine trout by this means, the only particular caution being necessary of keeping out of sight. He had discovered, also, that the lake had another species of fish, unknown to the inhabitants of its banks—a flat fish of the flounder kind, but exceedingly delicious for the table. They, no doubt, make their way up from the sea, as I have not unfrequently discovered them in the lakes of Scotland, where the communication was easy.[1]

The salmon and sea-trout had afforded him, during my absence, unremitting sport; and he expressed himself in terms of the warmest gratitude, such as a sportsman can really entertain for the amusement I had secured him in the communication of the secret of the infallible bait—the salmon-roe. He had not, however, been allowed to pursue the even tenor of his way at Waterville. His fame had for him too rapidly and too widely spread; and the calls on his humanity had become so

[1] This statement may appear of dubious veracity, but I can confirm the fact that flounders frequently ascend the streams for several miles and make their way into fresh-water lakes.—ED.

incessant, that he hardly regretted the return to his professional pursuits elsewhere.

We found the bay crowded with mackerel and gurnet, which afforded a good afternoon's sport, but it was of too monotonous a character to be worth the labour. The shooting was improved by the late gale, as it had brought to land innumerable flights of gannet, some of which we secured. The bay, however, having no harbour, is an unsafe station for a boat; and I ordered the crew to take her round again to Valencia, while my friend and myself proceeded next morning to Tralee.

Nothing is more fallacious than the opinion generally entertained, that the Irish are healthy on the meagre diet the potato affords. From the prevalent diseases of these mountains, as well as from the illness which I find in towns where the potato is the staple, I have arrived at the fullest conviction that it is not suited to human food for any continuance.

"The disregard to human life," said the surgeon, "exhibited in the hard measure of justice, dealt out by a British government to these unhappy islanders, is worthy only of execration. What is now to be done I know not, but it is impossible not to perceive that nearly all the fatal diseases among them originate in the absence of proper and generous nutrition. Wherever skill is applied to a failing constitution, we find it unavailing; there is no native strength to sustain a change, or to apply sanative resources. When sick from any cause, they generally die; and a disorder which, among a well-fed people, would bear no danger to them, brings death even in youth. You cannot but have perceived the rigidity of expression in the countenance of the youngest here. The prevalence also of scrofula, the sore eyes, and frequent blindness, are referable to the potato diet. Out of fifty, who at an early age meet death, more than half that number have expired, not from the ostensible disorder by which they were first attacked, but by that universal curse—the potato. Cobbett was quite right in deploring its introduction as an irremediable misfortune. It enabled the landlords to compel their vassals to subsist on a lower and less nutritious diet, from which they will hardly ever be able to escape but by a determined effort, which may, while it procures food proper for man, at the same time establish their independence as a people."

The drive to Tralee displayed to me more than I had yet observed of the terrible state of misery to which the rural population of this district is reduced,—children, literally without any covering, or, perhaps, only a ragged shirt, defying the rain and wind, and apparently not aware of the possible comfort of any superior clothing. At one cottage, where we stopped, we found nine children, all under ten years of age; the mother nursing two, and consequently herself helpless, while the father's wages did not exceed fourpence per day.

It is remarkable that the children, throughout Ireland, bear all the indications of strong health. This appearance is deceptive; the tendency to scrofula and consumption everywhere exists; and both these diseases need only some exciting cause to display their horrors.

The passage by the side of the mountain, on entering Castlemaine, is of the finest order of scenery; and, from a considerable elevation, the beautiful bay bursts upon the sight. The river which forms this bay is the Alang, composed of two rivers, the Flesk (not the Killarney Flesk), and another mountain stream of some volume.

The stream at Castlemaine is sluggish, but there will be found excellent fishing for white trout and the common trout, two miles from the town. There is also in abundance, in the river, what is called the *lob*-trout, which I have before described. Here they become large; indeed I found them quite three pounds in the tide's way.

Although the accommodation is not very good, yet a station might be made for shooting at Castlemaine during the winter. The entrance to the bay is safe, and the shores easy of access. It is crowded with every variety of sea-fowl, while the neighbouring mountains afford continual amusement in an undisturbed stock of grouse. I say undisturbed, for I believe they are seldom shot over. The only sportsman I could discover, resident at Castlemaine, was the exciseman. Of him I learned, and he affected to make a considerable favour of the communication, that there were abundance of grouse on the hills.

On inquiry of my landlord, I found that he was not deceiving me; for, having abandoned his rule, like a bold exciseman, on the first day of the season (a day not very scrupulously regarded) he had produced at Castlemaine more than thirty head of grouse. They are not esteemed by the residents; and there are no means of sending them to the other side of the island.

The entrance into Tralee is now so much improved as at once to inspire the notion, that we have as suddenly emerged from all that was wild and uncultivated to a high state of civilisation. The town is nearly all new, and has, I believe, been built within a few years; cottages and really handsome houses adjoining each other, in an agreeable variety. There are here, even, *rows* of houses, built in the English fashion, with the exception only of the usual inattention to the entrance; a disregard of which, either for cleanliness or appearance, the Irish, on this side the island, share in common with the Spaniards and Portuguese, their *immediate neighbours*, from whom no doubt many of their habits have been borrowed.

The bay of Tralee presents the most eligible site for building; but I am informed that the land cannot be leased for a less sum than ten pounds per acre per annum, an effectual barrier to anything like possible improvement.

The rapacious folly of these wretched landlords is worthy of reprobation. Thousands of acres remain uncultivated, producing nothing but the rank and useless reed, yet at such an elevation from the sea as would render the effectual recovery of them a matter of easy execution. Yet, I believe, a lease for lives—even of such property—can only be obtained on such exorbitant terms as to render the attempt hopeless. The land, therefore, remains uncultivated; the people are idle, and starve.

My friend, the surgeon, marshalled me into the head inn.

"This is my second visit to Tralee," said my companion. "I had once visited it under other circumstances, and such as made so deep an impression on my mind as will not easily be effaced. It was in this very room that I took my solitary dinner. On that day the assizes were held at Tralee; and, finding the accommodations in the way of lodgings all bespoken, I was necessarily obliged to resort to the inn. An Irish inn is a spunging-house, when situated in the capital of any district, where the charges are immoderate, the attendance bad, and the provisions worse.

"As I took my solitary meal, the door of what is here called the *coffee-room*—but, in comparison with such rooms as you are accustomed to in England, would be considered a tap-room—was thrown open, and in walked a person of some apparent pretensions. His whiskers were enormous, and his moustaches were of considerable growth. His appearance was of the inconsistent order; his countenance bespoke rather a bold defiance than any engaging interest. He bowed, however, politely to me; and inquired if there were any objects worthy of note in this dull town, which he professed not before to have visited.

"I explained my ignorance of the locale, and also the object of my visit, which was then made for the purpose of fishing. He also drew from me that I was unacquainted with any person in that neighbourhood, and then stated that he was similarly circumstanced.

"It is singular by what trifles we are sometimes induced to form an estimate of character. My first impressions were that this stranger was a gentleman; I, however, wavered when I saw him throw off an elegant and most expensive great-coat, and, for a moment (the error was immediately detected by himself), exhibit a marvellously foul shirt. This, however, might be a national inattention to the person. His conversation was shrewd, and by no means vulgar, though the chain of his watch was brass, and the gorgeous eye-glass, which was suspended round his neck, was gilt.

"He informed me that he had travelled nearly throughout Ireland, with a view of forming some opinion of the capabilities it possessed of more extensive trade and manufacture; that he had examined all the mines which had been opened, and that he had hope of introducing the iron trade to some extent. He familiarly referred to persons of high mercantile character, whom he connected with his views; and, having dispatched his breakfast, with an air of authority he demanded of the waiter what would be procured for dinner, and whether his horse was properly attended to, and fed.

"The first inquiry was easily answered, as the catalogue of an Irish larder is not difficult to be run through. This point settled, his next inquiry was relating to the lions of the place. The waiter informed him that, in addition to the church and the harbour, the assizes had that day commenced; and that there was a trial of some interest expected to take place, relative to a murder. Of this he expressed great indifference, and thought an Irish court of justice not likely to be very amusing. As he had little of the Irish accent, though in some words he uttered it was sufficiently marked, I concluded that he wished to pass for an Englishman. He said he was English, but that he had caught a little of the brogue from the frequent visits he had paid this country.

"He now invited me to join him in the dinner, to which I expressed my assent; and we both proceeded to view the lions, and thence to the court-house. Having found our way into the gallery of the court, and obtained good seeing-places, we found the jurymen already assembling, and answering to their names.

"The important cause was just coming on, and the prisoner was now conducted to the bar. He was an elderly man of fifty, perhaps more, decently dressed, and wore a brown wig. His face was expressive, though entire confidence seemed to pervade that expression. His appearance altogether, however, created no prepossessing effect. During the charge, he was in constant communication with his attorney, and frequently shook his head with a sort of smiling dissent.

"The charge was that, in company with others, he, on the night of the 14th of May, had murdered and robbed the Rev. ——— in ——— wood.

"The counsel for the prisoner now applied to the court for a postponement of the trial, on the ground of the absence of material witnesses, whom every exertion had been made to find. It was stated that a clear and convincing defence could be established in the form of an *alibi*, but that it had been impossible as yet to find the parties, whose testimony would effectually clear the prisoner of every imputation. This application was refused by the judge, and the trial proceeded.

"Witnesses now stated that, on the day in question, they were passing down the road which skirts the wood of ———, about one in the morning, on their return from ——— fair. They distinctly heard the cry of murder, and at first feared to enter the wood. On its repetition, the witness and his fellow-traveller, arming themselves as well as they could, proceeded to the spot whence the cry had emanated. They clearly saw two men rifling the pockets of the murdered man. They fell on them, and, after some blows, the murderers fled. Two others then rushed from the thicket, and joined the retreating party, who were soon out of sight; and the witnesses now directed their attention to the dying man, whom, on being brought to the road, they recognised as the Rev. Mr. ———. He was not dead, but faintly declared that he had been set on by four men, who had stabbed him in three places, and robbed him of one thousand pounds, which it was known he had that day received as tithes at ———. He particularly described one man, who was dressed in a white great-coat: that was the man the witness had seen running from the deceased—it was the prisoner at the bar.

"On cross-examination, both witnesses admitted that the dress was a considerable ground of their belief in the prisoner's identity. They both agreed that he had a wig, which corresponded with that he now wore.

"It was some days after the murder that the prisoner had been apprehended. He had only some silver in his possession, and professed his entire ignorance of the crime at the time of being taken. He added, also, that he was not in the country at the time the murder was committed.

"On re-examination, the witnesses swore positively to the identity of the prisoner, and adduced many circumstances to show that they could not have been mistaken. Indeed, it was impossible to shake their testimony; and, with this evidence, the case for the prosecution closed.

"The prisoner was now called on for his defence. He stated, in good language, that he had ever felt the utmost confidence in the providence of God, and his case was a signal instance of it. Notwithstanding all his exertions, and those of his solicitor, to procure the attendance of some witnesses, who could establish his innocence, he had failed in finding them; but at that moment he beheld a gentleman in the gallery, who could certainly give the court very satisfactory evidence.

"As the stranger and myself were now the objects of general attention, we both unconsciously rose, and the prisoner at once pointed out my companion as the gentleman to whom he referred. Hereupon the stranger addressed his lordship, and assured him that he knew nothing whatever of the cause, the crime, or the prisoner; that he had never heard of the murder itself, much less of the prisoner, or the circumstances connected with it; that he was there by entire accident, being on his way to the north of Ireland, and that he only waited in the town while his horse rested.

"The judge intimated that, as the prisoner demanded it, he must be sworn. Again protesting against the necessity of being made a witness in a matter of which he was wholly ignorant, he reluctantly descended, and was sworn. He was then examined.

"*The Judge.* 'Do you know the prisoner at the bar?'

"'I do not. To my remembrance I never before saw him. My being in this town, much more in this court, is purely the effect of accident. There must, therefore, be some mistake on the part of the prisoner. I never saw him before.'

"*Prisoner.* 'Look on me. Are you certain you have never seen me before?'

"'I am morally certain I never before saw you.'

"*Prisoner.* 'Pray, sir—for much depends on it—look carefully at my features. Do you remember no traces of them?'

"'None.'

"'Can your memory suggest no occasion on which we have met?'

"'I have distinctly answered that I know nothing whatever of you. I have no recollection of either your person, manner, or voice. I cannot, therefore, but wonder at the extraordinary accident or mistake which has forced me to stand here to repeat it, after the declaration of my entire ignorance of the whole business before the court.'

"*Prisoner.* '*Now,* sir, do you remember me?'

"The prisoner here took off his wig, and exhibited a head nearly bald, but with a large unhealed scar on the scalp. The witness, after carefully looking at the prisoner, manifested some confusion and surprise, and addressed the court.

"'My lord, I must beg pardon of your lordship and this court; I do now remember the prisoner, and more particularly by the scar on the head. The circumstance which recalls him to my remembrance is, that, on my passage from Liverpool to Dublin, this man, during the evening and night at sea, was exceedingly entertaining. He sang comic songs with great talent, and appeared in such bad circumstances that, among a few gentlemen in the packet, we made a trifling subscription for him. While he was receiving the amount from the hands of a gentleman who had much admired his singing, and had taken off his hat in returning thanks, a block which had been hanging loose from the rigging fell on his head. The fall inflicted, what we considered then, a very serious wound; but, after it had been dressed by a surgeon, who happened to be on board the packet, he recovered, and there were some jocular observations as to the cause of the accident—remarks on his being too polite —and, in the end, a second subscription was entered into for the purpose of purchasing a wig, when he might be quite as polite at a much less cost. This is all I know of the prisoner; as, from that time to this, I have never seen or heard of him— nor could I have at all recognised him unless he had removed the wig in which he first appeared in this court.'

"*Prisoner.* 'Now, sir, on what day was it that you passed over from Liverpool to Dublin?'

"'I cannot remember.'

"The Judge here intimated that it might be most important that he should accurately state the day.

"The witness said it was impossible, from memory, to do so; as, however, being concerned in heavy mercantile affairs, and travelling much, he had always regularly kept a diary of every day's proceedings, by a reference to it he could accurately ascertain the day. This journal, however, was at his inn, where he had that morning arrived, and, if an officer were directed to fetch his portmanteau, he would at once confidently state the day.

"This was agreed to, and the portmanteau produced. On opening the journal to which he had referred, he stated that he had passed over in the packet on the 14th day of May.

"*Prisoner.* 'That is the day on which I am charged with having committed this murder.'

"'There was a general murmur of satisfaction among the auditors, which was repressed by the judge, who asked to see the journal. It was handed to him; he went carefully through it; put a few questions as to other parts of it, which were satisfactorily answered; and he returned it to the witness, with every demonstration of entire satisfaction.

"After a few inquiries as to the witness's name, business, residence, etc., which were answered agreeably to the account which he had previously given me, the case was sent to the jury, and the prisoner at once acquitted.

"I now left the court, ruminating on so extraordinary a coincidence of circumstances, which had saved the life of a human creature, who was, doubtlessly, innocent of the crime laid to his charge.

"On arriving at my inn, I found the stranger had hastily devoured his dinner, and was already about to start. He barely wished me good day, and disappeared.

"The truth remains to be told. The 'mercantile gentleman' was the accomplice and fellow-murderer of the acquitted prisoner!"[1]

On my return to Cahirciveen, having taken leave of my excellent and philanthropic friend, the surgeon, I began to make preparations for my own departure. I had now spent three weeks at this lovely spot; and, I believe, three weeks of more unmixed amusement could hardly again, by any circumstances, be achieved. There had been no lack of society—the mild, modest, and learned priest, Mr. F——, had been always a resource; and between him and my hilarious and downright host, Mr. John O'Connell, all my unemployed evenings were pleasingly disposed of.

I cannot bid farewell to the Iveragh, without bearing testimony to the effect produced among the populace by a kind and judicious intercourse with their superiors. No part of Ireland will be found more tranquil or free from crime than this district—the very meanest of the tenants, poor though indeed they are, still cherish, in honour of their landlord, D. O'Connell, a jealous

---

[1] Since this recital was made, I am informed some of the outlines have been before published. The facts and particulars are, however, I believe, exactly those I have set forth.

regard to the general reputation. What I have elsewhere said of the Kerry peasantry will be found peculiarly applicable to this—here, indeed, are not seen any of those exhibitions of violence among themselves, so much to be deplored in many counties—here we shall not find, as elsewhere, a spirit of litigation, too much encouraged by the cheap law which the courts of the assistant barristers present. I have, indeed, been informed that O'Connell's tenants, by far the larger proportion of the inhabitants of this district, have a court of their own—a court of appeal personally to him, and to the settlement of their disputes—to an investigation into their wants, and an unremitting endeavour to alleviate them, is he, during his stay at Derrynane, chiefly devoted.

I cannot say that the peasantry are unhappy—their wants are of the simplest order, and they appear perfectly content when those are supplied. The proximity of this county to the lively inhabitants of the continent has also had its influence—and I was at first somewhat surprised to find men and women, without shoes or stockings, submitting to the instructions of the dancing-master and piper, evening after evening. I found, indeed, that the former was a regularly-paid official, and his labours were in continual demand through the summer. The Sunday evening is, of course, a general jubilee, in which all passers-by are requested to join. My prejudices were soon overcome.

How can the English suffer themselves to be so grossly deluded as to fly to the continent in search of scenic beauty or economy! This beautiful spot presents both, without the concomitant opprobrium of exile. What part of the continent presents the combined advantages of all wild sports to be indulged in, without the landlord's leave—good society, and cheapness that will erect a pittance into a handsome income? Where are our half-pay sojourners?—in Tours, Boulogne, or Bordeaux, where they are considered only intruders, and despised as persons necessarily expatriated. The danger of living in the remote parts of Ireland is a general suggestion. Danger? In no land is peace more profound—in none are the inhabitants more gentle and obliging than in the wilds of Iveragh?

Cahirciveen, farewell! Had not pursuits that necessarily call me to a varied intercourse with the busy world heavy claims on my exertions, I could be well content to erect my cottage on thy verge, and tranquilly eke out the remainder of life amid thy sports and beauties!

My movables being all safely stowed on board my little bark—my crew in high spirits at the prospect of revisiting their native town—we set off for Dingle, the capital of the extreme west of Kerry. This passage is sometimes effected in three hours, and abounds in objects of beauty; bold shores, skirted by lofty rocks, tenanted by innumerable wild birds of every species, while the surface of the bay is blackened with flocks of puffins and teal. The mackerel were now in the bay, and, with the glass, I could perceive the opposite shore dotted with black specks, formed by the numerous fishing-boats from Dingle. There was no lack of amusement in the passage. Our lines, out astern for mackerel, were productive, and we were continually under the necessity of altering our course to take up the produce of my double-barrel. I had by this time become skilful in shooting wild-fowl. It is not an easy acquirement. The boat's motion, being always crossed by the motion of the birds swimming on the rising seas, will render some practice necessary. They must be caught just as they attain the summit of the wave.

As we approached the Ventry shores, numerous boats stood towards us, and many and hearty were the greetings of the fishermen, who had so long lost their companions, constituting my crew. The attachment of these people to each other is remarkable—there is not even any competition in the sale of their produce. The hucksters, who attend their arrival every evening, for the purpose of conveying the fish up the mountains to Tralee and through the country, are always prepared to take the whole, and the prices rarely vary. They are generally at this rate:—whiting, 5d. per dozen, of thirteen; mackerel, 1s. 4d. per hundred; cod, or hake, 9d. per dozen; and all other fish in proportion. The mode of division of the proceeds is on a principle also that ensures unanimity. There are six men to a boat, which is generally hired of some large proprietor. For the boat is put aside two shares; the rest equally divided.

The harbour of Dingle is well adapted for yachting; yet, with the exception of a pretty vessel belonging to Dr. B——, a physician of considerable eminence, it has none of the advantages arising from aquatic amusements. The town is superior to those in other parts of Ireland of much greater pretensions; it affords excellent lodgings, and is surrounded by seats of resident gentry.

The inhabitants of Dingle appear to have more comforts —are better employed, and better paid than at most other places—while the improvements, continually progressing under the influence of landlords who take an interest in the management of their own property, have contributed much to the social advantages of the poor. The bay is a source of endless wealth, being never without abundance of fish of all kinds. Here also, with letters of introduction, good society would be found; and the open hospitality of Ireland, so fast disappearing from the more mercantile districts, would be fully recognised.

In addition to the sea-fishing, a white trout river will be found very abundant in the smaller kind; as, also, excellent grouse-shooting. I believe none of the mountains are preserved. I wish I could speak of the general state of this part of Kerry in the same favourable terms as of that on the Iveragh side. Here the chief landlord, as usual, deserts his domain—here the tenants are abandoned to the tender mercies of agents, while the proprietor dissipates in a foreign land the sums extracted from the extreme wretchedness of the poor.

What can be the object of the elaborate dissertations daily issuing from the press on the causes of distress in Ireland? The cause is as obvious as the remedy is difficult of attainment. No money is spent in Ireland. The produce of the soil, either in the shape of money or exportations, is transmitted to the original proprietors, who return no portion to the labourer—the whole is elsewhere dissipated. The only source of employment—tillage of the ground—furnishes no means of provision for a rapidly increasing population. Manufactures—the arts—all but the meanest exercise of man's faculties, tillage—are absent. Rents increase in the ratio of increased numbers, and the competition for land among those who must live—and live only by the labour applicable to it—has reduced the peasantry to the lowest means of subsistence. Money they have none—labour they can alone offer as rent—and it is by no means uncommon to find one hundred and fifty days of the year devoted to the payment of the rent for a miserable hut and plot of bog ground, that would not be valued in England at three pounds per annum.

What might not a patriotic spirit in the proprietors of the soil effect for the Irish people! Nothing is required but another direction for labour. Mills on the streams—manufactories on the coasts—ships for their naturally formed harbours—all not only within the means of the landed proprietors, but, offering certain success, might raise this country to a noble competition with any. As it is, neglected, or utterly deserted by those who should direct the people's energies, it presents only a scene of destitution and misery, which, with the number of the sufferers, must continue to increase. Poorer, however, they can hardly be—they are already reduced to the potato alone—braver and more determined they may be!

"Sure, and myself will spake to his honour; faith and it's I have the best right. Keep back, Paddy Shea—would you be 'truding to his honour's own room?"

Confused voices accompanied this remonstrance, till I gave out intimation that Owen should singly appear.

"Well, Owen, what do the crew want?"

"Faith, they want a holiday—it's a wake up the hill; and sure, sis I, his honour must go to the great wake."

"Whose wake is it, Owen?"

"It's the wake of a great farmer, your honour, and he fell down the other day."

"Fell down!"

"Faith he did, and died outright. His widow is making a wake for him that would do honour to the country, and has sent to beg your honour to be one of the howlers."

"But how can I assist? I never knew the deceased, nor the way to lament."

"Oh, it's no lament, any way. Your honour will be sure to be plased there."

Owen's importunities were not to be overcome; and, as it was quite clear that nothing was to be done without the assistance of my crew, I promised to accompany my *fidus Achates* to the scene of mourning.

We had to walk three or four miles up the mountain, a task I did not perform with the same ease as my attendants; and I really began to estimate, at the full value, the opportunity about to be afforded us of refreshing our griefs. On our approach to the door of the deceased farmer, a lamentation burst forth that at once showed the fact that our arrival was the appointed signal for the ebullition. The widow, with dishevelled hair, was at the foot of the bedstead which sustained the coffin, her head buried in her hands, which were only occasionally raised to beat her breast, which was nearly bare, and thump the coffin. Such demonstration of violence in grief was really painful, but remonstrance was in vain. The bystanders took no notice whatever of the hard thumps she inflicted on her bosom; her face, which one occasionally caught a glimpse of, was heated with her exertions in screaming

—every one joined—indeed, before my little band had entered the house, they had commenced with all energy, and entered howling. The din was distracting — as, in every variety of tone, men, women, and children, all seemed determined to show their affection for the deceased by the goodness of their own lungs.

The first impression made on the mind by the Irish howl is really a painful one. The tone of lamentation, so prolonged and loud, conveys the feeling of a sudden and irremediable grief; but, as my ear became accustomed to the sound, I ventured to look into the faces of the most sonorous of the party—there was almost an instant revulsion to the ridiculous. Not an expression of seriousness even seemed to accompany the howl—the muscles of the face were all perfectly quiescent; and so great was the philosophic bearing of some of the LADIES of the party, that I perceived they were examining and altering some parts of their dress, but in no degree relaxing in their stentorian efforts. One was deliberately putting on her stockings, which had been, as usual, carried with her shoes, not worn while walking to the scene of grief, and were to be put on only for effect on her arrival. Another was arranging the stray bands over her forehead; while here and there, amid the party, might be observed a steady and ragged old gentleman, who would suspend operations for a few whiffs at a short black pipe, and then recommence as a giant refreshed.

While the din was at its height, a person, obviously of some importance, stalked into the room — there was an instant cessation of the howl. Every one for himself; the widow arose and calmly headed the party, now consisting of at least forty, and led the way to the large kitchen. There were pipes, porter, whiskey, and a blazing fire. It was amusing to see Owen, who had howled as effectively as the best, entreating the ladies to suffer him to assist them to whiskey, and performing all the little offices of attention with an air that soon constituted him a favourite. Of course he took care of me, and I was soon seated, with a long pipe and a tumbler of whiskey-punch, in the best chair the kitchen presented. The conversation, which now became general, was translated to me by Owen, but did not at all refer to the solemn cause of the meeting. I learned, however, that the deceased had been one of the numerous victims of the "good folk"; that is, had been bewitched by some fairy. No greater or more satisfactory proof of the fact could exist than in the circumstance of his having been, previously to his death, utterly incapable of swallowing a glass of whiskey—an operation he had never for many years omitted. The man had really died of jaundice; I doubt not, indeed, by intemperance; but which, had it been subjected to medical treatment, would not, in all probability, have proved fatal. The impression, however, that he had been "banned" by the "good folk" was irremovable.

"Is it the good people?" exclaimed the steady old man, who now intermitted his whiffs and burst into tolerable English; "and if it was night, now, I'd tell the story of 'em."

This appeared to give proof of determination enough. These terrible GOOD people are powerless, it seems, in the daylight.

"Wasn't it myself escaped by a wondrous miracle?"

"To be sure and it was yourself, any way," reiterated numerous voices.

"It was night, and I slept alone by myself, only the childer and the pigs, when what should I hear but a knocking that would have aroused the dead. 'Oh, oh!' sis I, 'the whiteboys are up and doing, and it's meself will see the fun, any way'; so with that I got on my clothes, and looks cautiously through the door-cranks. The moon was bright—the divil a whiteboy there. Knock! knock! again at the door. 'Hallo there!' sis I, courageously, seeing there was nobody there, and open I throws the door. There were rows of little people all dressed in fine scarlet cloaks, and mounted upon small chargers, for all the world as complate as a regiment of foot, with drawn swords no bigger than a needle. 'Come on,' sid they, 'to the wood, Paddy

Brady.' 'And that's meself,' sis I, 'and here's for you.' Off went the elves at full gallop, and faith it took my best strides to keep up with 'em. Over rocks and bogs we went—never a sink for horse or foot till we halted on the ridge of a lake. There was a dead silence, and I wondered what next was to come; when a small fairy, with a long flowing red mantle, spoke to me. 'Paddy Brady,' sis he, 'if you are secret, you'll come to no harm.'—'Faith, and I'll be that same,' sis I.—'Look down on the lake,' sis he. Oh, the wonderful sight!—the bottom of the lake, clear as day, was covered with skeletons of men, all alive and kicking. 'It's the skeletons of the race that spoke of the good people,' sis he; 'and beware, Paddy Brady!' Hereupon began a dance, the likes of which one wouldn't aisily see again, though Murphy, the dancing-master and piper, should try his hardest. All at once a stop—and the little man with the red cloak again comes up to me. 'Read,' sis he, 'that paper.'— 'Faith and I can't,' sis I.—'Tim Murdock's wife,' sis he.—'Tim Murdock's wife,' sis they all, and fell to dancing again. The little man agin ordered the stop, and cried out, 'A cooleen!'— 'A cooleen! a cooleen!' cries all the band.

"There stuck I, wondering what the divil was the maning of all this—my knees began to totter as I looked into the lake again—there were all the skeletons, dancing as the elves danced, and doing in imitation all that they did.

"Oh, fear came upon me thin—my hair bristled up till it forced the hat off my head. 'What for is this?' sis I.—'Silence,' sis he; 'you're hearing the names of the *banned*.'—'Och hone!' sis I; 'I'll be after telling them,' sis I, unawares like. Crash went the rock—in went the moon—down tumbled I from crag to crag, an endless fall, till, after travelling in this disagreeable manner, cracking my ribs against rocks as I rolled, slush into the lake I fell—'twas there that Terry O'Rourke found me— and sure, haven't I the marks of the wounds I got in my fall?"

All signified perfect conviction in the truth of the events related by the ragged old gentleman, who resumed his pipe with a consciousness of dignity that greatly tried my ability to restrain laughter.

> Our life is twofold, sleep hath its own world.

The truth is, that Paddy Brady had doubtlessly got very drunk and had fallen down in his road homeward. Paddy Brady had dreamed the rest, and had recounted the story till he almost himself believed in the reality.

The whiskey and *porther* [1] had now progressed, and perhaps would have proceeded much further, but that a sudden *och hone* from the adjoining room denoted the recommencement of the orgies. Down went the glasses and pipes. "Och hone, och hone," joined all, and in two minutes all were again around the corse of the departed. At every cessation there was the same recourse to whiskey and pipes—the same fairy stories were told, only with less perspicuity; and it was one o'clock when, accompanied by Owen, I left the company, to fight out the remainder of the night (an exercise they had already begun), or to sleep off the effects of their inebriety.

Such was the Irish wake! the original institution was, perhaps, intended to have been expressive of grief and condolence. It is as much a custom with the mountaineers, and fraught with as little real feeling as the attendance of mutes at an English funeral. I must not, however, do these poor people the injustice of allowing it to be inferred that they are wanting in attachment to each other, or in sorrow for their bereavement; they are remarkable for both; but the custom of congregating their friends on the occasion of a death is one, by me at least,

> More honoured in the breach than in th' observance.

---

[1] Visitors to remote districts in Ireland who dislike Irish whiskey, will do well to remember that, in the humblest villages, it is nearly always easy to get the very best porter.—ED.

CHAPTER XIV

To the Shannon—Mountain Scenery—Profusion of Wild-Fowl and Hares
—Listowel—Extempore Dinner—Cheap Travelling—Excellent Sport
—Primitive Cooking—Mill Street—Extraordinary Cheapness of Living
—Extreme Wretchedness of the Inhabitants—First View of the Queen
of Irish Rivers, the Shannon—Athlone—Ballinasloe Fair—Onions and
Eels—Athlone Bridge—Lough Ree—The Shannon—Splendid Tract of
Country—Suitable Harbour for Shipping.

THE time had now arrived when I had proposed to try the celebrated Shannon, the Queen of Rivers. Discharging, therefore, my little crew (and, I confess, with extreme regret, as they had, by their unflinching industry, hardihood, and general temperance, greatly attached me to them, and contributed in a high degree to my amusement while lingering in the peaceful Kerry), I set out, accompanied by Owen, but to what point I should direct my wanderings I had not determined, leaving much to chance. The convenience of my pony carriage assisted my views of stopping wheresoever the scenery amused or the rivers gave intimation of sport.

After leaving Tralee, we traversed the base of the Stacks and Glanruddery mountains; immense ranges, which seemed to guard the island from the encroachments of the wide and cerulean Atlantic, over which, from the road, were presented splendid views. The immense concourse of wild-fowl, which here seem wholly unmolested, would perhaps have seduced a more devoted shot from his way; but I pressed on, only carrying my gun as we ascended the precipitous hills on foot. I found no difficulty in killing a few hares; plentiful, indeed, throughout Kerry, and of so little value that the extreme price is sixpence at any time. I found also immense flights of cormorants, wild geese, and swans, which evidently have, time immemorial, bred in these untraversed mountains. I could get no opportunity of securing any of them.

On our arrival at Listowel, I was resolved to spend at least one day in traversing the river, which passes through the town and falls into the sea at Mill Street. With this view we slept at Listowel.

The appearance of the town is in the highest degree wretched, presenting all the worst features of the Kerry villages. Civilisation has yet made no stride towards the skirts of the mighty Atlantic, for here nakedness among children seemed the prevailing fashion.

We had traversed with great difficulty the banks of the Feale without any chance of rest or refreshment, until we arrived at a few huts, dignified by the title Innsmore, which boasted only of a "public," of the poorest order. We were heartily wearied, as the banks were boggy and rocky alternately, the former compelling us sometimes to go a mile round before we could, with any safety, rejoin the river.

The result of our labours amounted only to a few trout, and those not of the best order. However, a selection of the largest among them soon furnished a tolerable dinner. It consisted of excellent potatoes, whiskey and water (which we had brought with us, uncertain that we could be supplied on the road), boiled and baked trout. The cost of our banquet was sixpence for potatoes, oatmeal, bread, and cooking, and a good turf-fire.

From Innsmore we pushed forward to the point about two miles from the village, where the Feale receives the river Gale, a shallow but rapid river, from the mountains. Notwithstanding the objections of Owen, I was determined to give this fall a fair trial. At a distance of some yards from the spot we lighted

"Good Cooking, any way."

a good fire, which may be almost everywhere among the rocks easily accomplished by the abundant supply of dry weeds and bog-wood, which the overflowing streams have lodged in the clefts. This arrangement first made, I prepared two rods, fitted with strong tackle, as the appearance of the water, the deep lodges which here and there terminated the streams, gave good token of a salmon. On endeavouring to decide on the depth, I was somewhat surprised to find my reel nearly naked of line. I am disposed to believe that it was above thirty yards deep.

We had no success with the salmon-roe, while Owen, pursuing the river, was busy with the small brown trout, which had doubtless belonged to the smaller river, and had come down from the mountains. They were worthless, as, indeed, are most of the mountain trout. At length, a tug at the end of my rod indicated the presence of some stronger antagonist. I called to Owen for his gaff, and began to reel up my prize. The first spring from the surface showed that we had a chance of a "good cooking, any way," as Owen expressed it; and, after a labour of some minutes, our prey was duly crimped and supported across the turf-fire by three triangular sticks, which presented a dish fit for a noble's banquet.

Perhaps I am travelling out of the record in saying a dish—if it constituted one, it was of easy manufacture, being nothing more than a large flat stone from the shallows of the river, polished by many an age of flood. Owen baked the potatoes, and my small wallet furnished the few condiments our desert journey rendered desirable.

While we were busily engaged in performing the last offices for the defunct salmon, I was again called to the relief of my second rod; it was a salmon again. I had in this pool three runs, and killed three fish; two of which, being about eight pounds each, we carried to Mill Street.

I had disdained to attempt the trout of this river; and, therefore, fished no part but the hole where the two streams meet. I do not doubt, however, but that this spot, after floods especially, would furnish almost continual sport through the year.

The rivers in this neighbourhood appear to have remained untouched. The fishermen of Mill Street being all seamen, the splendid supply which in fine weather they can command in the mouth of the Shannon, supersedes all attention to the minor rivers.

Mill Street is beautifully situated at the termination of the Feale, bounded on one side by a high range of mountains. There is, also, a small stream, which runs by the town, abounding in small trout from the sea, taken, not unfrequently, after floods, by the hand in the shallows.

Less, perhaps, is known of the inhabitants of this part of Ireland than of any other. The intercourse with any large town is confined to such communication as necessarily springs from the supply they receive of such articles as are required for the ordinary wants of life. There is not even a road by which the produce of the sea, their chief wealth, can be conveyed to any considerable distance. The consequence is, that every article which is of native production is sold at ruinously low prices. I saw a pig hanging from one of the cottages—killed to pay rent. It weighed eighty pounds, and was offered to me at six shillings. Of course the luxuries of life—that is to say, tea, sugar, and clothing—are in the same ratio, dear.

The miserable state of poverty in which the inhabitants pass their lives is almost indescribable; and if one had not beheld *destitution* even *more destitute* in the larger towns of Ireland, from a view of Mill Street, the traveller would be induced to say, "Surely life cannot be less life than here."

It was at four o'clock on the first dawn of a glorious summer morning that, on ascending a hill out of the town of Listowel, on the road to Tarbert, the wide expanse and magnificent waters of the justly celebrated Shannon burst on my view. The green surface of the land on either side, which now bore the appearance of a velvet carpet spread over the beauteous face of the soil, was reflected in the dark and silent stream with a brilliancy that no glass could imitate. Every object, however minute, was faithfully portrayed in the Narcissian mirror.

And this is the Shannon, whose course divides almost into natural provinces the vast regions through which its waters glide—the Shannon—Nature's canal—formed to convey to and from the inhabitants of a prolific land their manufactures and productions.

In the lower part of the river, however, there is little hope for the sportsman; the body of the stream is too large for the angler; with the exception, therefore, of the tributaries which fall into the Shannon, which, with no great success, I *en passant* tried, the sportsman would be ill employed who would follow this stream.

Packing up, therefore, our apparatus, we determined, without loss of time, to push forward for Athlone—the embouchure of Lough Ree, of which station report had highly raised our expectations.

Athlone, however, bears more marks of civilisation; it has a tolerable street; women occasionally wear stockings and shoes, and some of the children are clothed. I found it impossible to obtain lodgings, from the crowded state of the town, this being the Ballinasloe fair—perhaps the largest cattle fair in England or Ireland. The inns make this their harvest; and the reader will be surprised to hear that ten shillings and sixpence per night, for a miserable bedroom, was demanded at the meanest of them. As, however, my purpose was not to deal in cattle, I sent Owen to the little "public" situated on the mouth of the lake. Having made some arrangements, he returned to me, horror-stricken at some sights which had not very favourably impressed him with the population.

"It's impossible they should be rale Irishers. It's enough to condemn them all—eels, snakes as long as my arm, onions stuck in their mouths—and they offer to cook them, and give 'em as food."

I found Owen was right; there were, indeed, eels—and in such abundance, exposed at every shop, whiskey-hovel, or lodging window—eels of three, four, or five pounds, which would seem to imply that they constituted the chief food of the people. This turned out to be the fact. These animals descend the Shannon in such multitudes, that, in the autumn, after the flood, the rapids and falls in the narrower parts of the river need only be crossed by a purse net, and tons weight of eels are frequently taken in one night. Although, throughout Kerry, I could never prevail on the people to cook, much less to eat them —at Athlone, if one may judge from the abundant display, they are in the highest repute.

We now took possession of our little apartment on the borders of the celebrated Lough Ree.

The first thing that aroused my surprise at Athlone was the continued exposure for sale of trout of eight, ten, or fifteen pounds each, which seemed to excite no admiration among the people. I believe the Shannon produces the largest in the world; and, though difficult to capture, yet success in one instance amply repays days of disappointment. I was almost angry at the sight of such splendid creatures, sold for the merest trifle, and apparently regarded with less respect than the eels which satiated the town.

At the old town bridge there will be found a considerable fall in the river, which afterwards joins the main body of the stream below Athlone, constituting a little vortex. After having procured a boat, I first cast my line on this spot. Owen's labour and my own were without effect. Not a rise— not an appearance of a fish. We floated down the stream two or three miles, still accompanied by disappointment; nor was it till the evening began to set in, that we returned to the spot from whence we had first started. I now changed my tackle for the salmon-roe, and, having well loaded my hook, sent it off to seek its fortune in the whirlpool. The difficulty I found in fishing this spot was the extreme depth, at least forty feet; and, unless the roe was well put on, and wholly covered the hook, I found, before it had reached the bottom, the latter was frequently bare. As soon as I had corrected this error and effectually commanded the bottom, success followed. A tug, that nearly took rod and all from my hand, aroused my hopes of the new bait—new, indeed, to these fish, among which it had never been tried.

"Huzza!" exclaimed Owen, in an ecstasy; "here's the Shannon trout, any way; and it's your honour's the only man can catch 'em." But, alas! I could not hold them; fish after fish broke away, and, after an evening's hard work, we found ourselves only masters of five fish, from three to seven pounds each.

The day is unfavourable to Shannon fishing. Like other large animals of prey, their motion is too slow to enable them to catch the smallest fish in full light; twilight, therefore, is the time of their hunting, and should be that of the fisherman in all these rivers and lakes. Having returned to our little inn, I requested permission to accompany two of the Lough Ree fishermen, who lived in cottages close by our little hotel, and who principally supplied the inns and inhabitants of the town with fish. In this I had little difficulty; and, making preparations, therefore, for a night out, and not forgetting those essential portions of such arrangements, whiskey and tobacco, we set forth with muffled oars. The navigation of Lough Ree is dangerous in the extreme. My crew luckily knew every turn; and, as they prepared their long lines, I and Owen were busy with our flies. The success with the lake trout was trifling, not one having been captured of more than a pound weight.

The process of shooting the long lines was now begun. At every yard was a hook of the size of the whiting hook, and about two inches of a tolerably-sized eel, well twisted on each hook. I did not anticipate that such a bait would be effective for trout.

The number of hooks was two hundred, and the line was

cast, or, as the boatmen say, shot, just as has been previously described. The result, at daylight, was twenty-two trout, varying from three to five pounds, several large eels, and two very large pike. The amusement was not exciting, and, though we endeavoured to keep up the hilarity of the evening by Owen's songs and our boatmen's stories of their English wanderings, it

PREPARED FOR A NIGHT OUT.

must be confessed that fishing on Lough Ree is, to use the current expression—slow.

There is a change of character worthy of remark as we approach the more northern part of Ireland; Owen's disgust had manifestly assumed a more intense feeling, as he besought me not to remain on the Shannon; the inhabitants, he assured me, were heartless and cruel; that they had *larned* every kind of cheating; and that, for himself, he could have no chance whatever with them; even the boatmen expressed extreme dissatisfaction on Owen's presenting them, for their midnight company, three shillings, a sum that would exceed the produce of many a night's toil. I was not long in discovering the true cause of these peculiarities, for so I must term them, in the Athlone and Shannon "boys." At Athlone there has been long established a barracks, and it is now held as a station for several regiments. The officers have, in some measure, imitated the Killarney visitors; and I took leave of Lough Ree without regret, and abandoned all the joys of onions and eels for the better fare of Galway salmon.

The Shannon is, indeed, the queen of rivers; navigable for nearly two hundred and thirty miles through the interior of the richest tract of country in the world; abundant in every production that a river should present to the angler; but the sailing on the loughs is dangerous, and the river itself too rapid. Although, on all the loughs, vessels, or rather yachts of all kinds may be observed, like beautiful phantom ships, gliding over the dark waters of the endless lakes, yet the continual occurrence of hidden rocks, and those just emerging from the surface, renders the utmost skill of the pilot necessary; nor, indeed, without his assistance, should any one venture on the water. It were safer sailing on the wide Atlantic.

Upon the whole, I do not think the fishing of the Shannon agreeable. I say little of it, indeed, on that account; it is a style too much resembling sea-fishing; it must be long line sport or none, as the fly may in general as well be cast on the broad sea-shore as on these inland oceans. The river presents no better sport; a week's trial convinced me that nothing but the baited line at night, or the sweeping and execrable net, can be rendered available. I did not, however, try the tributary streams, where, I do not doubt, in the spring and autumn, great sport might be found; as, at those periods, the best fish are found in the shallowest rivers. It must, however, be remembered that nothing but the salmon-roe or the minnow will at those seasons succeed; with these the natives are wholly unacquainted, relying on the more wholesale methods of netting or night-lining.

In speaking of the splendid tract of country through which the Shannon flows, it is impossible to refrain from expressing deep regret that so little has been done to secure the advantages which ought to have been derived to Ireland. Nature, indeed, seems to have pointed out this tract as the harbour for shipping, commanding the whole continent of America by a direct and safe passage. If to the lower harbour, formed by this splendid river, could be cut a railroad, either from Dublin or Cork, Ireland would at once become a new country, and commercial prosperity would begin to relieve the oppression of a now too abundant population.

CHAPTER XV

Galway—Mr. Keogh—Fishing in Lough Corrib—First Failure of the Infallible Bait—Its Causes—A New Acquaintance—The Monastery—Claddagh—Its Antiquity—Forms of Marriage—Dress of the Females—Respect paid to the Dead—Prevalence of the Cholera—Benevolence of the Rev. Father Fay—Protestants and Catholics—History of James Lynch Fitzstephen, the Mayor of Galway.

Having left the valley of the Shannon, the country again assumes the barren and uncultivated garb; masses of rocks, with scarcely a spot of verdure, arising abruptly from amidst the deep green plains of bog, over which, as the coach rolled on, might be observed, for hundreds of yards, a succession of undulations that carried somewhat of fear to the inexperienced traveller, lest the road, the only firm spot over the boundless morass, should at any part give way and entomb the voyagers. The entrance to Galway, however, gave back all the beauties of land and ocean; at one burst from a hill the broad Atlantic presents herself, covered with white dots, the boats of the Galway fishermen; and the white smoke, extending along the shore of the creek, indicates the approach to what is still a large and considerable city; but what, alas! was once the capital of Western Ireland.

I cannot easily describe the sensation of pleasure I experienced in my first walk through Galway, a spot to which my highest hopes of success in angling had been directed; the town, through which a salmon river still runs, and in which the silvery tenants had not, through a succession of ages, decreased.

Taking my stand on the venerable bridge, through which the trembling waters of Lough Corrib, a lake of sixty miles extent, fall into the bay, I gazed steadfastly on the transparent stream; masses of black, here and there, covered the bottom, forming the appearance of seaweed, gently moved by the course of the waters, till occasionally by a silvery flash, here and there, was seen the delicate white of the salmon; those masses were constituted of fresh-run fish, congregated in preparation for their annual voyage to the vast lake.

Having marked the spots where they were thus clusteringly placed, I betook myself to the inn, soon unpacked my tackle, and, presenting myself at the gate of Mr. Keogh, the liberal renter of the river, requested his permission to try my fortune. This was promptly given, and in a few minutes I was on the wall which divides the stream from the weirs. Mr. Keogh accompanied me, but did not give me hope of success. A short time convinced me that his knowledge of the habits of the Lough Corrib salmon exceeded mine; not a rise to the most attractive fly I could present cheered my expectations; and, after two hours' hard labour, during which I had cast over the very heads of some thousand salmon, I retired in disappointment.

This was not to be borne, and I immediately sought the acquaintance of a gentleman, to whom Mr. Keogh recommended me, as a thorough fisherman. I record what I consider my good luck, because it may be serviceable to any sportsman who may follow in my track. With that gentleman, at a very moderate price, I immediately domiciled; having, for twelve shillings per week, an excellent furnished drawing-room and two bedrooms, with all necessary attendance. I lost no time in making my permanent arrangements for a sojourn in so interesting a town.

I now learned that the only chance of success on the river was at the dawn of day. At that time the fish, unscared by the continual view of objects moving over the bridge, were on the feed; but that, in fine weather, any attempt during the day was fruitless. Furnishing ourselves, therefore, with a gaudy fly, such as fresh-run fish are most likely to be attracted by, before daylight in the morning my host was with me.

Early as we were on the scene of action, we had, nevertheless, been anticipated. Two anglers were there, and had well thrashed the stream before us. My companion introduced me to one, the Rev. Mr. F., who expressed his regret that he had not known my intention to visit the river, as he would undoubtedly have left it for my amusement. This was so kindly said that I was immediately prepossessed with my new acquaintance, and requested his company to breakfast. In accepting my invite he pointed to a fine salmon of nine pounds weight, which he had just landed, as an addition to our commissariat.

It was necessary to allow the river some quiet before the fly was again cast, and, changing our tackle, we threw for white trout at a spot higher up than the salmon lodges. Success quickly followed here; but with the humbler species of the salmon I was dissatisfied; the nobler game had already possessed me, and I longed to try my chance with the roe. Candour obliges me to record that in this river, for the first time in Ireland, I was foiled; for, although I was convinced I so managed to present the bait that it must have passed the noses of the fish, not one noticed it.

The cause of this I at length discovered; in this river the fish do not spawn; they proceed through the lough to the mountain streams, and, being fresh-run from the sea, they have scarcely recovered from the violent transition from which they necessarily suffer. The truth of this opinion was well established by my subsequent success in the tributaries to the lake; in those, the roe was the most effectual bait for the salmon.

On resuming the fly, however, I was successful, and my companion not less so. In twenty minutes we had landed two fine fish, which I was assured and found was the extent of the sport we should meet; as the river, once fished down, was generally no further productive for the day.

On my return to breakfast, I had the pleasure to find that my new acquaintance, the priest, was my opposite neighbour; being the head of the monastery, a plain, though extensive building, situated on the banks of the river. The establishment consisted of twelve monks, and himself the prior. Their incomes arise from bequests, and were about fifty pounds per annum each. They all had separate apartments, a common hall for dining, the means of which were amply supplied by the presents of the laity.

There was, indeed, abundance—but an abundance well directed—at a certain hour, daily, might be seen the aged, the destitute, and diseased, knocking at the door of the monastery, and each receiving a portion, from the hands of the priest himself, of that which charity had supplied.

We are greatly misled in estimating these institutions. The services of the monks are, like those of the priests, services of hardship; nor is it uncommon for them to be absent among the mountaineers for days, visiting and consoling the afflicted and the dying. In this country, also, where no regulated provision for the poor exists, they form the authority for the judicious direction of charity; while themselves, independent of the world, and having no claims on their assistance but those of duty, are free to bestow all that is not necessary to the sustaining their institution.

The prior had, as was the case with the rest, been educated at Rome. Seven years had he passed within the walls of a monastery, wholly devoting his labours to literature of all kinds. I need not say that he was highly learned; for, in addition to that ordinary education which a college affords, he had traversed the whole Christian world. I shall not easily forget the happiness I derived from his society, nor be ungrateful for the advantage it afforded.

Perhaps one of the most interesting features of Galway is the fishing village called Claddagh. The name signifies in Irish the sea-shore, on which it is situated. It is irregularly built, and intersected by several narrow lanes, and contains about four thousand inhabitants, who are exclusively employed in the bay fishing. It has, like every part of this curious town, strong characteristics of antiquity, and by some is assumed to have been the original site of the earliest settlers' first habitations. It constitutes a perfect colony; and has, time immemorial, been ruled by one of their own body, periodically elected; he is dignified by the title of mayor, and, though a ragged representative of the municipal power, satisfactorily settles all disputes, and propounds laws by which the whole population are governed. To him are all disputes referred, civil as well as criminal; and by him are they generally decided, without any apparent disobedience to his decree. It appears they still remain exempt from all government taxes, have no party feeling, and never interfere with politics. In short, so perfect a specimen of the *imperium in imperio* will nowhere else be found.

The forms of marriage among these singular people are worthy of notice; they have no connection with the townspeople, to whom they appear to entertain a decided dislike, and their own marriages generally take place at a very early age: fifteen being the usual time that is recognised for the man. Having made his choice, the young couple elope, and, having been two or three days absent, return, are pardoned, assigned a dwelling, and commence as independent members of the community. It is remarkable that infidelity is unknown among them; nor, from all I could gain from my intelligent informant, the priest, could I understand that jealousy was ever known to exist. The fortune of the wife is the share in a boat.

The dress of the females, as among those of the inhabitants of Galway and Connemara, still retains the characteristic of their Spanish origin—the blue mantle, and red body gown, petticoat of the same colour, and a blue or red cotton handkerchief bound round the head. Sometimes the gaudy ribbon may be observed, but the regulation among the Claddagh people is strict, that none shall be allowed the use of this ornament who cannot speak English. There is no difficulty in selecting the lady one would address, though I should by no means advise any brother sportsman to cultivate any particular admiration of the Claddagh damsels; the consequences might be more direct than those of damages in an action duly recovered.

The respect shown to the departed friend is manifested in an especial manner, by adjournment to the whiskey-shop; and the measure of grief is ordinarily established by that of the inspiring liquor served out to the survivors. The lamentations continue the whole of the night, which is consumed in carousal with the party attending the funeral. It has been observed that this peculiarity seems to connect these people with the Arabs, whose peculiar constitution it is to rejoice at the death of their friends. There can be no doubt that the Irish wake ever has been and still is a festival; whether established for such an occasion by sound philosophy or not, is still a problem I am unable to solve; this, I think, is certain—life is not made for happiness—death may be so.

It is to us laymen, who presume to understand nothing of the matter, but who are happy enough if we do all that we can in the fair and right way, and can, as Izaak says, obtain health and strength and leisure to go a-fishing—it is to us sometimes amusing to listen to the opinions one set of reverend priests express of priests of another class—it is amusing to hear the Rev. Sydney Smith, the mouthpiece of all that is liberal in the Church, in his bold and round manner lay down this position:

> The Catholic faith is a misfortune to the world.

Yet can no one step into the humble habitation of the dying labourer in Ireland, whose life, as it has been without comfort, so the loss of it is attended with little to regret—yet whose sorrowing relatives surround him in all the bitter anguish of the parting hour—no one can step in and view the consolations offered by the priest, consolations not of forms, as too often are all the solaces of the Catholic faith supposed to consist of, and say the "Catholic faith is a misfortune to the world." To the Protestant world, our reverend friend and militant should have said; and to the Protestant world, small as it is in Ireland, in particular.

But let us see how the Catholic religion is a misfortune to the world.

In the summer of 1832 the Claddagh was more than any other spot in Ireland the resting-place of the destructive and horrific cholera; then might be seen in one house the dying father laying out the lifeless corses of the mother and her children; the physician, even the druggist doctor, had abandoned the place; and death in his most frightful form, unchecked, held on his way of devastation. The cholera was by no means exclusive, nor made it any particular favourites, either with the Protestant or Catholic—if one may be allowed to personify so *deep a blue*, it may be well observed that the lady swept all before her in Ireland; and even the decencies of life, which protected as it was thought the rich in England, were here unavailing.

Galway has its Protestant church, and takes all the tithes; but the Protestant clergyman, seeing how useful his services at that moment might become elsewhere, bid adieu to Galway as the cholera entered. Why should I hesitate to name the man who has entitled himself to the love of all his parishioners. It was the Rev. Father Fay, who, so far from abandoning his post, he being at the time in the cure of the fishermen's city, ordered a room to be fitted for himself in the very midst of destitution, that he might be at hand to administer to the wants of the countless sick and dying. Here was not only religious consolation, but also for the exhausted and the fainting all the comforts and restorations which the active priesthood had accumulated from the general contributions of the people.

Nor were the inhabitants of the convent idle—not a call was disobeyed—the habitations of wretchedness, disease, and death, were alone entered by the priests; their whole labour, and even their slender means of support, were generously devoted to the succour of the poor; at the hour of midnight would the wearied inmate of the convent obey the summons, to traverse the mountains during the descent of rains and floods, to give, as they *thought then,* and believe now, consolation to the sick and wretched. From such communicants could be obtained none of those ENORMOUS fees which excite the indignation of the Protestant clergy. No! the fee, by which their exertions through this terrible and destructive time were remunerated, was the affection and confidence of their flocks, which can never be removed.

Preach to the peasant the villainy of Catholicism—show him how vile a faith he follows, and bid him remember the conduct of the Irish priesthood during the cholera, and recall that of a reverend rector of ——! The result might possibly be that the attentive listeners would, because it would be very impolite to do otherwise, admit the proposition of the Rev. Sydney Smith, that "the Catholic faith is a misfortune to the world," but he might at the same time insinuate that it is useful in times of cholera!

I am no Catholic, but I reverence the religion which produces humane feelings and cherishes the exercise of kindness of heart. What is it that some—slight enough—distinctions are to be made, in those nobody seems agreed—shall such a cause take from the deserving labourer in the vineyard of generous devotion all the honour which his sincerity and exertion challenge! Protestant England—alien in blood, language, and religion—having seized for the propagation of her own religion, which is not and cannot be that of the people, all the funds originally intended for far other and more useful purposes, would at length strip the Catholic priesthood of the influence which their merits have created. It will be easy to curse the power of the Irish priesthood; but, to destroy it, the same means must be used which have created it among the people; let me see the Protestant clergyman vie in good deeds to his fellow-men with the priest; let me see the same absence of all personal motive, of pride, of state; let me see the same conduct adopted, and the Catholic power will be in jeopardy—*not till then*.

The singular good fortune of the priesthood, throughout the prevalence of the terrific scourge to which I have referred, is worthy of record. I believe not one fell a victim to the exercise of his office and the discharge of his difficult duty. The veneration now expressed by the populace must be to them the proudest reward, and obviously exceeds that vast amount of wealth which is delivered to the tender mercies of the aliens in religion. Father Fay, whose courage in casting his lot amid the dying fishermen has been spoken of, may be found in simple guise, with an unassuming and quiet demeanour, peacefully casting his fly on the stream that runs through Galway; as ready with any information he can afford a stranger who seeks it, as he is in the performance of the high duties attached to his office.

The scrupulous reverence which is paid to the ancient habitation of the Lynch family, though now occupied by meaner tenants, will, necessarily, excite the inquiries of the stranger; nor shall I deem any apology necessary for giving the whole of the story with which it is connected. The romance of history greatly exceeds that of imagination; and, while the stern deeds of a Roman Father have been for ages extolled, the still firmer mayor of Galway has fallen into oblivion, and nothing now remains but the skull and cross-bones reverently preserved to indicate the spot where the most terrible sacrifice of feeling to justice was once made.

James Lynch Fitzstephen, an opulent merchant of Galway, was elected mayor in 1493, at which time a regular and friendly intercourse subsisted between the town and the several parts of Spain. This mayor, who from his youth had been distinguished for his public spirit, had, from commercial motives, on all occasions encouraged an intercourse that proved so lucrative as well to his fellow-townsmen as to the Spaniards; and, in order the more firmly to establish the connection between them, he himself went a voyage to Spain, and was received when at Cadiz at the house of a rich and respectable merchant named Gomez, with the utmost hospitality and with every mark of esteem suitable to his high reputation, and to the liberality of his entertainer. Upon his departure for his own country, wishing to make some grateful return for the numerous civilities he had received from the Spaniard, he invited his son, a youth of nineteen, to accompany him to Ireland, promising to take parental care of him during his stay. Young Gomez, who was the pride of his parents, was rejoiced at this opportunity, and seized with ardour the kind offer of his father's friend.

On their arrival at Galway, Lynch introduced the young stranger to his family; he was kindly received, and especially taken as a companion to the son of his host, a young gentleman of great acquirements, and enjoying the general respect of his fellow-townsmen. His popularity was so great, indeed, that he might at any time have become the leader of the Galway men, and could even have commanded the affections of his choice among the Galway ladies. There was, nevertheless, some disposition to freedom in his attachments, which had in some degree afflicted his father, who had ever been remarkable for the purity of his life. The latter had, however, conceived hopes of an entire reformation in his son, from the discovery of the fact that he was deeply attached to a lady of great personal beauty and accomplishments, the daughter of his warmest friend.

Anxious as he was that the mayoralty, an office which had been thrust on him the year of his return from Spain, an office of high importance and dignity, inasmuch as he was invested with the full powers of judge, both in civil and in criminal matters, should be sustained with unsullied honour, the prospect of his son's succeeding him gave new pleasure to his life.

The attachment of the young men was matter of general observation; they were seen together on all occasions; and, even in the visits to the beautiful Agnes, they were seldom separated. At length the English youth conceived a jealousy of his companion's attentions. It was confirmed by watching, from the house of the beautiful Agnes, him who had been his nearest friend. It was night: the streets were dark: his dagger was buried in the bosom of the stranger, who, though wounded unto death, staggered some distance towards the shore, whither the relentless assassin pursued him, and cast the now lifeless body into the sea.

On the coming morning the body had been cast up by the tide, and the whole town was in consternation; the mayor had been summoned—a dagger was found on the shore, red with the blood of its victim—one was only absent—it was he to whom the dagger belonged—it was to the son of the mayor, who sat in deliberation on the murder!

On the discovery of the criminal, he made no denial of the deed, but avowed himself the murderer amidst the deepest exclamations of remorse for the frenzied act. The disconsolate yet determined parent consigned him to a prison; public disgrace awaited him, should he shrink from the performance of his duty; the violated laws of hospitality must be vindicated. The rigid severity he had, during the discharge of his functions as mayor, exercised towards an unhappy criminal guilty of a similar act, shut out the possibility of compromise, and sealed the fate of his son.

Once only in the annals of men had so terrible a scene been witnessed; and it was left for the upright magistrate of a small town in the west of Ireland to revive the glory or the horror of consigning to death the son of his affections, as a sacrifice to public justice.

On the promulgation of the inflexible sentence of death the people became tumultuous and violent: they surrounded the house of the heart-stricken magistrate; and, incensed by the belief that justice was second to the feelings of nature, determined on the rescue of their admired fellow-townsman. Some suggestions were made, in order to pacify the people, that mercy would be extended, and that the actual execution of the son was not contemplated by the father. This was effectual, and prevented the outbreak, which had become otherwise irrepressible. It was at midnight that the stern father entered the cell of the criminal —announced to him the certainty of his fate on the coming morn, and banished from his mind all hope of escape. The father wept and prayed by the side of his prostrate son, who spoke no word: the exhortations of the priest were without effect—with hope had departed reason; still the father watched, till the first ray of daylight warned him to act. At that moment, looking into the vacant countenance of his son, the heart gave way, and he fell on the upreared body, overwhelmed by his feelings.

At length he arose, gave the necessary orders to the guards, and, between the files of the soldiery, who had formed a strong guard by the orders of the mayor—the priest supporting one arm, and the father the other—the subdued culprit was conducted to the place of execution. Who shall paint the concluding scene?—a frantic mother, heartbroken sisters, met him at the spot—the reproaches of the frenzied parent were loud against the sternness of the magistrate, but ineffectual.

Demonstrations, however, among the populace arose; shouts from the armed mob of relatives, whom the wife had excited to the rescue, surrounded the place of execution: it was amidst the threats of the crowded thousands that the mayor took his son in his arms. "My boy," said he, "thou hast only a few moments of life. God may pardon thee; I dare not. I may end my life with thine, but cannot save it." And, before the multitude could be aware of the intention, with his own hand he placed the deadly cord round the neck of the criminal, and launched him into eternity.

In the full expectation of instant death, from the fury of the mob, the calm magistrate, with a dauntless countenance, presented himself to their threatened vengeance: they were stayed by his determination—a sudden sentiment of awful admiration prevailed, and all peaceably retired. It was his last public act. The father was never again seen but by the members of his secluded family.

The house which was the scene of this terrific tragedy still exists in Lombard Street, Galway; and, though now tenanted by more humble citizens, is still a spot regarded with reverence. Over the window from which the unhappy culprit was suspended may still be seen the monument which was erected to record the deed. A skull, carved in stone, and cross-bones beneath, are all that remain to mark the public virtue of the mayor of Galway.

CHAPTER XVI

Fishing in Lough Corrib—Enormous Trout—The Weirs—Perch and Pike—Productiveness of the Weirs—Arrival of the Major—Difficulty of getting a Fishing-Boat—Independence of the Fishermen—Herring Fishery—The Mayor of the Claddagh—The Prior—The Priesthood—Preparations for Sport.

On the second morning after my arrival at Galway, I took care to be early on the wall. It is, perhaps, hardly credible that, with dressing-gown and slippers only, I daily stepped from my lodging, crossed the bridge, and secured a salmon—sometimes two, and, not unfrequently, white trout of a good size. The latter are considered of little or no value, but are, nevertheless, of most delicious flavour.

During one of the autumnal floods, when these fish run in shoals into the lake, I was surprised by one of extraordinary magnitude. I had two flies on my line, the dropper had been chosen, and, in darting towards the bottom, a salmon took the stretcher—I was close to the bridge—one fish took one arch, downwards, and the other made a different choice, and, for several minutes, so stout was the tackle, that the two fish were suspended between the arches—a stream of immense volume bearing on each.

My friend and host, seeing my difficulty, hastened to my relief, and with one blow of the boat-hook, which was close at hand, so stunned the salmon, that, though by the concussion freed from the line, he was easily taken by the landing-net; the other, being the stronger of the two, dashed down the stream,

"I was close to the bridge."

and to him I abandoned my rod, which easily passed through the arch to the dark pool below. Having with some difficulty recovered it, I now began a fair contest, and, in a short time, succeeded in landing a white trout of sixteen pounds. This size is not unusual, and, when they are taken so large, exceed in value the best salmon; although, I believe, very few of this class of fish are seen in London. Indeed, they seldom attain such a size but in lakes of enormous magnitude, such as Lough Corrib.

From the lake to the weirs there is a long, flat river, in which the more contemplative and unambitious angler may find excellent sport, should he be adept in perch fishing. I believe the whole of the river, at least, wherever the waters form a still pool, is crowded with perch, and, with a common stick, and the coarsest tackle, hundreds may be taken from one spot in a day. They are not, however, esteemed, and the style of angling is below the noble game the glorious lake and falling streams should suggest. Pike are also taken with great ease, either by trailing from a boat, or by the long line, baited with eels. So abundant, however, is the supply of sea-fish from the noble bay, that, when taken by the few fishermen who frequent the lake, they are considered valueless. Threepence is considered a great price for a pike of ten pounds.

Really, this is mortifying. The English angler, who, by a due application, has at length extracted leave for a "day's fishing" in some dull ditch or putrescent pond of an English landholder, exults in having captured a pike or two; nor is there any lack of broad direction on the basket he fills, addressed to his nearest friend or most liberal patron. The prize is spoken of as worthy of record. Visit Lough Corrib, and fill your boat daily, without the mortification of having asked a favour from the selfish owners of the water whence the supply comes. The broad expanse of Lough Corrib—as are all the lakes of Ireland, with the exception of those which are situated in the desert of Ireland, Connemara—is open to all.

I must not, however, fail to notice that the river leading

from the Lough to the weirs presents admirable sport throughout the summer and autumn, when the salmon are, as it is technically called, running; nor is it at all preserved. The fishery is below, and at the weirs—all that escape the traps are free game, while the salmon season lasts. So productive are the weirs, that, I believe, the present rental is from £300 to £400 per annum.

According to an engagement made with the major, I deferred my sea-fishing till his arrival at Galway, where we had appointed to meet for the purpose of exploring the coast of Connemara. I had written a full account of my success at the weirs and on the lake, the relation of which so hurried his arrangements that I was surprised by his presence some time before his promise.

His greeting was that of an old friend—obviously excited, nevertheless, by feelings of strong jealousy—jealousy at the advance I had made without his tuition and superintendence. My friend, the prior, readily joined the evening party, to which was added mine excellent host, whose society was really an advantage, not included in the small sum which had been fixed on as rent. His knowledge of the locale was invaluable, and I owed much of the enjoyment I experienced, in my Galway visit, to his assistance and direction.

The difficulty of getting a fishing-boat was discussed. We had already visited the Claddagh, but, such was the independence of the fishermen, that there was no hope of obtaining, at any reasonable remuneration, assistance from them.

The Claddagh men look upon the bay of Galway as their inheritance—one which they have defended with a courage which speaks better for their determination and spirit than for their knowledge of law. They have, however, up to this period, effectually prevented the use of the trawl, although frequently attempted by gentlemen who had possessed yachts. Their opinion is that such a mode of fishing is destructive of the spawn, and that the disturbance of the shallows would end in the destruction of the deep-sea fishing, from which, for a great part of the year, they draw their subsistence.

At the herring time, however, the nets are in requisition, and in this fishery all are joined. They have not the same mode of taking the herring as will be noticed in the Scotch fisheries. Whenever a shoal is indicated in Galway Bay, every boat is at sea; the nets are all fastened together, forming a circle of nearly half a mile in circumference; these are gradually drawn together, and then begins the work of sport. The herrings are literally scooped into the boats, as solid masses, and many tons are frequently the reward of one night's toil. This is the harvest of the fishermen, and, from the immense profit derived from the short period of the herring visit, they are sustained through the dreariness of the winter, when the sea-fishing is attended with considerable danger.

But the Claddagh men are a noble race of independent fellows, innocent in their lives, and determined in character. Of their honesty, generally, there can be no suspicion; and if they do not possess the polish of citizens, they, at least, are not deficient in the sterner virtues.

"The divil take the selfish loons!" said the major: "not take hire for their beggarly washing-tubs of boats? Maybe it's a high market they want."

"I think not," said the prior. "There is little to tempt them in money. They are wholly free from the characteristic vice of the towns."

"Oh, by the powers, Father, they want to be in a regiment; a little military law would aid them; but they have at least the satisfaction of being free from the patronage of a rascally government, from which I draw a paltry pay quarterly."

"No doubt they purpose to remain so. Although neglected now, many a family among them has suffered deeply by the ruthless demands of the state, which, if applied to in their affliction, is tardy in affording assistance. You know not how many widows and orphans are there whom the pressgang has rendered such. Finer sailors were nowhere to be found. But they were not enslaved easily; and in the contest for liberty many a life has been lost. Although these people would resist to the uttermost, even to blood, the impost of a tax, or the subjugation to municipal authority, they are open to all the feeling of gratitude which kindness can inspire. What is it you want?"

I explained that we had determined to try the sea-fishing of the bay; to visit Arran and Connemara; and for that purpose our intention was to fit up a good boat, such as the fishermen used, with some additional comforts.

"It can immediately be obtained," said the prior; "I will write to the mayor—not of Galway, but of the Claddagh."

The note was soon dispatched, and as soon answered by the presence of the mayor himself. He was an elderly man, of the roughest exterior; the tanned complexion bespoke a long life of exposure to the roughest breezes; but there was an intellectual boldness that might, under other circumstances, have raised him to eminence among a community more powerful than the Claddagh fishermen. He bowed as he entered the room, and his countenance brightened at the prior's presence.

"What can the Claddagh do for your reverence's honour?" said the sturdy official.

"Not much, Michael. My friends, here, are anxious to have one of the fishing-boats that happens to be unemployed, and a good hand to attend them in their excursions. I am told it is difficult to find a boat."

"Difficult! Sure is it your reverence that talks of difficulty in getting a boat? the whole fleet is ready."

"It is not for myself, Michael, but for these friends I want it."

"It's enough, your reverence; when shall it be ready?"

"To-morrow."

"Your reverence would have two hands any way to the boat. The sprats are in the bay, and there will be glorious sport to-morrow with the white fish."

"Take a glass of whiskey, Michael."

"Oh, long life and blessings to your reverence!"

He was impatient to be gone, bowed with profound respect to the prior, and retired.

A short time only had elapsed before we were literally beset with applicants for the honour of attending us. A selection had been made, and several of the best hands, anxiously hoping to become the choice of the prior, had been permitted to present themselves. The two first were at once appointed to the office; and, though full intimation was given that the choice had been made, nothing could repress the anxiety of the poor fellows to secure the happiness of obliging their kind pastor.

"You must offer these lads no money for their services," said the prior; "they will really feel aggrieved if they have not the opportunity of serving you without being suspected of any mercenary views. While in your service I know you will treat them well; but give no wages. I will contrive that you shall not be without the means of rewarding them, but it must be done with delicacy, and through the medium of their families."

"By my soul, they are noble fellows," said the major. "Why the devil was not I a priest? I shouldn't then have been paid by a rascally government."

"There would certainly be no chance of that," said the prior, smiling; "we are not *the paid* of any government; but our usefulness, I trust, is not the less on that account."

I suggested that it was probable the strong prejudices of the English would one day yield to the irrefragable proofs of the importance of sustaining the influence of religion amongst a people whose education and improvement were so much the apparent objects of parliamentary solicitude, and that an adequate remuneration would be ultimately awarded to the services of the priesthood.

"Remuneration!" said the prior, while a blush of excitement mounted to his cheeks. "I trust I shall never be one of the body that could be induced to accept it. Nothing can be more untrue than the suspicion that, as a body, the Irish priesthood aim at any state assistance. We war not with the tithes; if they were collected from the right sources, they would become nothing more than burdens upon the tenure of the land; we would scorn to accept any part of them, if offered. Our influence and our usefulness might date their downfall from the moment the Catholic priests condescended to be sustained at the expense of a Protestant government."

"Condescend!" said the major; "faith, and we must all condescend; and whenever I draw my quarterly — this is quartering upon the inimy, says I."

"The priests," said I, "have no enemies to quarter on, but those who have not known them."

"And," said the prior, while he took my hand in token of a grateful cordiality, "it is not from strangers we would derive the reward of our labours; we are content to receive it, humble though it be, from those who know us."

Our evening was spent as an angler's should be. The subjects discussed were indeed various, but none were passed by the prior. We learned the process of education adopted in Rome for those intended for the priesthood; the discipline is severe: seven years of absolute confinement within the walls of a monastery; the utmost labour exacted, each hour bringing its appointed task; while the personal comforts awarded to the novitiate are of the most meagre order. The range of the studies, however, is extensive, comprehending not only the learning of the ancients, but the controversial productions of the fathers, whose voluminous tomes would alarm an English collegian. Nor is modern literature neglected; the priests are generally excellent linguists; their manners subdued and amiable, affected, doubtless, by the severity of their education; but the reward attendant upon the sacrifice of all the worldly happiness of their youth is, when viewed in reference to other professions, of a very inadequate amount; there must be, therefore, other motives than the selfish ones too liberally ascribed to them.

Having taken our leave of the Father, the major produced his basket; it contained a supply of every sort of tackle calculated for deep-sea fishing, an art very little understood, as the mere pot-fishers of the coast pursue it in the cheapest and, therefore, the coarsest manner. The science of sea-fishing has indeed been wholly neglected where nets are not available; but it is a science that will repay the trouble of acquirement.

The ordinary coarseness of the tackle used by the seamen is very ill adapted for the better sort of fish, such as turbot, ling, and cod. The hake, indeed, is a very voracious creature, and partakes of the qualities of the dogfish, although the former, properly dressed, forms by no means a contemptible dish. Galway Bay presents, however, sport of every kind, and, on the approach of the herrings, which is indicated by the arrival of immense shoals of cod, ling, and halibut, there is, perhaps, no variety of the northern tribes, some of whose fraternity do not appear on the coast.

Preparing, therefore, for impending business, we selected the finest tackle. Our mackerel hook-lines were composed of good twisted gut, instead of the heavy hemp lines of the Galway fishermen, and our whiting crosses were made of the same material, *vice* the common tarred string. To each of our long line hooks, which were an inch and a half in the diameter, was affixed a swivel to preserve the tackle against congers; villains who abound on the coast, and whose dishonesty is so intense that on the discovery of any fish fast hooked, no matter of how large an order, they never hesitate to convert it into an extempore meal, politely, however, leaving the head to communicate the intelligence when the line is drawn. If, however, by any accident, he should also take a fancy to the head, or should himself be induced to attack the original bait, and find no accommodation for his contortions, in the way of a swivel, it will not occupy him long to destroy a whole line.

Although this difficulty may be guarded against by the use of the swivel, there is no such thing known among the Galway fishermen.

Our long line prepared, and hand lines duly stretched, we appointed an early hour in the morning for our essay, determined to visit Arran in the evening. Full of anticipation, we separated for the evening, the major having drained the whiskey bottle to the dregs, declaring that there was nothing in the Galway Bay, or on the coast of Connemara, that could come near the *riding a salmon ashore*.

CHAPTER XVII

Dress of a Sportsman—Embarkation—Wild-Fowl—Appearance of a Grampus—A Haul—The Conger and Dog-fish—The Herring—"Heads, heads, nothing but heads!"—Accident to the Major—A Splendid Halibut—A Sea-Dinner—Islands of Arran—Costume of the Arran Peasantry—Cordial Reception—A Dance—A Beauty—Amorous Propensity of the Major—Smuggling—Coast of Connemara—Magnificent Scenery—Return to Galway.

THE morning was glorious; the grey tinge, which covered the mountains and amalgamated with the cool and unbroken clouds, gave token of a goodly day.

The major's voice was my alarum. "Hallo; is it yourself that keeps the fleet waiting?—Daylight, and a fisherman asleep"—and thump went his heavy fist at the slight panelling of my chamber-door.

There was no time lost. The canvas dress was soon shipped; and, on opening the door, I could not refrain from immoderate laughter. There stood the major; a pair of coarse well-tarred trousers ensconcing his nether man, and a rough pilot jacket over all; a tarred straw hat, lined with green silk, while the wrists betrayed linen of the most delicate texture and hue. It is odd, but no disguise of dress removes a certain air of refinement—it is inseparable from the possessor. It was impossible not to see that the major was a fisherman in masquerade only.

Owen stood behind, loaded with baskets, from some of which might be seen to peep certain corks, indicative of an attention to the possible privations of a sea-voyage. All was hilarity; the freshness of the morning air, the anticipation of success, amid scenes of novelty, and, above all, the merry companionship I had secured, conspired to make such opening days little gems of remembrance.

The guns had not been forgotten, and the major, a second Robinson Crusoe, had slung them behind his back, forming altogether a most picturesque figure, while the gravity with

Leaving the Claddagh.

which he sustained the metamorphosis did not constitute the least amusing part of the scene.

We were soon at the Claddagh: here a surprise awaited us; a huzza from a long lane, formed by double rows of fishermen, at once evinced the cordiality with which we were to be received; our two visitors of the preceding evening quickly unloaded Owen and the major, and conducted us to our boat, which, though of the ordinary kind, that is, about twenty-five tons, half-decked and sloop-rigged, had been thoroughly cleansed and ornamented by all the means the poor fellows possessed. On our embarking, the admiral of the fleet, who is also the mayor of the Claddagh, paid us his respects, and wished us good sport.

The major said not a word, but seizing one of the bottles, and breaking, by a dexterous blow, the neck, without losing any of the contents, proceeded to hand round the whiskey in an ecstasy of delight. As he shook hands with the mayor, there was another shout of the fishermen; the hawser was loosened, and, in a few minutes, we were gently gliding with the tide out of the harbour of Galway.

The rising sun illumined the bay; the bold and rocky coast of Clare now opened, till the broad Atlantic, obstructed only by the shining spot called Arran, presented a gorgeous picture. The surface of the sea, for miles, was spotted by the white sails of the returning fishermen, or those putting out in search of prey. The fresh ocean breeze soon caught our sails, and we formed one of the group which completed the morning picture.

The scream of wild birds of every kind, congregated on one spot, put every sail in requisition; and in an instant might be seen a fleet of five hundred vessels, with all canvas spread, dashing forward, as in a race; we were not behind, but, to our gratification, discovered that the vessel selected for our accommodation was one of the fastest sailers of the fleet. Our two boatmen were in the bows, each armed with a long pole, at the extremity of which was a deep bag-net, for the purpose of scooping up the sprats, which, at this season of the year, constituted the only bait.

The major and myself, each with a double-barrel in readiness, were silently watching the approach towards the mass of birds. It was a perfect trial of the fleet. The breeze was fresh, and the shouts of the different boats, as they passed through the shoal of herrings, and scooped up a basket of them, did not disturb the wild-fowl, which seemed perfectly aware of the purpose of the visit, dashing a yard or two under the water, and again appearing on the surface at the stern of the boat.

A space of a hundred yards was dense with ducks, teal, widgeon, gannets, gulls, and cormorants. Within twenty yards of the spot our four barrels were discharged; all in an instant disappeared for a few seconds; first one quietly rose and rolled on his back; another, another, and another, were scooped up by the nets, till we steered into the midst of the mass of fish, so thickly crowded together as to give the appearance of discoloured water. At that moment two other boats dashed through, and, as we were all closing, the appearance of a third party put a sudden stop to our proceedings; up went the helm of every boat, and blanched became the cheek of every boatman; the shout of hilarity was in a moment changed to the silence of utter terror. The monstrous grampus had arisen in the very midst of the shoal, and, within three yards of the boats, opened his frightful jaws, entombing hogsheads of the small fry at one gulp.

The view I had of the monster was distinct; the head was completely out of the water as he opened his expansive jaws, which were lined with sharp teeth, in several rows, of about an inch long. On sinking, he flourished his tail on the surface; and this, it seems, was the great object of danger.

On our escape, it will be supposed, inquiry was soon made. The grampus is a continual visitor of the bay, on the approach of the herring season, and is regarded by the fishermen as the most deadly of all foes. Boats have frequently been sunk by one dash of his tail; and it was not without reason that the sailors expressed so much terror at his proximity to our little bark. The major was for setting up means of capturing him, a sport in which I begged not to be associated; but as my dissent became positive, the major's courage increased, till, having seized the gun, he fired at the spot, in the overboiling of his valour, where the monster had disappeared. This seemed to appease the major's wrath, and, threatening a future attack on this monarch of the bay, he betook himself to preparation for the deep-sea line, which was now ready for the bait we had taken.

Upon sounding, we found twenty-five fathoms a good depth for the larger sort of fish; and having prepared our hooks, upon each of which was a sprat, and on some two, we proceeded to sink the long line, attached to a buoy.

This done, and the bearings taken, we stood over towards the Clare shore, where we found the water deeper, and in thirty fathoms cast anchor.

We now let out the hand-lines, each person having the management of two. These we continued to sink and draw, but not long, as we soon found a dash at one: then commenced the real labour of fishing. Thirty fathoms of line, with a cod of twenty pounds weight at the end of it, was not a light amusement; but we got through it manfully. No sooner had we unhooked the fish, re-baited and set off the line, than the other was ready. This continued for an hour, till one of our new friends, the boatmen, cried out that it was time to up anchor.

"Oh, the divils are here, your honour! Up anchor, or our tackle's done."

He was right; we were all busily engaged. The major declared he had nothing less than the grampus at the end of his line, and we were all in glorious expectation of a simultaneous haul. Up they came, indeed, writhing in all directions; running foul of one another, darting across each other's lines; congers and dog-fish all—and of so terrific a size, that nothing but the sledge-hammer made any impression on their skulls, or could reduce them to any reasonable conduct. The scene was ridiculous in the extreme: each bellowing ineffectually for the assistance of his neighbour.

In the *mêlée*, however, it was discovered that the major's was really a ling, a fish of great value on this coast, and apparently of forty or fifty pounds weight. Every man, therefore, abandoned his own difficulties to remove those of the major:

he was landed—our estimate was not incorrect as to his weight. One conger was also landed of enormous size, but the rest were sent adrift, as we thought it better to cut the hook than endanger the safety of the boat's bottom by their violence.

The congers, I know not why, are never used by the Irish for any purpose. There can be no doubt that they form, well cooked, excellent food. In Jersey and Guernsey they constitute the staple of the inhabitants. Here, however, they are held in detestation, as is also the dog-fish, which, at Boulogne, and at the other fishing ports of France, one may see daily exposed for sale, at no very cheap rate.

The intimation our last haul had given of the invasion of our quarters by the congers and dog-fish soon put us again under sail. The produce of our long line now became the object of our solicitude. In the present disturbed state of the bay it was impossible to conjecture what would be captured, as it was obvious that every part of the bottom was covered with fish of some order.

What the herring eats no one knows. There are not wanting fishermen who record the catching of these spiritual creatures by the exhibition of a bright hook, without bait; but it never fell within my observation that they were in any way addicted to the gastronomic vices.

However involved the means by which they are sustained may be, it is certain that the purpose of their existence is no matter of doubt. They form the chief food of all other sea-fish; they are an unlucky set, go where they will; from the whiting to the whale they are diligently followed, and if the enemies of their own element are not sufficient, they have an ample assistance in the population of every country they are unhappy enough to visit. He who never before fished, but who hath spent the year in attendance on his flocks, is called on in the herring time. Common cause is made to prosecute the war against the unoffending visitors, who appear to migrate from one shore to another, for the sole purpose of affording a general chance to all. But the herring is a capital fellow, and must not be quarrelled with, forming, as he does, the only security against utter famine among the poorest, and the most delicious dish possible for the opulent.

Whenever the herring can be obtained, let no sea fisherman attempt any other bait. The flavour of the herring is omnipotent among the villainous community which inhabiteth the deep—I say a villainous community, because in it is no respect of kindred or of genitorship. The father, remorseless, devoureth the son; and the mother her own spawn, the moment it has become enlivened. I have no pity in consigning such ruthless savages to the bottom of the boat, especially when in doing so a noble revenge presents itself in devoting them to the mosaic equity of mastication.

The breeze was still fresh, and enabled us to come up with the buoy without difficulty. It was the first draught in the Galway Bay, celebrated throughout Ireland as the beau ideal of piscatorial achievement. The major drew the buoy, it was heavy, and he swore there must at least be a ton weight of fish on the lines. Our two boatmen coiled the line as it was drawn in silent doubt. At length the first hook appeared.

"A head!" cries the major.

"A head!" cried the boatmen; "the divils are here again." It was the head of a fine cod.

"Fifty pounds, if an ounce!" says the major.

"A good cod!" said the fisherman.

"A head!" exclaimed the major, as the second hook appeared.

The boatmen crossed themselves, and wished the bay wasn't spoiled by the carrion.

"Oh, by the powers," cried the major, "your prayers are heard. Cross again, ye spalpeens; here's a flat gentleman, at any rate."

The boatmen crossed themselves.

"Cross again," says the major, "as if it was pay-day, when every man must make his cross."

"A turbot."

It was one of the largest order; he had not, however, been unassailed; the marks of teeth in his side were visible.

"Cod!" cried the major.

A cod was landed.

Then followed a long list of empty hooks, or rather strings from whence the hooks had been broken.

"Cross again, ye spalpeens!" cried the draughtsman. The rite was performed, and a fine ling made his appearance. "Heads, heads, nothing but heads."

"Halloo," said the major. "We are done! the divil himself is in the line"; all rushed to his assistance—it was stationary—no power could move it. "On a rock, by St. Pathrick!" as he threw down his hat, and stamped in a violent fury on the crown. "All lost!—we are on a rock."

"Will your honour allow us to try," said the boatmen.

They took the line, and, having jagged for some minutes, the obstruction gave way.

"A fish—a fish."

"What divil of a fish," cried the major, "couldn't I move! hold on, hold on."

All hands now seized the line. The boatmen implored us to stand clear, for, should the prey once get his head downwards, the danger to all was great, from the numerous hooks which the line would run out, and which ought to be clear. They were right. The fish gave a sudden dash downwards, and, in an instant, all the line which had been previously hauled in and coiled in a basket was thrown overboard.

The major stared in astonishment. "What! let the monster go, out of pure fear? Faith, it's meself that would have held on any way—haul in again."

The process was soon recommenced, and as quickly abandoned.

"Hould on, ye spalpeens," screamed the major; "hould on, for the love of the Trinity!"

We all ran to his assistance—it was too late; one of the

hooks had caught his hand, and, although what by the sailors is termed a round turn had been taken, it was impossible to prevent the accident.

The line was now seized by all.

"Oh! for the love of St. Pathrick, hould on the fish; here, help my hand!"

Without using the least ceremony, and with none of the surgeon's skill, I thrust back the hook, which had penetrated the major's hand. It was but one effort, a strong one, indeed, and he was free.

"Haul in," cried the major, "I have a hand still"—I had bound the lacerated one with my handkerchief—"haul in, and let every spalpeen that has a hand to spare cross himself."

There was, however, no crossing now, the tackle was too good to yield, and we soon found on the surface of the water a splendid halibut. The size is unknown in England, but will be imagined when I say that it weighed upwards of one hundred and twelve pounds—a magnificent specimen of the tribe, not valuable, but still convertible to the purposes of sustenance. We resolved, therefore, not to lose him. The boat-hook was in requisition; blows with the oars, large hooks stuck into the body and the tail, all contributed to reduce to subjection the overgrown tyrant of our line.

He was secured, safely slung at the stern (for we did not dare to introduce him to the boat), the rest of the line was hauled in, and, the major's hand dressed *secundum artem*, that is, bathed in salt water and properly bound, the fore-sheet was hauled to leeward, and we directed the boat's head to the beautiful speck on the ocean, which was our destination.

This was the signal for all culinary preparations. The fire was resuscitated, the potatoes put on—a bushel, at least—the finest cod, whiting, and smaller fish selected, split, and washed in the sea, ready for cooking.

The dinner was splendid. It is absurd to say that a man makes only a gastronomic journey who records his eating. So

P

indissolubly is this necessary process bound up with our happiness, that I cannot think him a fallacious philosopher who sets forth the necessity of strictly providing for that which constitutes the chief act of every day, and, therefore, the prime purpose of our lives—dining. I have no respect for a man who dines *ill*. It is a proof of bad taste, and ought to be resented by his stomach, the source of all our enjoyments. Commend not me to the philosopher who eats not, or who eats in *bad taste:* he is ungrateful to the powers of Nature, and unjust to the energies of his constitution; he is ever cynical, surly, severe, and segregative; but to him commend me, and to him alone, who, in glowing gratitude, pays that respect to his organs of resuscitation which is due to the happiness they engender, and to the sound doctrine they inculcate.

No doctrine is sound which hath not its basis in a good dinner. The kind sympathies of our nature then burst forth, the best acts of our lives are attributable to its influence. It is poverty, *i.e.* the absence of a good dinner, which teaches misanthropy; it is a false philosophy which exists not among the children of plenty. A lean, squinting abortion may be sometimes seen, contorting his detestable visage into an expression of general hatred of the convivialities of man—he is an impostor. Poverty and special pleading have destroyed the powers of his stomach, and he no longer feels that the remedy is timely—that man has no digestion. Put him on the Galway bay, let him see the happiness of a sea-dinner, and, though he may be an adept in other matters, he will confess that he is none of the real happiness of man, or of the purposes for which a good digestion was accorded to beings of intellect.

Retournons à nos moutons, and our *moutons,* on this occasion, consisted of broiled sea-fowl, split, and washed in the salt water, broiled haddock, whiting, and cod, with a splendid corollary of potatoes, cooked in water from the Atlantic. Those who have never partaken of the "fruit" thus prepared, know little of the real *goût* which may be imparted to it. The occasional interruptions, which stopped the course of the feast, arose from the frequent crossing of gannet, geese, and gulls; scarcely had one a fair chance; the moment all appeared arranged for the due exercise of the knife and fork, they were changed for the double-barrel.

Arran now began to assume a specific form. The sandy shores shone brightly in the sun, and we could distinguish the little pier, which the poor inhabitants have constructed, covered with moving dots; they constituted the chief of the inhabitants of this strange spot. As we still neared the landing-place, we could distinguish shouts, and waving of handkerchiefs, or rags so estimated; but we were all at loss to conjecture the cause of such joyous demonstrations. Our boatmen smiled, but at length confessed that they were in honour of our arrival; some of the fishing-boats had already apprised them of our approach, and the people of the island had all assembled to bid us welcome.

Having moored our bark, we were hailed on landing by about a hundred men, women, and children, the whole of the inhabitants the island could boast; and, certainly, so strange a concourse had never been beheld forming a part of a community which considers itself civilised.

It has been ridiculously said that the only true fashion of the Irish peasantry is a blanket, two burnt holes for the arms, and a wooden skewer for the waist. Such a costume would be really luxurious. Here the women were covered from the waist only—some rag thrown over their shoulders; while the men, with old pieces of sack or sail-cloth, carelessly tied round the middle, and children literally naked, altogether formed so strange a group that it would, in persons less accustomed to such a sight, have occasioned some alarm lest they had arrived indeed among savages.

There was, nevertheless, no lack of hilarity; joyousness and the piper go hand in hand; nor was the procession towards the huts impeded but by the want of discretion in the major, which occasioned a general huzza. A fair girl, whose hair was hanging over her naked bosom, just covering a countenance of extraordinary beauty—her large blue eyes, constantly fixed on us as in astonishment—at length attracted the major's observation. Whether the sea-air or the whiskey had aroused the elderly militant, I know not; but he burst forth into rapturous exclamations, caught the unconscious beauty in his arms, and inflicted divers kisses before the poor girl was at all aware of his intention.

"That's for luck!" says the major, as the girl regained her liberty.

"Huzza!" cried the crowd; "Kate's the gentleman's partner."

There was no more to be said: the piper struck up, each roughly seized his particular favourite, and, in one minute, the whole island population, shoeless, were jigging on the sandy shore. The major availed himself of the happy incident—soon wooed his former favourite; while I, more modest, am ashamed to confess that a lady offered herself to my notice as a partner.

How long this kind of welcome would have lasted I know not; but the major exhibited symptoms of breaking down, and began to puff so audibly that I thought it a good opportunity to desist, and save the major's reputation. He took the hint, and we quietly proceeded to the huts.

The largest was selected. The whiskey which the major had brought was put under the command of Owen, who, as master of the ceremonies, had acquired a high character already among the islanders.

We now strolled round this interesting spot, having, with great difficulty, shaken off our new acquaintances for a time, under a promise of joining the evening dance.

There can be little doubt but that these islands once formed a long neck of land at the mouth of the bay of Galway, and stretching to the coast of Clare. The Atlantic at last burst through, and the remnants of the highest lands may be now viewed as the three islands of Arran. The remains of wood, which are still to be seen, favour this notion. The ruins of a very extensive monastery may be still viewed, and the burial-

THE ISLAND DANCE.

ground, which is attached to them, furnishes records of a once extensive population. The writer of the life of Kierian sets forth, in reference to Arran: "in quâ insulâ multitudo virorum sanctorum manet et innumerabiles sancti, omnibus incogniti nisi soli Deo omnipotenti ibi jacent."

From the burial-ground is a splendid view of the Atlantic on one side, and the whole coast of Connemara on the other. The lofty Twelve Pins seemed to bury themselves in the heavens.

The few persons who now inhabit the island seldom visit any other land, and many of the women have never left their native sward—bounded, indeed, in their notions of the world, which to them this little tract encloses, their manners were simple as their lives; and, but for the occasional visits of the coast-guard, they have learned nothing of the restrictions of law. They are, it is said, very naughty in sometimes assisting two or three poor fellows, drenched by a gale of wind, in burying certain packages; nay, I believe some of the Arran men have been known to pollute their pipes with the very contents of those packages, for which no duty had been paid. A few of them had been sent to Galway prison for a year, convicted of this appalling crime.

In the evening, the assembly had greatly increased in numbers; the fishermen had arrived, and soon joined the dance, which now had attracted the whole population. The major's spirits never flagged, and Owen had become a perfect Lothario, and seemed to have for a time shaken off the sad reminiscences which had so strongly marked his thin countenance. It was indeed a jubilee for the islanders, with the joyousness of which they were unwilling to part; and, long after I and the major had retired to the pallets which had been prepared for us, the dance-shout still continued to ring in our ears.

Having divided the whole of our fish among the aged and helpless of the island, and left some little gratuities among the rest, we set sail for Galway, determined to shoot our way along the coast. The weather was still fine, so that we could direct our course as we chose. Having made, therefore, for the high coast of Connemara, we crept along the shore, so that the vast projections concealed our little bark from observation till we were in the midst of the numerous flocks of wild-fowl which bred there. We were very successful, though it is an amusement of danger, for, should the voyager have the ill-luck to be caught on this shore by a westerly from the Atlantic, his chance of ever landing again, otherwise than by the gentle assistance of the waves, would be little.

Magnificent, indeed, is the scenery of the Connemara coast. Immense masses, of greater height than any part of the shores of Ireland, still present their dark fronts to the wide ocean's roar. The unbroken Atlantic rolls its immense mountains against these bulwarks of nature, which, still unscathed, sustain the shock. The deep and thunder-like echoes add to the solemn grandeur with which the whole scene is invested.

The prior was awaiting our arrival, and we had again to go through the gratulations of the Claddagh men. The major shared the last drop of whiskey with the high functionary, who received his portion with a becoming dignity, and informed us that our crew would be ready at all times, and the boat would be considered as wholly devoted to our service. We repaid all this with our thanks alone—the prior had forbidden that we should do otherwise—as good Christians should, we submitted to the Church.

AN IRISH STREET PIPER.

Facing page 214.

CHAPTER XVIII

Superstition of the Fishermen—Execution of Lynch for the Murder of his Wife—General Sympathy for the Murderer—The Priest—His Disclosure of the Circumstances of the Murder—Villainy of R——.

ALTHOUGH on the following day nothing could be finer than the weather, or more calculated for fishing, on my arrival at the Claddagh, I was astonished to find all the fishermen standing about in clusters—not even a net spread to dry, or a needle plied among the wives and children—their common and almost endless occupation. There was a deep feeling of sorrow pervading the expression of every face, as though some common calamity had befallen this segregated horde. Not even the offer of gold could, I believe, have tempted any one to get under way for the lovely island of Arran, which, as one looked towards the broad Atlantic, seemed like a diamond sparkling in the sun, and set in splendid emerald.

Having at length found my own *compagnon de voyage*, I questioned him as to the cause of this sudden idleness of the fishermen. Owen shrugged his shoulders.

"Faith and it's all up, this day, your honour—we'll have the lake, any way, if your honour rows up yourself against the stream—and we may have some pike and perch, but the divil a sea-going fish we'll take."

Disappointed by this sudden refusal, my preparations having been of a very laborious kind, I answered pettishly, which Owen immediately felt.

"It's true, as your honour manes to say—there's no use in it

—if the man must die, he must die—and faith it's not of their work, anyhow—but your honour's considerate—the poor deluded people of this place will neither wet an oar nor set up a sail to-day—and, perhaps, it wo'd be as well for your honour's self not to do the like—your honour knows what is a sudden squall off the coast opposite—divil a man can tell when it will come, but it will come, and like enough to come at the moment of murder ashore!—There would be a curse upon the man who should go to sea to-day."

I could not but perceive that in the attempt to conceal the effect of this delusion, there was also much of belief in the reality in poor Owen. His devotion to my service, however, prevented his at once declining to accompany me on the lake.

At this moment two of the sturdy sea-fishermen came up. The eldest, as if he had been acquainted with the subject under our consideration, "begged his honour's pardon—he might be too bold, but his honour would do a great service to the men if he wouldn't any way go to sea to-day—perhaps his honour would spake to the priest."

On this day the execution of a Lynch was to take place in front of the gaol—solemnly and sacredly was such a day to be held, as the parting spirit of the dying man should pass amid the sympathy of all.

Unlike the sight-seers of our more enlightened population, who regard the violent death of a fellow-creature as an occasion worthy of a holiday, that their unfeeling and heartless curiosity may be gratified—nothing here was observable but a solemn grief that did honour even to the prejudices and superstition of the people.

The crime of the condemned man was that of murder—murder, too, at which the best feelings recoil with extremest horror—murder, the most determined and ferocious, of his own wife—her whom it was his duty to protect and sustain.

I was, indeed, astonished at the general interest the fate of such a malefactor seemed to have excited, and expressed my surprise to Owen, after having assured him that it was by no means my intention to violate the feelings of the fishermen by persisting in going to sea that day.

"'Tis true, 'tis a bad murther, your honour, and I suppose the law must have it murther; but, if I was judge, I wouldn't harm a hair of his head—faith, but it's murther—he's guilty, no doubt, of murther; and it's myself, and everybody else, will be sorry to see him kilt after all."

I inquired the reasons Owen had to become the apologist of so hateful a criminal; he referred me to the priest, who had attended him all night—who, regardless of rest or food, had preferred the damp and cold cell of the doomed wretch to all the comforts his convent afforded.

On reaching the gaol I beheld a concourse of persons, evidently comprehending the population of many miles round, and exceeding, in number, twelve or fifteen thousand. All was perfect silence. There was a dignity under even the rags of this multitude which commanded and received respect. With some difficulty I made my way to the gaol-door, and sent in my card to the Rev. Mr. —— I was admitted to the outer room, leading to the gallows, which was before the gaol-door; there stood the condemned man; his lip curled; his eye still bright in dogged resolution; he leaned carelessly against the wall, and seemed to be little excited by the horror of his approaching fate. The kind sympathy of the priest—the sympathy which every word carried with it—seemed to give an unnatural vigour to the nerves of his auditor; he was steady, attentive, determined, yet was he within a few minutes of death in its most frightful form.

I was not permitted to hear the last words whispered into his ear by the father; but they excited a calm smile in the features of the condemned, who let fall his head upon the bosom of the priest in token of the strongest affection. I wondered at the cool deliberation of that man—while I, and all around me, felt that some terrible and unnatural shock was impending—while the horror of contemplating so sudden a death in another unnerved us; with a firm and unflinching step *he* mounted the stairs leading to the fatal window.

"Father, you will not forget me in your prayers;—you know all."

As he spoke this, he stood upon the platform. To measure the dense mass of heads which surrounded it would be impossible; yet was there the most awful silence; the stillness of night alone could equal that dreadful pause; it was but for a moment—a crash—and then a simultaneous groan among the people, so dreadful in its tone, so terrible in import, that I needed not to lift my eyes to the spot to be convinced that he, whose words still rang in my ears, had passed into eternity!

I met my friend, the priest, as he came forth from his long and painful duty; he was pale and fagged, and would hardly reply to my questions concerning the effect of so immense a concourse of persons. On his way homeward, however, he assured me they would separate peaceably—that a word from any of the Fathers would disperse them. I could not refrain from pressing on him the expression of my surprise at the sympathy which seemed so generally to have been felt in the fate of so atrocious a murderer; at last he replied:—"I cannot now divulge all that I know concerning that unfortunate being; but, in the evening, I will do so; meanwhile be satisfied. Murderer though he was, he is entitled to our deepest commiseration; he has been more sinned against than sinning."

"Your anxiety to know the facts of the murder shall now be gratified," said my reverend friend, as he seated himself by my turf fire; "and though it is not often we disclose what is under the strictest confidence revealed to us, yet the circumstances of this case are so extraordinary that justice demands the disclosure. Nor need you hesitate to attach to the tale entire credence. So perfect was the conviction on the mind of the malefactor, that he had, by fully revealing every fact relating to the horrible act, as much as remained in his power, atoned to his Maker for its atrocity; so entire is the belief among our followers, that confession is an indispensable ingredient in the means of salvation, that, trembling as he was on the grave, I am certain he has not in the minutest point deceived me. It is under circumstances alone of this awful character that we may penetrate into the real feelings of the heart, when all hope in this world is gone, and disguise becomes a crime: a crime too, that would shut out futurity. It is then we find the real motives, and sometimes, alas! the real facts of a case, in judging of which mankind have greatly erred.

"Lynch, who this day expiated his crime on the scaffold, was the son of a poor cottier, and was born and brought up amidst the mountains which divide this country from Connemara. He was not possessed of more than very ordinary talents, but was inoffensive in his manners, and affectionate in the highest degree towards those who reared him.

"The poverty of the district in which he was bred is, perhaps, hardly conceivable by you who have not yet passed through the drear and neglected tract, which has depended wholly upon the attentions of the priesthood, unaided by the expatriated and dissolute lords of the soil, even for the common information that its inhabitants are of the human order. Any employment to be obtained, therefore, among those whose means promise comfort, is, among this destitute class of beings, looked on as a provision of fortune: and it was with the utmost joy that this poor lad, whose age this day does not exceed nineteen, accepted an offer of engagement as working-gardener on the estate of R——, a resident magistrate, and agent for some absent proprietors.

"R—— is a person of great influence among the extensive community around him—to him the ragged and half-starved cottier pays his hardly-hoarded rent—to him it is he looks for compassion and forbearance, under inability and misfortune; and when I tell you that he is the only resident in the district of several miles, above the rank of a turf tenant, you will easily believe that his will is law.

"I will not say more of his character than you may gather from the circumstances. At the time to which I refer, he was living not very respectably with one of his own servants—a young female, who had exhibited symptoms calculated to disclose to the world the nature of the connection which had existed between them. A circumstance of this kind could not be concealed; and R—— was, at that moment, under an engagement of marriage with a lady of considerable fortune—a matter of great import to him, who, notwithstanding his seclusion, was deeply involved in debt.

"After Lynch had been some days in his new employment, the dreadful train of occurrences which have closed by this day's awful execution commenced. In the evening, on returning from his work, he repaired to the small study of his master to report his labours, and to take orders for the next day. On entering the room, he there found the girl to whom I have alluded—the door was shut and locked. Screams of murder echoed through the hall.

"R——, attended by his bailiff, who was constable of the district, rushed downstairs from an upper room, burst open the door, and there beheld the woman, with her hair dishevelled—her clothes torn and disordered—struggling with Lynch as in deadly contest: they were instantly separated; the girl fell screaming to the ground, while Lynch, freed from his antagonist, stood apparently in a state of stupefaction.

"Explanations were soon made by the recovering female, that Lynch had come unexpectedly into the room—had locked the door, and had proceeded to accomplish too fully a diabolical purpose. Her solemn assertions of the completion of the crime by the still amazed and silent Lynch were vehement and repeated. By the orders of her master she was removed to bed. Lynch was immediately taken into custody by the constable, who proceeded to bind his legs and hands. The lad protested, as soon as he could be made to comprehend the nature of the charge, against its truth—his denial was regarded not, or was overborne by the denunciations of his master, who threatened death to the accused. An interview, a short time after, took place between the girl, the constable, and magistrate: before them she made a statement on oath, that the crime of Lynch had been completed.

"On communicating this statement to the accused, all the horrors of a legal execution were painted; he was made aware of the certainty of his conviction on such evidence, and the necessity the master was under of forthwith consigning him to a gaol to take his trial, was fully set forth. Overcome by terror, the apparently kind suggestion that there was still a mode of saving his forfeit life was caught at eagerly by the accused—it was the usual amends—the girl might be persuaded to marry him. After suffering hours of agony, between love of life and strong disinclination to the means of preserving it, the priest was sent for, the sudden license procured, and Lynch became a husband.

"During the ceremony he was passive and cool, uttered no word beyond the necessary responses, nor betrayed any feelings either of satisfaction or dislike. On the completion of the form, R—— was the first to speak. He generously offered to provide a supper for the bride and bridegroom, and forthwith ordered his people to be sent for to mix in the festivities. He encouraged the bridegroom to be gay, to shake off the impression of his recent troubles, and to show the happiness he ought to feel when his master declared his intention of providing for the young couple.

"To all this Lynch answered not a word; but, on the return of the bailiff, who was loaded with viands for the evening's cheer, he stood boldly up, and demanded to know if he were relieved from all charge, and if he were now free. Both master and man assured him he was so, whereupon he thrust his wife from his side, darted out of the room, and disappeared.

"It was some weeks after this circumstance that R—— was

married, previously to which event the widowed wife of Lynch had returned to her mother's cottage. On receiving, however, some money from her late master, she set off in search of her fugitive husband.

"The difficulty a stranger finds in obtaining even the common necessaries of life by employment in a part of the country in which he is unknown, perhaps would hardly be conceived by the English, where poor-laws always present relief to the destitute stranger. In these wild, though over-populated countries, the appearance of a stranger begets jealousy and distrust; the observation is common to them, that as they have too little employment for themselves, they need not strangers. Lynch had, however, been fortunate; he had traversed the mountains of Connemara, till he had found on the borders of Galway the means of comfortable living. His employer had overcome the prejudices to which I have referred; and, approving his quiet industry and inoffensive behaviour, had even promoted him to a place of trust.

"The good fortune this situation seemed to constitute was suddenly obscured by the appearance of his wife. She had previously presented herself to Lynch's employer, and bore in her arms an infant, which she declared was the first of their marriage. She had represented her husband as one who had been dismissed from every employment in his own country, in consequence of his dishonesty; that he dared never show himself in Connemara, in consequence of the prosecutions for theft which hung over him. She declared that he had first seduced, then married, and abandoned her and her child.

"Much, I believe, of the attachment which exists among families, even in this wild population, is the offspring of necessity and destitution—the crime of deserting their wives and children is of uncommon occurrence in this country, as it is held to be one of the deepest iniquity. The utter dependence of the child upon the father, where neither the poorhouse nor the hospital exists, renders the connection more indissoluble, and the reciprocal dependence of the parent upon the labour of the child repays the devotion of each.

"It will not surprise you, therefore, to hear that this statement had already determined the mind of Lynch's employer: he was dismissed. Silently receiving his sentence, and without bestowing a look on the abusive woman who had thus sought and maligned his character, he departed.

"The jeers of the wife at his discomfiture rang in his ears as he sullenly directed his steps over the mountains—jeers that spoke of a revenge at his neglect, which no bosom but that of a slighted woman could entertain. Need I repeat the accumulated wrongs the enduring wretch suffered? Why should I say more than that he found rest nowhere. Employment in every place denied—stigmatised as a thief—conscious of the deepest wrongs —believing himself destined to perish by the calumnies of a fiend —weary and stung with hunger—he was making his way towards Galway, having been that day again dismissed from employment by the appearance of his wife, in the hope of finding some vessel that would convey him to a foreign shore.

"Unhappy chance! he was too late; the very path he was treading the figure of the to-him-tormenting fiend crossed—it was his wife—waiting his arrival with the savage vengeance of a successful conqueror. On his approach she assailed him with loud and insolent laughter, took her place by his side, and ceased not a moment her threats of spending her whole life in marring his peace wherever he should go. For some time the inflamed mind of the wretched husband was kept in control; for some time he bore the exasperation of the fiend-like tongue of the woman with fortitude; till, at length, as struck with a sudden thought, he turned upon her, and, ere reason could regain her power over his maddened brain, his clasp-knife had penetrated the heart of his wife, and her warm blood was reeking from the ground!

"The rest is soon told; the proofs of the act at the trial were undoubted—not even denied by the prisoner. His fate this day has closed the scene to him for ever. But there remains yet one, who, buoyed with the hope that his villainy is buried with the wretched malefactor, yet remains for the exercise of retributive justice. It was R—— who instructed the wretched girl to make the charge of violation against the unsuspecting Lynch; it was he who had promised much, if she succeeded by that plan in gaining him as a husband, who would relieve the real seducer from the suspicions which might have obstructed his scheme of marriage; it was he who had placed the girl in the study, had sent for his bailiff to be witness of the scene, that the terror of the threats of the law might accomplish the view of the master!

"He has not dared to remain in the country; of that I am glad. I will not—dare not name him; but I trust there is still an honest pen that will not fail to set forth the truth, which, if ever he should see it, will bring on him the heaviest punishment justice can claim. I was right in saying, that the dying malefactor, who perished on the scaffold to-day, was entitled to our deepest commiseration—that he was more sinned against than sinning."

CHAPTER XIX

Departure from Galway—Coasting—The Coal-Fish, or Bace—Aground on Roundstone Flats—The Harbour—Protestant Clergyman—The Major's Reminiscences in America—Catching a Sea-Serpent with a Shoe.

I DID not leave Galway without sincere regret; to a sportsman, it presents every attraction, while the social kindness of those to whom I had the good fortune to be introduced had contributed highly to enhance the amusement I had enjoyed. My landlord, indeed, expressed deep sorrow at our parting; and I must in justice say that I had never before met, in any country, a more disinterested and obliging one.

But the advance of autumn warned me of approaching term; and pictured the necessity of movement over the unbeaten track which the Irish map presented.

Our preparations were soon made, having resolved to coast it round to Connemara, and then cross the mountains on foot. For this purpose our boat was in readiness, and our *compagnons de voyage* still on the alert to attend us. Transmitting, therefore, all our baggage to Belfast, and putting our wardrobes in travelling order, we sailed from Galway, our kind friend, the prior, attending us to the water's edge. We had determined to shoot our way round to the Connemara coast; and certainly never did more abundant sport present itself. But we had long since given up all hope of rendering the produce of our guns available to the commissariat; the abominable toughness and fishiness of flavour which all sea-birds have forbid their use, except after very adroit culinary preparation.

The coast, after leaving the Black Head, which is the extremity of Galway Bay, though in part traversed by us before, presented continual objects of admiration. The picturesque is, indeed, here concentrated, and the wildness of coast scenery unapproached by the shores of any other country.

As the breeze was favourable, we were soon among the cluster of rock islands which are scattered as breakwaters along the Connemara coast: to some of them we approached with perfect safety within twenty yards, sending our four barrels amidst the cormorants and gannets, which stood on the points of each rock, fluttering and drying their wings in the air, unconscious of any danger from the boat.

While we were listlessly viewing the varying beauties of the coast, Owen started from his seat in the stern of the boat, seized the boat-hook, and plunged it into the sea—the effect was instantaneous: a large fish floated in a few moments on the surface: we could not, however, stop to take the prey on board; but, looking over into the wake of the boat, the major and myself were greatly surprised at perceiving thousands of a large kind of fish, which I immediately recognised as the coal-fish of the Scottish lakes—bace on the Welsh shore. They are of the salmon size, and not unlike the salmon in form, and average about eight or ten pounds each. In bringing the boat to, for the purpose of getting tackle ready, they immediately disappeared. They had followed our course as in pursuit, and the moment our way ceased they sank.

This did not prevent immediate preparations: our swivels were soon ready, and the only bait at hand was a piece of cormorant's thigh. This we soon attached to a double hook, and bound it with white silk. The major was in a ferment of haste, and Owen commenced snapping his fingers and dancing the Irish fling in undisguised delight. As the sails again filled, we watched at the stern with great care. First, one appeared in the wake—another and another, till the vast shoal had become as numerous as before. Out went our two swivels—the baits were instantly seized, and our tackle as instantly smashed.

We had forgotten that the rate at which we were going through the water added enormous impetus to the original strength of these strong animals, against which we had to contend. It was curious, however, to see the very creatures which had thus discomfited our preparations swimming close to the boat, having the double gut visibly hanging from their mouths, in utter disregard of the danger they had passed. Swivels were out of the question. The common sea-line was resorted to; and, whether with or without bait, was a matter of perfect indifference to these voracious animals. The bare hook was sufficient: one after the other snapped at it under the very stern of the boat. The amusement was, for a short time, highly exciting. Owen had attached large salmon-flies to a line, each of which was instantly seized, and the fish securely hooked.

While the bustle of this new mode of fly-fishing was occupying our attention, we had not perceived our approach to Roundstone flats. Our Claddagh sailors, being themselves fishermen, had abandoned all look-out ahead, convulsed with delight at the drollery of our sudden captures. One shock, however, while excitation was at the highest, recalled us to more sober contemplation. We had run up the shoal all standing, and had become safely moored in the sands, eight miles from the coast, and as equally situated as possible between two ranges of rocks. Luckily, we had run so far up the sands that our boat was wholly motionless, and the sea between the ranges of rocks was not high.

The two Claddagh men became eloquent in the exchange of complimentary anathemas, each throwing the whole blame on the other. Owen let down his rod in consternation; while the group, which the major and myself completed, might have formed a subject for a painter. The Claddagh men knew the extent of the danger: it was, perhaps, as well that we did not. Having appeased their reciprocal wrath, and represented that it was as well to try some remedy, we at length got down the sails, lightened the boat, and got the anchor astern. The difficulty, however, was this—that we had no sound bottom to work on. Oars and spars buried themselves in the sand, and required greater efforts to release them than could be devoted to the impetus necessary to clear the boat. Once having, however, moved her, by all bearing on one side, and just as we supposed she was about to float, a roll came in and set us higher than ever up the strand.

There was nothing for it now but our all getting overboard: this was effected by first securing her to an anchor astern—tying on to our feet the boards ripped from the lining of the vessel, and ranging ourselves along the side, up to our arms in the surf.

After continual slippings from the gunwale, and one or two immersions, the major threw himself into the boat, and gave up the affair as useless.

It was not so; the tide fortunately assisted us—and in two hours we were again safely under sail: shipwrecked mariners indeed, but shipwrecked in the finest weather which could have ever invited a voyage.

We now resuscitated our fire. The coal-fish were prepared, cooked, and—thrown away; for more execrable creatures were never presented for food. This addition to our meal was attempted and rejected by all; not, however, without the drollery of our Claddagh men, who knew and avoided these pests of the coast.

It appears that these creatures follow the herrings, and make sad havoc with the nets; they are sometimes taken in extraordinary quantities, salted, and sent to England, where a sale is found for them, in Lent, under the disguise of salted cod. They must form a very inferior substitute for that excellent fish.

The harbour of Roundstone now opened to us, in all the

majesty of a fine, deep bay, well protected from the Atlantic gales by numerous islands of rocks, forming a natural breakwater. The passage up to the rude quay, which the natives have constructed, was easy; the regret that accompanied the view of a harbour, by Nature's hand alone constructed, capable of receiving ships of almost any burden, but uncheered by a single mast, save from the wretched turf-boats, was inexpressible.

A few straggling houses along the quay formed the town—the town of Roundstone—the capital of this immense tract, where, from the park gates to the house of the proprietor, it is boastingly put forth that fifty miles may be numbered.

Having secured our lodging at the little public on the quay, the only one the town afforded, our first care was to provide for the poor Claddagh men. Their wants were easily supplied: a pipe and the eternal iron pot of potatoes satisfied their demands. But our own were not so easily complied with—the major's bustle, and Owen's importunity with the landlady, however, soon extracted the important information that a dinner was preparing—but it was for the clergyman, the Protestant minister, who lived *at the public*. We were soon admitted as guests to the only boarded room in the house, and permitted to share the preparations of the reverend pastor of the Roundstone flock. But, without this permission, we should have had nothing but the smoky kitchen, and the humble fare of eggs, potatoes, and butter.

Our new acquaintance was communicative. It is not difficult to remark the effect of want of society—the change which the constant absence of intercourse with our fellow-men will engender. The order of our friend's conversation was that of monologue—we had scarcely a chance of a remark—and yet, so long had the *small* things of Roundstone achieved *greatness*, in the estimation of the segregated minister, that he never doubted all the little affairs which related to himself were fraught with the highest interest to us.

It appeared, however, that his stipend was fifty pounds per annum, which was awarded him by the bishop of the diocese, not as a curate, but as a missionary, whose business was to convert from the fatal errors of Popery the inhabitants of these wild coasts. His success he himself recounted—appealed to the great increase of his congregation, and solicited the honour of our attendance on the following Sunday; on which day, we hoped to find ourselves near Belfast.

His church was the very room in which we were dining, and his whole congregation consisted of the police and the coastguard. They were, I believe, ready-made Protestants, provided by government regulation; but I could not discover that he had gained one communicant from the inhabitants. Our meal soon finished, and the major having dozed through the ecclesiastical politics of Roundstone, "the matarials" were the signal for the sportsman's evening; and, willing to get some information from the major's travels, I gently excited his reminiscences.

He had travelled in America, when serving in the British line there, and he had not arrived at the fourth tumbler, when, aroused by a reference to the *salmon horsemanship*, he took umbrage at the bare hint of that story being deemed extraordinary.

"What think you of catching a sea-serpent with my shoe?"

We all begged to have the story.

"I can assure you, sirs, that the fishing of America is beyond all that could be conceived in a country like this, whence monsters have been long since banished. Would you believe in a salvation from a shoe?—Faith and the thing happened."

"Salvation from a shoe?"

"Be aisy—you're too much in a hurry, any way"—and the major settled himself to a story. I endeavoured to give every demonstration of absolute attention.

"I served in the British line, in America, during the last war. We were stationed up the country—a few detachments of outposts, on the borders of our American possessions. The divil was always in me for a fisher, and the regulations could never restrain my wanderings wherever a fish could be had. One of my peregrinations was interrupted by a tribe of Indians, whose purpose was politely that of depriving me of any necessity of again dressing my hair for parade, or any other purpose. I was to be scalped; and nothing but showing my fish, which a good day's sport had afforded, and the tackle, which I always carried with me in abundance, saved the natural covering of my head. Such delight did the savages express at the delicate manufacture of my flies and hooks, that they immediately formed a circle and danced around me. I was invested with all the honours of the tribe—a detestable compost was thrust into my mouth, in token of kindness and patronage; and, though I understood no word of their speech, I had little doubt of the *maning* of the ladies. Oh! it's the ladies will get an unfortunate out of difficulties!"

This tribute was heartily responded to, and the young clergyman was by no means backward in the expression of his conviction of their power.

"It was soon intimated to me that there was a place full of fish, to which I was to be led. I followed with alacrity enough, glad of the possession of that organ by which I signified my ready consent—I mean my head. I was conducted by the two chiefs to a splendid waterfall, into which two rivers emptied themselves. The constant dry weather had so exhausted the streams, that the fall had become gentle, and nothing but a dull and undisturbed basin presented itself. A boat was soon procured, my flies were soon ready, and the divil may tell the rest of the sport, for I'd hardly be believed."

I protested that nothing but the most perfect conviction followed all the major's assertions. He was appeased, but not without some misgivings; for I could observe that, in the particular parts of his narrative, his attention was addressed particularly to me and Owen; every startling point being accompanied by a close examination of our countenances.

"'The huchos were there. The hucho is a fish, half pike and

half salmon; they are known in Norway and the lower rivers of America. Och! it's impossible to tell their number. It's enough to say, that each cast had its fish; and, as I threw the monsters ashore, the Indian chiefs danced round them in an ecstasy of delight. This went on till my arms were tired of reeling up. In a moment there was a solemn silence; not a fish rose; the water was clear as crystal:—' What's up in the infernal community?' thought I. It was then I looked down to the bottom; the whole was as clear as daylight; the sun shone with extraordinary brightness, and I could distinguish the minutest stone—not a fish was there.

"At length I observed something black, and of an extraordinary length, exactly like the sunken trunk of a tree, tapering towards the end, and the tapered end waving, as though in a current. 'The deuce a current is here,' thought I, and, while I examined the form, two red eyes struck me with terror. The trunk gradually rose to the surface; och, it was terror then that seized me; the red eyes showed a monster, that made me heartily wish myself ashore—it was the work of a moment—I jumped up in the canoe, over went the execrable craft, and myself was in a moment precipitated into the basin. You needn't doubt but that I struck out like a frog; the monster rose to the surface; away swam I, in all the horror of impending death—I was seized by the foot—fortunately, my shoe came off; the monster struggled with it in his throat, so tough was the material, that, before he could recover his power of a second attack, I had reached the shore.

"It was then the Indians embraced me, took out their red betel, and marked my face in extreme kindness:—'To the ford,' said I; but the divil a word they understood; but, brandishing their tomahawks, we followed the stream to the shallows—there was my monstrous antagonist struggling in all the agonies of death—hatchets and bludgeons were in instant use, and the red-eyed vermin was chopped and beaten into submission—he measured fifteen feet, with his head off."

"That was a surprising adventure," said the clergyman.

"It was a terrible one," said I.

"By the powers, and saving the major's presence," said Owen, as if awakening from a train of ratiocination, "but that was a fishing, any way!"

"It's more than surprising," said the major; "it happens to be true, and this is the tooth of the brute that was caught by my shoe."

The major produced a large ivory tobacco-stopper, held it up, placed it in the bowl of his pipe. The fact became indisputable!

CHAPTER XX

Connemara—Serving a Writ—Mr. Martin's Permission to Fish—Rags, Rags, everywhere Rags!—Character of the Inhabitants—Departure—Bad Roads—Desolation of Connemara—Cong—The Subterranean River and the Lady White Trout—Mountain Accommodation—A Strange Adventure in the Gorge—Its Satisfactory Result—Bog River Fishing—The Wilds of Lough Mask—The Desert Lands and their Proprietors—The Major's Run and Catastrophe—The Prize.

It required no great trouble on Owen's part to rouse us from our beds—they were bad enough, and constructed on the most approved plan for preventing rest. Our Claddagh men had taken their leave the preceding evening, and were far on their journey homeward. They had parted with us in regret—having entreated us, in any future visit to Galway, not to recount the adventures on the sands.

With good spirits the major and myself, burdened with nothing but a wallet strapped across our shoulders, our fishing-rods and baskets, strode over the rugged masses which constitute the entrance of this almost unexplored country.

Connemara is the most desolate waste on the face of the civilised globe! Many have spoken of it, yet few have dared to enter the savage dens which are here and there scattered along the undrained bogs—one continuous mass of rocks, piled on each other by some extraordinary convulsion of nature, till they overhang their base—here and there patches of green alluringly presenting themselves between the abrupt projections, on which, should the luckless traveller place his foot, he is buried for ever!

Fifty miles from the lodge-gates to the proprietor's house!—that is, from the first mud hut that stands on the domain of Ballinahinch — lodge-gates!— description is beggared; holes dug in the bogs by the road-side, broken rocks for a floor, and turf for a roof, at once furnish the habitations of the tenantry, and the lodge-gates of Connemara!

This is the free desert into which it has been said that the king's writ never but once came; how, on that occasion, it disappeared, ought to be no secret.

Two officers, more daring than their brethren, undertook to serve a writ on a proprietor. Having entered the confines of Connemara, suspicion as to their purpose was soon awakened; the wild inhabitants assembled, and, as the luckless strangers proceeded, they found their retreat cut off by hundreds of followers, whose numbers increased at every turn. The attendance continued to their arrival at the destined spot, when the people closed around, with every mark of civility, offering their assistance. They were surrounded. The officer's credentials were produced, which, on the spot, he was compelled to swallow, seal and all, himself crammed into a sack, and precipitated over the bridge into the river. The other escaped. Hundreds were present at this inhuman act, but not one was ever betrayed.

But the writ has, I believe, run into Connemara, nevertheless; and the power of the law is vindicated in the wretched poverty and destitution of the inhabitants, whose welfare is under the immediate guardianship of the receivers of the rents appointed by the law.

As we approached the bridge which leads to Ballinahinch Castle, as a wretched white farmhouse is termed, we observed girls and lads, almost naked, watching our progress from behind the rocks, and peeping, as it were, in terror of our appearance. Whenever we turned our full gaze on them, they ran from their hiding-places up the rocks, evidencing all the agility and timidity of the savage, who had, for the first time, seen a new animal. Our observers increased as we advanced to the bridge; men stayed their occupation to gaze on us; while here and there clusters of human beings might be seen, fully intent on examining our strange appearance. Six miles had we traversed without having discovered a dwelling beyond what a night's labour might construct. Those we did observe consisted of holes cut in the bog, and covered with the dried turf; the staring inmates regarding us with astonishment and suspicion.

The little cottage of Kelly at length presented itself; he is the fisherman in the employ of the proprietor, as he is termed, Mr. T. Martin. I presented my permission from that gentleman to fish the lakes. We were utterly astonished to find that the permission was of little avail; it was indeed a permission to fish, but the means were in other hands. We found the boats in the hands of some vulgar person, who took umbrage at our expectation of leave to fish being regarded if coming from any person but himself. The boats, he said, were his own, and he cared not for Mr. Martin's leave; he should do as he liked. Our error was in not having solicited the permission of this official receiver of the rents. Hitherto, however, the liberality of the Irish landlords had utterly disarmed us of suspicion. Throughout the south of Ireland, even where the rivers were rented at high sums, no obstruction to the angler had ever been offered. It was left for our entrance to Connemara, to which dismal region the visit of the tourist would bring more advantages than could be returned by the hospitality of the inhabitants, to find all the laws of proprietorship strictly enforced. It excited only a smile to look around the wild morasses, the herbless rocks, the uncultivated plains, and remember that leave was necessary to angle in measureless lakes, from which the combined wealth of the inhabitants would hardly supply the means of capturing a single fish.

It is but just to Mr. Martin to say that he was not in Connemara, and it is equal justice to say that he was ill represented in the authoritative person who assumed his power.

Disappointed in the use of the boat, we nevertheless pursued our purpose; but the lake-fishing was difficult; the sides were composed of bogs, and could with difficulty only be approached. We did not feel that security which had elsewhere attended us; and, as the evening approached, having met little success, we set out on our return to Roundstone.

Rags! rags! everywhere rags! The singular ingenuity with which those are held together astonishes, and the only means of keeping them on the limbs would appear to be the veritable wooden skewer. The beings who had in groups assembled as we retraced our steps, presented most grotesque figures; standing up to their ankles in the wet bog, they regarded us, apparently ill-disposed, unlike the Irish of other districts, to exchange the civil recognition. Had they been met anywhere but in Connemara, it would have been impossible to have restrained from laughter at the various devices which had been resorted to for the purpose of covering parts of their bodies. But the Connemara peasants are not to be ridiculed. Their deeds have been deeds of seriousness, and we remembered them as we passed.

It was a matter of wonder with Foote what the beggars in England did with their cast-off clothes, for at some time they must be worn out even for beggars; yet one never hears of their ultimate destination or use. Foote had never visited Connemara, or his difficulty had been at once solved—they must be bought by the Connemara freeholders!

But Connemara has indigenous wealth; its natural productions are marble, tin, lead, and coal; all which invite the labour and enterprise of civilised man. Alas! there is neither talent to suggest, means to prosecute, nor safety to complete the undertaking!

We lost no time in preparing for our departure; having, with some difficulty, procured a cart, which was dignified by the name of a car, we rather sailed than bounded over the roads. The undulations, occasioned by the unfixed bogs, over which the roads pass, being formed only of a wood foundation, would create alarm, and not, in some places, without cause.

These roads, which have been constructed at immense public expense, are continually giving way; rendering the journey through this dismal region a work of exercise, as every five minutes the traveller is warned to alight, to avoid the danger of being entombed in the morass. The major's industry prevailed; he was our driver: and an unintermitting disciplinarian, as the gentle mode of persuasion made no impression on the sullen brute on which we depended for our arrival at a lodging better than the bogs presented.

Oughterard at length appeared; the major thanked his stars that he had at length got out of such ruthless dominions; and Owen crossed himself, in token of gratitude that he had passed the dangers of a visit to Connemara.

I cannot dismiss this neglected district, however, without expressing my high admiration for its scenic beauties. They are various as the productions of nature, and call loudly for the interposition of the skill of man. But, until the habits of the uncultivated creatures who dwell amidst them are greatly changed, however vast the natural advantages, there can be no inducement for the capitalist to risk his energies among a people who have long been trained to consider themselves above all law.

So general and so great is the apprehension of the lower orders of other districts, that, even where employment has been offered, they have declined to undergo the danger of fixing their habitations in Connemara. The jealousy entertained by the aborigines is sufficient to deter new-comers; while the secrecy with which the most atrocious crimes have been committed, and the utter fearlessness of the law's visitation, have given a long-fancied impunity to their conduct.

But Ireland must not be blamed for Connemara, nor Connemara spoken of as Ireland. Once over its borders, and the civility and courteousness so characteristic of the Irish, in general are at once recognised. Nor, if I were plainly to give my opinion, would I throw too much blame on the inhabitants of Connemara themselves; when the time shall arrive that may give to many proprietors this now neglected tract—and that time we may hope is not far distant—instruction and improvement will contribute to place these unhappy and hitherto hardly-treated people at least on a level with the rest of their countrymen.

To Oughterard the civilisation of Galway has extended; and accommodation and comfort may be procured. I should certainly never advise the English tourist to trespass farther into Connemara than this post. There is nothing to invite the angler; as no place of rest, from the laborious lake-fishing, is anywhere offered; nor, indeed, do I believe the fishing itself good. The white trout we secured were of no very inviting size; and the one salmon, which by accident we had captured at the bridge, was of a bad colour and quality. It is a preserve; and the preservation, I doubt not, will continue to be easy, at least as far as English tourists are concerned.

Our boat to Ashford, a small creek of the Corrib, was ready—we were already denuded of all personal incumbrances—the major had tightened his wallet, Owen strapped his sack—travellers indeed; and now prepared for the worst that a desert could inflict. Our greatcoats and cloaks, however, which had been sent on to meet us at Oughterard, were now not forgotten; and the tent, which had long been the theme of the major's laudations, was well packed. The morning was fine, and, luckily, the wind was in our favour; the beautiful islands which cover the lake—each having, in the rising light, its peculiar and distinguishing hue—formed an addition to the scenic charms of this splendid expanse. But the major saw no beauty in it, and declared that he never knew anything come of the picturesque—if there was no fishing there was no beauty—and Lough Corrib was beneath his contempt, harbouring, as it did, the detestable destructionists of all waters, the vermin pike. His indignation, indeed, was great at my proposition that we should trail over the Lough; and he expressed surprise that a rale fisherman could be induced to stoop to such a profanation of sporting. I submitted—and we shot our way over Corrib.

It was mid-day when we arrived at the creek, and we had some difficulty in procuring assistance to transport our luggage to the main road. This, however, was at length found, and a rough pony and a lad hired. The route we purposed to pursue prohibiting any vehicle, the tent was slung across the animal, which a little ragged, but good-humoured fellow, who spoke no word of English, was to conduct. We soon reached Cong, a village of a few huts, if it may be so dignified, about midway between Lough Corrib and Lough Mask. A river connects these lakes—but not a river to be traced—one of the most extraordinary freaks of nature has sent the full stream through the earth; it disappears for a considerable distance and again bursts forth, in the neighbourhood of Cong, in an enormous whirlpool, the object of general curiosity, as its depth has never been clearly ascertained. It is no matter of surprise that such a place should be the scene of much superstitious and romantic invention. The river, where it was suited to the angler, did not present much attraction, and we passed on, with a hope of reaching, before evening, Craigh, on Lough Mask.

"The divil a white trout did I see in the cave, Owen."

"Nor I."

"Your honours didn't look long enough—maybe she's there still."

"Well, tell us of the white lady."

"Faith, and it's a doubtsome story, any way—but the ould woman swears it's true—and it all happened in the time of her own particular grandmother, that lived at Cong, and kept a potheen shop, where the identical sergeant was billeted. There's many accounts of her, poor lady."

"Tell us the old woman's."

"It was in Irish she tould it; it mayn't be *quite* so believable in English."

We protested that should make no difference.

"Why, formerly, all the rocks here—and the deuce a bit of anything else there is now—were beautiful praty fields, all smiling like; and there was, on the top of that kill devil range that covers the road, an ilegant house entirely, of the great king of Connaught. It was his daughter. Oh, she was just what your honour would call beautiful—with long hair and a muslin cap, for all the world like the fairies themselves. Well, there comes a great king of the Connemara bogs—bad luck to 'em and the divil mend them!—and makes a great to-do about marrying the beautiful young crathur in white; and a bargain was struck, and the day was named, and the portion paid, and all were joyful like, except the beautiful young crathur herself, who did nothing but grieve because she had lost her choice in battle, and wouldn't be comforted anyway. Just as the priest was going to pronounce the benediction, a fine little crathur, exactly like herself, appeared, but nobody but the lady could see her. Oh, it was thin they had the private talk, which nobody heard but the priest. 'Save me,' sis the lady.—'Och, it's meself that'll do that same,' says the fairy; 'your husband's to be no king of the bogs, but a noble soldier, home from the wars.'—'Go on,' sis the father, sternly like, to the priest. 'To be sure I mustn't,' sis the priest; and, just at that moment, the book fell from his hand, and away *vanished* the beautiful lady, all elegant *to behold*, in the shape of a white trout. Splash went the fairy and she into the stream, and under ground they wint together; and sure that's the rason she'd never be caught, but comes out, once a day, to look for her soldier—never caught but once."

"How was that?"

"Faith, and a long time passed, and a great big hulking sergeant came to be quartered at Cong; and, hearing what had happened, he swore he would have the lady, for he was the soldier waited for. Oh! the spalpeen! with a beautiful fly he tempts the darling from her dark hole—she caught at the fly—

the soldier landed her without any play at all at all, and ran up to the potheen shop, where he determined to have a capital dinner off the lady trout. There she lay on the table, saying nothing for herself, as if she was really a dumb crathur like, while the soldier takes the knife and gives one score down the side of the fish. Oh, then was the bother entirely—a cloud of smoke and a room full of fairies scattered the soldier's brains—the room turned around, and the roof fell off, and out flew the beautiful white trout and the whole band of the *good* people to the dark cavern again. Oh, it's many have seen her since, with the red stripe down her side, peeping into the daylight."

"Is this all the story of the Cong white trout?"

"Faith and it is."

"Then it's a confoundedly bad one," said the major.

"Whisht," said our companion, "I was thinking so myself—but we may as well get out of the country of the good people before we say so."

Ridiculous as this account may appear to the reader, it is, nevertheless, of such high credit among the ordinary travellers who stay at Cong, that they generally visit the cave of the white trout, with a view of catching a glimpse of her ladyship. I was unable, by any inquiries, to explain on any reasonable supposition the groundwork of the belief that trout do inhabit the subterranean river. The absence of light would probably prevent it.

We halted at Craigh—the major being obviously wearied, and having too much calculated on the resources we should meet on the road. Here, beyond a turf fire and potatoes, was nothing: and we had to dispatch Owen some distance to procure eggs. I regretted that we had not fished our way, or preserved some of our birds, all of which we had abandoned as useless addition to our luggage. Luckily the major had his flask, for the whiskey we procured was what the Irish call a "durthy drop." Our pallets, which were of straw, did not exactly suit with the recent good accommodation we had met, and we required little inducement to proceed early in the morning. A little warm milk refreshed us, and we set forth on a dull misty daybreak, resolved to traverse the wilds of Carragh.

We soon came in sight of the lake, which leaving to the right, we pursued our way on the Westport road. The Aghagower mountains contributed to increase the gloom of the day, and shut out from the dark waters of the mountain lakes the view of the Atlantic. The road now crossed the two rivers which lead from the very sources of the broad Corrib; and we halted to resolve. I proposed following the mountain river, while Owen and the major should try the lake, and join me down the stream. This plan was adopted, and the boy with the luggage was directed to follow me over the rocky masses as well as his stiff-legged pony would allow. It had rained during the night, and the water was slightly coloured, giving goodly expectation of sport. The trolling tackle, therefore, was adopted, and not long ineffectual. The white trout were up the rivers, attracted by the unusual height of the stream—they were not large, but, in our perishing condition, I secured all that gave me the least chance.

There is, between the road and the first fall of the river into the great Lough Mask, a magnificent gorge; the rocks on each side were nearly perpendicular, overhung with brushwood. Its darkness was awful, while the angry stream dashing into the basin below sent forth a hollow sound, that was re-echoed from the many walls of rocks up which the sound ascended. I paused at the attempt to descend, but, lured by the prospect of finding here a maiden fall, which, in all probability, the line of the angler had never yet polluted, I consulted my young companion, as far as signs could be called a consultation. He shook his head; but I cheered him on to the attempt, fastened the pony to the brushwood, and showed the way. The boy followed with my rod, which, however, it was found necessary to abandon in the descent; and, in a fit of determination, I let it down to the bottom of the gorge: where the rod goes, thought I, the angler must follow; and, supporting myself amidst the stunted trees which lined the sides of the rocks, and never daring once to look downward, scrambled along the ledges. At some distance down, when return was hopeless, we discovered that there was a blank in the ledge; the whole view of the country, and the splendid cataract at a dizzy height, were presented: but the precipice was not to be descended.

Mortified and fatigued, I rested for some time undetermined how I should proceed, and regretting my hasty determination in having dispatched my *avant-courrier*, the companion of so many and so cheerful scenes. "Hurrah!" cries my little ragged attendant. I turned suddenly, and beheld him suspended from a branch, and about to drop on the lower ledge. There was joy in his countenance; I followed him—the ledge on which he had descended was the first of a series which led to the gulf. It was a dangerous journey; but what angler could resist the dark and boiling basin, in which, during a partial flood, the trout and salmon would necessarily be congregated in their peregrinations upward. It was but an effort, and we were both landed on the rugged rocks, which formed the bed of the winter stream. My rod was soon recovered; nor was I long in making my way towards the fall, which now became almost deafening. I directed my little Mercury to bring round the pony to the lower part below the precipice, where I should be able to join him.

It is not easy to describe the sensation of loneliness I felt. Pictures of a new country are nothing to the reality of such a spot as this. Though it was day, there was hardly sufficient light to enable me to direct my steps with due care, while the slippery surface of the rocks contributed to divers prostrations, not claiming the respect of religious rites, nor accompanied by that resignation which excluded some short exclamatory apostrophes. But the basin was at last achieved. It was about one hundred yards in diameter, and required no great strength to command it. The fly was useless: the short but darkening

"I Shook off the Butt."

Facing page 245.

trees reached nearly to the surface; no net ever could have been used in so deep and irregular a hole, if even the superstition of the natives would have allowed the attempt. Having well loaded my line with lead, I passed it gradually down the foaming fall into that part of the pool which formed the deep and boiling eddies. The run was instantaneous, and I was immediately rocked by a large fish. I had now gained some experience in this kind of resistance, and determined to give time to the enemy, who seemed disposed enough to take it, as, with all my jagging, he remained immovable. I now set up a second tackle, laying my rod over the rocks, determined not to lose a first fish by any want of temper or management. By the time I had completed my second tackle, up sprang the fish at the lower end of the basin: I seized my rod; and, I believe, never had a more determined or spirited enemy to combat. He yielded, however, and I was drawing him gently to land, delighted with the success the adventure promised.

As I turned towards the shore, I encountered the face of a man close to mine, whose lineaments can never pass from my remembrance. He was enclosed within a mass of rags: the hair and beard covered the whole of his face, with the exception only of the high cheek-bones, which, protruding through the matted locks, gave an awful effect to the deeply sunken face; the eye was quivering in alarm; and there was an agitated expression, which evidenced some terrible emotion under which he laboured. I caught the infection. I saw nothing but death in such a spot, beyond the possibility of assistance, and opposed to a being whose state could not be rendered more desperate. I threw down my rod without a word. The fierce eye of the stranger pursued my every act. I shook off the butt, and took an attitude of defence. A slight smile passed the features of the man, as he drew from under his dress a pistol.

"You are here in search of me?"

"No."

"You are no Irishman."

" None."

" Then, for the love of God and your own life, tell me—am I sought for—will you betray me?"

" I will not."

" Thanks, Englishman, you are safe; I will take the word of the Saxon, though the Saxons are our oppressors. How could you descend these rocks? I believe no man has, before myself, attempted to penetrate to this dark and dangerous hole—a sudden flood and you are swept away without the chance of escape—this pool has chambers underneath the fall, that would bury for ever the creature whose step should slip.—I heard a gun an hour ago? are the bloodhounds on the track?"

" It was my rifle—be satisfied, you are perfectly safe, as far as I am concerned: shake off the horror that seems to have unnerved you. What, in the name of Heaven, can have rendered you so desperate?"

" Your honour shall know. Look into this cavern"; he led the way into a fissure of the rock, which was wholly obscured from the view by the thick clusters of brushwood and short oaks. At one end of the cave were a heap of rushes and the smouldering embers of a turf fire, over which had been suspended an iron pot; the aspect of the man, as he leaned over the fire to restore its flame, was ghastly, and I involuntarily drew back from so uninviting an apartment. My new friend followed, and, familiarly laying his hand on my shoulder, as if to detain me, " Sure, sir, it's yourself will listen to my miseries. I'd show you hospitality, if I could, here; but maybe ye'd rather not sit in the cave." I declined that honour, while he pursued the train of his narrative. " You see, sir, an outcast—if the bloodhounds once caught him, would hang a thousand times, if a thousand lives he had."

" A criminal? Say no more—I wish to hear nothing of your life or deeds—as yet you are safe."

" Safe! I *am* safe. I have continued safe, even through the bloody butcheries of Rathcormack. Even where the widows—

made so by the Church—send up their morning's curses on the murderers. Through all this I am safe; yet, by this hand— you see it is a strong one—by this hand four villains of police fell; their blood is unatoned, and I am free." I shuddered at the wretch who could so exultingly make a declaration of horrors. "They were upon my track once; you see my *pistol*"—he grasped it—"the leader of the party gained on me; I fell; as he was about to bind me, a ball passed through his heart—you are one of the hunters—you are seeking me—beware—I have a load remaining."

Bloodthirsty villain!—I had determined now to await my opportunity and seize the ruffian—the only difficulty was the pistol, on which, during his exclamation, he continually laid his hands. I could not but remark that his language little accorded with his appearance; the former evincing an intercourse with persons of the higher order. Although tinged with the brogue, his expressions were sometimes even elegant. He took an evident pleasure in the concern which my manner indicated. There was a pause for some moments, during which I had collected my tackle, the salmon having long since made his departure.

I began, within myself, heartily to regret this adventure, as putting upon me the necessity of a very serious duty, besides spoiling my fishing, the duty of delivering a murderer over to the laws. My own safety was hardly ensured in the *rencontre*, and I was deeply calculating by what stratagem I should manage to betray him into my power.

"Sir," said the man, confidentially approaching me, "you have heard of the affair at Rathcormack—fifty murders in one day will hardly be forgotten—the police were the murderers— the police, pushed on by the parsons—they were told to spare nor man nor child—they spared none. This is a dark place— the light of day sometimes hardly penetrates—the viceroy is, at this moment, in search of me. I heard it from some emissaries; I would meet him at once, but that there is a difficulty about the passage to the road, and the ground is better here. When, therefore, the fight comes, my dagger will pierce his heart. I have sworn that a thousand times to the saints, and there are plenty to help me."

There could be no doubt of the danger which encompassed me. I had, therefore, arrived at the fixed determination to arrest the monster in his lair. The only difficulty was the mode of disarming him of the deadly weapon which he held in his hand, and scarcely for a moment seemed to relinquish. Stratagem was necessary. I found it hard to restrain my natural impetuosity, which directed the attack at once. I resolved better, and proceeded to fish the fall again with an assumed calmness.

The horrible stranger took his seat near me as I rested on the rocks attending to my two rods. The familiarity and boldness of his manner disgusted me. I was rising to an ebullition, when he again gently seized my arm:—

"You have heard of the murder."

"What murder?—The noble lord who fell by the pistol-ball?—I have heard of that atrocious act."

The wretch smiled — and, standing erect, exclaimed, "'Twas I!"

"Then it shall be your last!"

I had the advantage—he was seated—I fixed my hand on his throat, and he was prostrate. I found my strength greatly superior to his struggles. At the very moment he was lifting his hand to discharge the deadly weapon, I seized and wrested it from his grasp, and threw it on the rocks. Great, indeed, was my surprise to find that no further resistance was offered. Anticipating some deep design in this, I bound both his arms together by a silk handkerchief, so tight, indeed, that he became utterly motionless.

All this passed so rapidly that the time of the narration seems tedious. The moment I felt my triumph, and that I had secured one of the most atrocious malefactors, I scrambled towards the opening at the end of the fall, the point to which I had directed my little attendant with the pony. On emerging into the light, I was greatly relieved by the view of the major and Owen, picking their way in great haste through the bog; they had with them two strangers. Having hailed them, and enjoined their haste, I returned to the prisoner, who had done no more than raise himself against one of the rocks, and, to my astonishment, was in a convulsion of laughter. I paused to behold so blood-stained a wretch, and could not refrain from uttering the reproaches which so naturally suggested themselves.

"Sir," said he, "you would laugh, also, if you knew all—will you accept my confession?—by St. Patrick, you shall have the truth, if you will undo this confounded handkerchief—listen—come nearer—it is a secret that the world is dying to know—the great truth which is kept with me and me alone. I am—come nearer."

"Speak whatever you please—I will faithfully report it."

"I am the Pope himself."

As he uttered this he drew himself up, pinioned as he was, with a degree of dignity; his eyes again assumed that peering and anxious look which had at first so powerfully struck me:— "Hear—if you are a good Catholic—I am the Pope himself—fall down and worship."

As he uttered this, the major, Owen, and their companions, had forced their way through the pass. The greetings were mutual, my exultation complete.

"There," said I, "is the atrocious malefactor who has so long escaped justice—there is the monster whose murders cry out for vengeance."

"Oh! be aisy, there," said one of the strangers; "all a mistake—this gentleman is a friend of mine. Hollo, W——, why what the divil brings you to the fairy's fall?"

"I am the Pope," said the malefactor.

"Oh, Pope be bothered! you're Lieutenant W——, any way, and you've got a greater crack than ever in your unfortunate head to-day."

The whole mystery was explained; the poor fellow was, indeed, a half-pay militia officer, who, having dissipated everything he had possessed, had been consigned by his relations to the care of the person who now addressed him. A full and clear explanation followed. It was frequently the case that, after having procured by the false kindness of friends any quantity of whiskey, he would disappear from the house of his host, and hide himself in inaccessible caves. This had happened in the present instance, and he had been missing two days.

"But," said I, "how can such a man be entrusted with firearms? he had a pistol, which was directed to my breast."

"A pistol!" exclaimed the farmer; "a precious pistol! one of his own manufacture."

I produced it; a general laugh followed; a blackened piece of bent iron was all the weapon which had occasioned me so much real terror.

"Is there no truth in the murders in which he avers he has been concerned?"

"Murther!" exclaimed the farmer; "the poor fellow wouldn't injure a worm. Come, W——," continued he, "we must go."

He took him by the arm, all his former violence had vanished, he became perfectly docile, and, without uttering a word, went off in care of his friend, who gave us an invitation to his cottage, about a mile distant. It appeared that the two strangers had been in search of the wanderer when they met the major.

That veteran had been more successful than myself, and produced a couple of fine salmon, which were really acceptable. I led to the *penetralia*, where turf and the iron pot were ready. Owen soon made up the fire, and we enjoyed a hearty meal, enlivened by the store which we had brought on the pony, and our appetites suffered nothing from their being ministered to in the madman's cave.[1]

[1] I learned subsequently the death of this unfortunate; in one of his wanderings he had died, no doubt, from cold and hunger. Although

"Is there such a swamp in England as this?" said the major, as the whole plain broke on our view, in following the river between Lough Mask and Lough Corrib; "look about you—not a blade of grass—here and there, indeed, upon the rising grounds, a few patches of oats, the rest bog and reeds— nothing but bog and reeds. Misery in this uncultivated waste is at the highest sustainable point; the want of food among these cottagers daily forms the theme of your newspapers, and sometimes the ground of your subscriptions. A villainous robbery of the English—those subscriptions. It is only another way of putting money into the pockets of the landlords. Here, amidst thousands of uncultivated acres, a wretched patch is let for three times its value—the poor crop fails, for even the small tracts that are cultivated are ill managed—all is seized for rent, and the crathurs die, or would die but for a subscription; and the liberal landlord, who views this desert, puts his own name down for a trifle, and expects the public to do the rest; while he reaps all the benefit, and showers his favours among the inhabitants of London or Paris. Among all the estates you have passed through, what landlord have you found at home?"

I was grieved to be obliged to admit — not one of the higher order.

"It is to the higher order that these enormous tracts belong. Give me a grant of a thousand acres of this morass; in two years you should see smiling corn-fields where now you behold nothing but reeds. Just view the depth of the bed of this

the persons who attended him appeared to show him every kindness, I cannot but think his friends, if such a creature of affliction had any, should have taken more effectual means for his restraint. Although generally harmless, as I learned, his passions and feelings were all connected with murder — a tendency in a disordered mind that should certainly have suggested the necessity of confinement. We found he was well known among the cottagers of these mountains, among whom he had been some years located.

river; several feet below the bog-surface. The whole moisture of this bog might be conveyed into the stream; the shallow passes might be with little labour deepened; employment would be given to the poor, and wealth would be the result to the landlord. But, no! the landlord knows nothing of the soil, or has nothing to spare for its improvement."

"May not this neglect be attributed to other causes?"

"The accursed restrictions of the tenure," said the major. "Why, half of them have no power to grant leases to those who would undertake the recovery of the land. Then, there is the still more iniquitous act of agistment. The instant a plot of ground is drained, and turned to the purposes of agriculture, the tithe-owner comes in; but there must be an end of that."

"Is it possible," I exclaimed, "that so splendid a country as this should be unknown or neglected? I see before me expanses of water, crowded with every kind of fish; land, capable of the highest production, and a climate of great mildness and salubrity; but, when I look at the wretched hovels of the thinly-scattered inhabitants, I cannot but believe that some great error exists. What can be the inducement to emigration to New South Wales, while millions of acres here are untouched by the hand of the agriculturist?"

"Push on," said the major; "these are reflections that bring no good effect. We are in a wild country, but its wildness is our sport; that river, noble and bounding as you see it, knows but *one angler*, a poor fellow whom we met at the top of the rocks, with a hazel rod, a stout string, and flies of the coarsest texture; he, I believe, is the lord of this stream."

"And can catch a fish, any way," says Owen.

"Millions of salmon pass this stream annually; they are never touched or sought for until in the shallow tributaries: a villainous system of poaching is carried on when the fish are spawning. This evil arises from the poverty of the people, and their ignorance of the proper art of fishing."

"There is, it appears, no enforcement of the penalties."

"Enforcement?" cried the major; "all the enforcement here is about a pipe of tobacco and a drop of potheen; by neither of which do the government lose a farthing, for, if they were not both smuggled, they could never be consumed. To the bottom of the lake, say I, with their coast-guards and excisemen. *Here*," continued he, striking the sod with the butt of his rod, "here is the real wealth of the country; here is employment for their trumpery coast-guard and their poor. But the prevention of crimes committed from necessity is never regarded; it is honour to a government if it punishes them with rigour. It is pleasing and satisfactory to find all the noble lords of the United Kingdom, in one burst of virtuous indignation, exclaim against any lenity in the punishment of crimes, which are the offspring of ignorance, and to which their own neglect of the unhappy criminals has mainly contributed. Where are the capitalists who affect a fondness for wild sports? where the numerous classes who yearly transport their dependants for interfering with the game, the object of all their solicitude and care? Let them behold this void—view those lakes."

I confessed to the inviting nature of the scene, and could not but join in the wonder expressed by the major, that these attractions had never yet been sufficiently known to cause the erection of a single edifice. The economy of such a location would be no small consideration; labour is abundant at sixpence per day for an able man; stone of excellent quality only for the bringing; lime everywhere produced. A small income, judiciously invested here, would be wealth in comparison with a residence in any other country in the world!

"Hould on," cried Owen, in the midst of our apostrophes; "he's here, your honour." He had hooked a fine fish on the flat.

"Faith and there's corn still in Egypt," exclaimed the major; "where the deuce is my fly-book?"

He was soon prepared, and as soon rose a salmon—another —he is hooked.

"The landing-net," cried Owen.

"The landing-net," cried the major.

I stood between the two combatants, knowing not which to assist.

"The gaff," cries the major; "let the spalpeen hould on."

At that moment a magnificent fish leapt from the water—down went the major's rod—"and that's a fair one, any way," said the major; "he'll give us a run, yet. A hand, for the saints!"

I assisted him to disencumber himself of his coat and hat. "Now we start fair"—but the fish was lodged; it was the largest salmon I had seen, and I confess I shared all the sportsman's anxiety with the major. "Off again"—he was off, indeed; and it was impossible to follow, so ludicrous a figure did the major present, puffing down the stream, utterly unable to guide his steps, his whole attention being on the reel which was running at a fearful rate, notwithstanding his own exertions to follow the fish.

"Gone, by St. Patrick!" exclaimed the major, dashing the rod into the stream, and falling squat into a bog on his face. I hastened to his assistance; and Owen, having landed his fish, was before me. We raised the major in anxiety—he scraped the mud from his eyes and mouth, and, as quickly as he could, exclaimed, "Never mind me; follow the fish—I'm done——" and, in a pathetic but earnest manner, made out in signs what the masses of mud in his mouth would by no means allow him to utter.

We were both sportsmen too well seasoned to hesitate; but the rod was gone, and a long run we had to overtake it. There it was, in the middle of the stream—nothing but the top to be seen, the weight of the reel sinking the butt; and, to our mortification, a slack line.

"That's a misfortune, any way," said Owen; "the fish is gone."

"Gone!" cried the major, who now came up, and who had

by this time so well effected the process of cleansing by his pocket-handkerchief, that he had succeeded in well covering every part of his face, hair, hands, and clothes, with the brown bog mud—he looked like an animated masterpiece of Vandyke.

"Give me your rod"—with a dexterous cast he covered the top, and caught the line with the flies of Owen's apparatus—"gently, and don't disturb him if he's there." It was a moment of real suspense—the rod was recovered—the line reeled in, which had at least one hundred yards out. It was now found to have taken a different course, and the fish had again turned up the stream—the line was fixed.

"He's here," cried the major.

"Huzza!" exclaimed Owen, in extreme delight; "this is a fishing!"

"Now, major, for your skill—if you lose that fish——"

"Be aisy," said the major, "the time's against me—he has not been idle all this time—he has been busy enough grubbing at the bottom, to get the hook out of his mouth—faith and he'll give us another leap yet."

As he approached the spot where the fish was sulkily ensconced, I could perceive the paleness of the cheek—the quivering of the lip—both so indicative of extreme excitement, that I began to question my own nerve. I was not much more calm—this was a prize. The major did not venture to hint at the weight, but it was obvious that he felt he had an enemy worthy his utmost skill.

The fish now gradually and gently moved up the stream; a steady but tight strain was kept on the line, which the reel gradually received, giving token of an approach to the surface. He came, like a log of wood, to the top. A fish, indeed—for one minute I had a perfect view of him as he broke the water with an enormous tail.

The major grew still more nervous; yet the steadiness with which he held the rod was admirable. "Beware now," says he. Up went the fish, at least five yards into the air!—the rod was again down, and recovered at the moment of the splash occasioned by his fall. "He's safe," whispered the veteran—"that last spring has tired him." He struggled with some violence for some minutes—I was ready with the gaff—he came gently to the shore, turned two or three times on his stomach, and I plunged the hook into his side.

It was well that I did so at that moment—the fly had worn out of his mouth, and he was free from the line. "Huzza!" cried Owen and the major, in which I heartily joined—up went our hats, in token of our triumph—the monster floundered on the shore.

"Salmon," cries the major—"the devil a salmon at all!"

It was, indeed, no salmon, but one of the great lake trout, the largest that had been seen for many years, even from the broad waters of Lough Corrib. Its weight exceeded thirty-three pounds. The memory of this fish has not passed away—it may still be heard of among the cottagers, many of whom saw it.

Although fish of this size are very rarely taken, I can have no doubt but that they are abundant in the Lough. The mode of taking them is not yet discovered. In the lake itself they are rarely captured but by night-lines, which must always be a very inartificial mode of taking so timid a fish as the trout. Yet the expanse is so immense that it is hopeless to traverse it with flies or the trailing lines:—the small brown trout are continually infesting the former, and the pike the latter. Nor am I certain that the large lake trout would be induced to rise at all at a fly on the lake. In the river, when making their annual migrations to the tributary streams of the upper lake, they may be lured by the fly; but it is a sport of so uncertain a character that I should hardly recommend the angler to pursue it beyond an hour or two.

We had now two fish—one seven pounds, a salmon; the other thirty-three pounds, as we afterwards proved. They were really a load; and, from certain intimations from Owen and the major, I found an appointment had been made to spend the

"The monster floundered on the shore."

P. Chenevix Trench.

night up these dreary mountains which surrounded the bog. But there was some suspicion of me—why, I know not; and Owen was the spokesman, while the major looked on in a quiet but peering manner, that indicated some doubt of the effect.

"We have five miles, your honour, to return to the road."

"Well, we must trudge it—there is the pony."

"But your honour's weary; and the major is not an over-fine figure for a gentleman to make among the roaders; there's a good resting-place across the bog."

"Well, Owen, I'm for the resting-place."

"But maybe your honour will be disturbed."

"By what?"

"That's it, your honour—you may be disturbed, you see— but the major will tell how."

"Oh! you're a rale Kerry man to make out a case. By St. Patrick and we'll have a fresh drop to-night, anyway—leave all to me, and we'll keep clear. With the big trout no bad luck can come to us."

I protested, that after such a day's sport, I feared nothing.

"Give me your hand—you are a sportsman worth coming to the land of the floods. On with you, Owen, across the bog— look out."

This was no easy matter; the pony was the only and the best guide. Not a step would he take that he had not well examined; and we had only to follow the route he made for us. It was amusing to see the little ragged animal pawing every spot which was in the least degree suspicious. The boy had no control when the pony had entertained doubts; and not unfrequently were we compelled to retrace our steps, at the suggestion of our mountain guide. At length, by numerous crossings and recrossings, we reached the base of the rugged masses of rock, among which there was an ascent. The major gloried thereat, for he was really overcome; nor can I boast much of my own endurance, which had given way marvellously under the difficulty of recovering one foot, while the other was at least two feet immersed in the bog. The rough and rugged ascent was, therefore, a relief, and we acquired new spirit, as we found the foundation firm.

A shrill whistle was now heard, and as immediately replied to by Owen. It was clear that the major was in the mystery, for he smacked his thighs with a peculiar satisfaction, an indication of his perfect approbation, to which I had long since become accustomed. Some yards farther a mountaineer appeared; he was of the roughest order, but had on the veritable brogues, the great characteristic of the inhabitants of the mountains. We stooped to enter between two masses of rock, the passage between which had been well roofed with turf, but still showing evident symptoms of a hasty and recent erection. He spoke in Irish to Owen, who translated for us a thousand welcomes.

There were two apartments: in the first was a noble turf fire, rough seats made of bog wood, and a table in the centre. Here were also plates ready prepared—and roasted hares were soon produced. Our companions had increased to four, and we sat down to the game with excellent appetites, while one prepared the fish for a broil.

The repast finished, the major intimated that I should have a drop of the *rale*—a jar was brought in, covered with mud; it had been dug from the ground, and from it the major prepared my tumbler. It was smoky stuff, but anything was acceptable in a country where absolute starvation would by no means constitute an impossibility. Pipes were produced, and all joined in the fumigation which filled the cabin.

Owen soon warmed into a toast: "Here's the honest drop that a poor man may drink, and parliament be none the wiser." The loud huzza that followed this toast explained the whole affair: just then, also, I caught a sight of the inner apartment, and did not fail to observe that there was a huge fire in it, as also a singularly long chimney flue; there was also a very particular flavour. It was a mountain distillery. I now professed myself in the secret, and begged to see the apparatus. There was no disinclination expressed; and it is worthy of remark that there was entire absence of all suspicion. I was suffered to examine the apparatus, which was then at work, and consisted of a large still, which could easily, at a moment's notice, be removed. I found, also, that one of the party was absent, and that he was relieved by another about every hour.

"Do you never deviate?" said Peregrine to the Cornwall Dan. "No, I always whistles," replied he of the Red Cow; and whistling was the order of telegraph here; for while we were all enjoying the luxuries of a good fire, a long pipe, and fresh whiskey, a blast so loud and shrill was sent forth, that needed not a prophetic soul to understand. The still was out of the hut in an instant. Perhaps it was the sudden excitement which prevented any due estimation of the enormity; but the fact must be recorded that we all joined in this. It was not difficult to remove the apparatus a distance of twenty yards, where, by some accident, there was a hole ready cut to receive it, and even covering of turf and wood, as though Fortune, blind as she notoriously is, had foreseen the necessity. The quiet was wonderful, as all drew round the fire in the cabin.

"Stand fast," whispered the major; "we may get into trouble if we remove."

I took the hint, and endeavoured to look as simple and composed as my friend Owen, who puffed away with all the philosophy he of the tub would have exercised while enjoying his pipe, had he known that luxury. There were some slight under-skirmishes in Irish, but I considered the major a sufficient guard, and did not interfere to have it translated.

"There are strangers up the mountains," said an authoritative person to the simple Paddy outside the hut.

"Faith, and ye may say that," replied he, "and rale gentlemen, too, and small blame to 'em, Mr. Exciseman, for coming where they could find a good fire, and a respectable cabin like ours."

The stranger entered; we perceived he was armed; two others followed: they bowed to the major and myself, and then addressing himself to the veteran, he begged to know who and what he was.

"You are little likely to know," replied he, "unless you first give us your own birth and education, and more than that, your authority to make me pass my examination before ye."

"Hurush!" said our friends, in an undertone, "he's got it there."

"I am the appointed exciseman of the district—there is my authority."

"With all my heart, and a very well appointed exciseman you seem. By the powers, I would have appointed you myself."

"You must be aware, sir, that our duty compels us to examine every hut in these mountains: we know that there are stills regularly at work."

"Stills!" cried the veteran.

"Stills!" re-echoed all voices.

"The thing's impossible," replied Owen; "a still!"

"Faith, and the likes of a still has never been seen for many a day up the mountains," added one of our party, with imperturbable gravity: "where would the poor crathurs get a still, except from the bottom of the bog, where our forefathers may have left it?"

"The still, sir, is a very good thing to make whiskey with," observed the major, "but I carry my own; my name is Major ———, and this gentleman is ———, and that's Owen, our attendant, and the divil a drop he'd taste anyway that wasn't rale parliamentary—would you, Owen?"

"Saints forbid!" replied he, as he removed his black pipe from between his lips.

"Good-night," says the exciseman, "good-night."

"Oh, the bist of nights to you," said the hutters, bowing in mock gravity, " and give you a snug berth, where the nights last for ever "—*sotto voce*. They departed.

Another whistle in a few moments, and the still somehow recovered its lost dignity, and was again spluttering and steaming in the inner cabin.

CHAPTER XXI

The Friar's Visit—The Monster of the Mountains—The Mystery Solved—The Whiskey Store—The Unparliamentary—Traversing a Bog—Process of Grabbling—A Brood of Otters—Castlebar—Wretched State of the Inhabitants—Annual Subscriptions—Ludicrous Adventure of Owen—Following a Salmon—Decency on Entering a Town.

As we were congratulating ourselves on the comfortable housing we had found in so dreary a night, and our good fortune in having escaped the gauger's lengthened visit, we were again alarmed by a knocking at the door.

The scout had given no intimation, and the host expressed less apprehension than ourselves; he went fearlessly to the door. An old man wrapped in a blue cloak presented himself; there was an immediate reverence awarded. Every man rose from his seat as the stranger entered. It was not difficult to perceive that he was a priest—one of the mendicant order of friars. He bowed to the major and myself, and took his seat with an air of subdued humility. He was obviously weary, and exhibited no great disposition to stir from the comfortable quarters which the cabin presented. The torrents descended with increased violence, while the cottiers shuddered at the peals of thunder which echoed through the ravines. The reverence that the friar's presence inspired restrained any observation; the major, however, girded himself up to another glass, and ventured to offer his congratulations that we were so well housed.

"Come, worthy father," said he, "it is by no means necessary that we should sacrifice to drought while the elements set us the example of drenching the earth."

"I have seen," said the friar, "the Monster of the Mountains."

All crossed themselves, while some whispered to each other, as though struck with melancholy forebodings: the pipe was taken from their lips, and each centred his gaze on the friar's countenance.

"You need not be alarmed," said the friar.

"Faith, and the alarm is all their own," said the major; "we are strong enough for any monster of the mountain or flood. Let us know who he is."

"I shall relate the history, because I think it right to instruct all in the facts. I have had some difficulty, indeed, in the explanation which should always be the business of those who relate wonders, lest the superstitious effect of their recital should produce some of the many evils which have arisen from the Monster of the Mountains.

"Four hundred years have passed since the enormous and terrifying being first appeared in these mountainous wilds. For centuries has he continued to assume a form sometimes of a mile in height, of varied colours; and whenever this apparition takes place, there are few of the inhabitants of these wild districts who do not anticipate some terrible evil.

"Roderick O'Connor was the earliest king of the mountains of Maamturk. In his time war was unknown; the peaceful flocks were fed without interruption on the mazy surface of these boundless tracts. Beloved was he by all; the service the people paid was a service of the heart. Never did the wanderer pass his noble castle unrefreshed; nor did the follower of Christ fail to find in him a patron and a help. He paid neither service nor suit to any; and the protection his people enjoyed was effectual even against the Saxon invaders, who had penetrated to all other, even the remotest, parts of this suffering land. There was but one greater than he—it was the Monster of the Mountain!

"It was on the eve of a splendid day, when the produce of the cultivated tracts had been secured—when all within the dominions of Roderick were assembled at the castle—when the joyousness of plenty and happiness enlivened the countenance of every being—that Roderick led his new-married bride in front of the concourse. She was the loveliest of the daughters of Erin. Her dark eye beamed with the sweetness which was inherent in her nature, and as she smiled in recognition of the cordial shouts which greeted her, the beauteous sun shone forth as if in unison with the splendour of her charms. The cup was raised to every lip, as the O'Connor stood forth by her side. At the command of the chief, the harpers struck their instruments, and, joined by the well-skilled voices in the native songs, the noble pair gave their blessing to the crowding thousands who surrounded the throne of the open avenue.

"Suddenly there was a stillness—the harpers ceased, as if by a magical command, while every eye was turned upon a tall majestic figure, who, dressed in knightly armour of a brilliant green, a plume of feathers of the same colour nodding over his helmet, with a firm and solemn step advanced towards the throne of the O'Connor. The chief arose to receive the stranger, who, having arrived within a few yards, plucked from his hand the gauntlet, and threw it on the ground. The beauteous bride uttered a piercing scream, and threw herself on the breast of her betrothed.

"'It is enough,' said the stranger, 'I have been wronged. Not the tears of the fair can wipe off the dishonour.' Unaccoutred as he was, the O'Connor descended, took up the fatal gauntlet, and, brandishing in his right hand his shining blade, offered the other to the stranger.

"'Let no man offer violence to this knight,' exclaimed the O'Connor; 'he dies who interferes between us.' The multitude, which had already risen in token of protection to their lord, were suddenly awed by the voice of their chief, and every sword was sheathed.

"'The wrong thou hast done me,' said the stranger, 'death can alone repair; thou darest not refuse my honour a fair contest. I gave thee credit for as much.'

"'Thou shalt have it.'

"'That syren fair whose hand this day crowns thy bridal feast is, as thou knowest, my affianced bride—thou hast known the pledges that have passed between us.'

"'Never!'

"'Let me whisper to thee, then, thy madness and thy misery. She hath been mine already.'

"'Liar and braggart!' exclaimed the chief; and ere the stranger had time to draw, he was prostrate with the blow from the heavy gauntlet, and the blade of the O'Connor was sheathed in his heart. The stranger threw back his vizor; the O'Connor staggered back a few paces, and fell on the lifeless corse of a murdered brother.

"He was borne unconscious to his castle chamber, while the clan, excited by the unexpected issue of the meeting, seized the body of the green knight—ignorant of his rank or name—but attributing to his sudden and unexplained appearance some deep injury to the house of O'Connor, conveyed it to the mountains, and threw his still quivering limbs among the rocks.

"Years rolled on: the beauteous bride of the chief had brought him three sons—finer lads the light of heaven had never shone on. The green knight had been forgotten—his bones had whitened in the sun, on the desert recesses of the mountain cliffs. It was the anniversary of the wedding-day of the O'Connor, and the clans again assembled; revelry and feasting again elated all hearts. In the midst of the shouts, silence once more suddenly occurred. The green knight, accoutred as before, stalked boldly up the avenues formed unconsciously by the terrified people—his vizor down, and the green plume waving in the air. The O'Connor alone quailed not, but descending boldly from his throne, took up the gauntlet which the stranger had cast at his feet, and, as before, offering his hand to the knight, passed through the wonder-stricken crowd.

"'Not here,' said the stranger. 'I would meet thee if thou hast the courage, alone, on the mountain, where the blue craig thou seest overhangs the precipice: thou hast courage, or thou wert no O'Connor.'

"'I pledge myself to meet thee.'

"'Enough,' said the knight, who disappeared with almost incredible swiftness.

"The O'Connor returned to his bride; she spoke not, but, trembling, caught her partner in her arms. But there was a foreboding in her heart, that could not find utterance.

"The people were dismissed, and the gorgeous sun was fast falling over the mountains. Just as the O'Connor, having fixed his armour, had received from his attendant the sword which had once before dispatched his rival, 'Go not,' cried one, who, in breathless haste, seized the arm of the chief, 'go not to the mountain—I have seen with my own eyes the slain knight—green as the moment thy sword pierced his heart—swollen into a monster of immeasurable size.' 'Go not,' said the lady, on whose countenance a terror of an unearthly kind was visible.

"'My honour is pledged, and I go.'

"At that moment, they looked towards the mountain. The form of the green knight was there. His head reached the very top of the highest promontory—the wild birds screamed around him. At the sight, the chief, for the first time, trembled. The lady fell horror-stricken at his feet.

"'The young knight,' exclaimed she, 'is my son! Forgive me—I was betrothed to the father, whom thou hast slain. He forsook me—you know the rest.'

"The chief gazed on his beauteous bride for a moment—his cheek blanched with rage—the white lip trembled, as he thrust the sword through her heart. The gigantic figure of the mountain was still there. Casting the body on the ground, he rushed forth to the combat; the green knight awaited him;

the mountain no longer sustained the monstrous form—he was slight as before.

"'Thou art come,' said he, 'to meet thy doom. The murderer of my father shall never triumph. Long have I waited till the years of manhood came, that I might deal retribution on the cowardly assassin.'

"'Thy guard!' cried the chief.

"'Know first thy injuries, that thou mayst bite the dust in bitterness. Thy faithless wife—she who saw and directed my father's murder—it was she who bore me. Thou wast dishonoured ere thy bridal night.'

"'Thy guard!' cried the chief; and he fell on the upraised sword of the knight without a blow. 'Thou art avenged!' exclaimed the dying O'Connor.

"The attendant, who had followed the chief, hastened to the clan; the war-cry was raised, and a thousand armed men rushed forth to the scene, burning with determination to revenge the fall of their chief. They had attained the foot of the mountain, when the monster again rose before them: even while all were struck with consternation, the knight descended with five hundred bowmen, rushed among the panic-stricken crowd, of which none escaped the sword. Frightful was the slaughter among the inmates of the castle; the two sons of the chief were among the first who fell. The very morass was tinged with the blood of the slain.

"Over all, the Monster of the Mountain presided. His form was visible till the English had laid all waste. The green knight, the recreant O'Connor, was the general of Strongbow, and from that hour have the English held dominion over those beauteous wilds; from that hour have the noble race, once the proud and manly attendants of the O'Connors, sunk to mere wretched cottagers, without liberty or spirit to achieve it; from that hour has every inhabitant of northern Connemara trembled at the appearance of the Monster of the Mountain, believing that some further ill is to fall on their devoted heads.

"'The explanation of all this," said the friar, as he regarded with a stern look the terrified distillers, " is not difficult ; it is certain that thousands will never be otherwise persuaded than that they have seen some spiritual being of enormous dimensions upon the mountains. Often, indeed, have I reproved those who repeated this story; but they were themselves deceived, and had no intention to deceive others.

"It is in one month of the year only that the Monster of the Mountain appears; that is in September, when the sun sets about six in the evening. Should there be a cloudless sky—a circumstance not uncommon at this season—the shadow of the opposite rocks is reflected with a peculiar strength of outline on the high mountain, and, the glare of the Atlantic falling on the sunny parts, presents the exact outline and form of a man in armour. The peculiar greenness of the mountain furnishes the origin of the story. It is by no means wonderful that, to persons little accustomed to examine into the causes of things, and suddenly coming on the sight of so peculiar a picture, the approach of night adds to the delusion; and many who were strangers to the country, on reaching the brow of the opposite ridges, have sunk under their apprehensions. That the destruction of that once noble pile took place in the time of Strongbow is true; how much of the rest of the tale may be relied on I know not. I have repeated only the tradition of the country."

"Long life to the Monster!" cried the major, as he gulped down another joram of whiskey, "and thanks to you, father, for the tale; but it is day, and we have many miles yet to traverse of this river ere we meet a breakfast."

The friar bid us a hearty farewell, which was accompanied by as hearty a blessing. We took also a cordial leave of the whiskey manufacturers, and begged to have a drop of the "bran new" to fill our pocket bottles.

"Whist," exclaimed the architriclinos, "would you be after drinking the fresh rum! I'll show you some ten months ould, as mild as mother's milk, without a headache in a hogshead."

He led us on our way till we arrived at the base of the rocks, and, rolling a large stone from the mouth of a well-concealed hole, displayed several large stone jars, out of which he furnished our store, and bade us farewell.

I believe a man may be benighted, and knock at many a park-gate entrance, and find less hospitality and amusement than we experienced at the hands of the lawless distillers of the *unparliamentary*.[1]

I cannot tell whether dyspeptic people ever become fishermen, or whether fishermen can ever become dyspeptic; but it would be as hard a trial as any I can conceive—even to one of the guards who finished at the battle of Waterloo the tender discipline of the Peninsular war—to drink whiskey punch all night in a cabin, and set forth at daybreak, for the enlivening purpose of traversing a bog, of twenty miles extent, saturated with rain. If the powers of digestion are a little irregular and fastidious, perhaps this would be an occasion to call forth some of those extraordinary antics their defective subordination so frequently suggests.

Owen's face looked, if possible, more lengthy than ever; and I thought I could discover the major's eye somewhat of the golden tinge, which, though in the main rather a pretty colour, is not highly esteemed even by gentlemen from India, who come to drink Epsom salt water at that pleasant vortex for invalids —Cheltenham. But I was afraid to venture an observation, fully impressed with the conviction that the *Tu quoque* would form a just rejoinder. I won't say that I was quite well, or that a good bed, with a nice clean-capped chambermaid, lighting me thereto, and fumbling about the clothes with an old fryingpan, with holes in the lid, would not have o'ertopped the hopes of the fresh in the river. But here was nothing but the wild heath, the resounding river, now charged to its banks' edge, bursting through the chasms of solid granite, and in the stillness of the dawn roaring through the glens. The mists still covered

[1] All whiskey which has paid the duty is called parliamentary whiskey.

the tops of the mountains, and showed forth the dreariness and desolation of an unexplored expanse.

Nature has made some little confusion in what philosopher Square calls "the eternal fitness of things"; the heat without is by no means in a proper ratio of that within the body; for, though both the major and myself had taken especial care and used considerable diligence in fortifying the inner man with all the warmth which new whiskey could possibly excite, it is a curious fact in physics, for which I am wholly incompetent to account, that the exterior man did shiver most intolerably. There was a disinclination to parlance also—at other times little to be charged on the major; and I believe, friends as we were, nothing would have been more easy at that moment than to have concocted a very nice quarrel. None of us were quarrelsome, but the discourse was monosyllabic, and our words were chilled; but neither dared confess the discomfort under which we all three laboured.

I thought of nothing but the twenty miles, and continued to occupy myself in ratiocinative deductions, arising from the fact that a man had been known to achieve the distance even without once throwing himself horizontally on a wet bog—an inclination, however, which ever and anon assumed considerable force. Not unfrequently did I persuade myself that I could walk, and sustain the dignity of the *ad sidera vultus*, with my eyes shut. Nothing could be seen; the bog was level; nor was I roused from the favourable view I had been induced to take of this very pernicious fallacy but by the practical squash into the morass, which generally invited the other foot to the rescue of the offending member, which it was not then exactly convenient to amputate. There was no inequality of wretchedness, therefore, both feet being well saturated with the porter-like overflowing of the bog.

As to Owen, I had conceived hopes that he at least would break down, and give me some colour for following his example. The imperturbable villain had secured a piece of lighted turf, and, as I looked behind to observe how he got on, I had the mortification of witnessing a countenance of the utmost complacency, in the principal feature of which was stuck a short black pipe, and out of which very principal feature issued long volumes of detestable-looking smoke. There was no chance from him. There was nothing for it but to push on.

The river was swollen to a flood; but, as the rain had now ceased and the fall was rapid, we anticipated a good cast by mid-day. The major grumbled at the disappointment, as he had determined to carry into the town the wherewith of a good dinner. I found in this state of the water the roe useless—the fish were scattered by the extended volume of the stream. We were at least three hours too early, as the major ventured to observe after a few casts.

"It's a glorious morning, however," said he.

"Splendid."

"The fresh morning air is very refreshing."

"I daresay it is."

"This is a grand specimen of the fisherman's life. Now, I just observe to you that nothing gives a greater relish to a breakfast than the mountain air—it's perfectly astonishing what it will do for the health."

"And the comfort too."

"Why, I was thinking that the smallest drop of whiskey might do no great hurt, and help us onward."

This was the point the gallant officer had been aiming at ever since our departure. I could not resist the temptation of assuring him that it was, of all things in the world, the proper thing: the stimulus should be kept up when there was no sport to enliven the labours. The major's draught was not loud but deep; and there was a manifestation of enterprise almost simultaneously engendered.

"Huzza for the lob-trouts this day!—the thick water will be off in an hour. It was just after such a day that I grabbled fifty of the best salmon I ever saw—all fresh run from the sea."

"What is the process of grabbling?"

"After a fresh flood, the salmon come up in shoals to the falls, and there rest till they are sufficiently recovered to make the leap. They are then sulky—will take neither bait nor fly, but stick like logs under the fall. I then quietly take a dozen large cod-hooks, tie them back to back, and, with a stout stick, a strong cord, and heavy lead sinker, let down to the bottom, every now and then twitch to the right, then to the left, then upwards, and in-wise, and outwards. Fifty of the silvery villains fell victims to my industry, till the proprietor of the fall came personally to pay me a visit, and had the audacity to question both my right to fish and the fairness of the style of it. As to the fairness of it, said I, all is fair in love, war, and fishing; and as to the right, you'll particularly honour me by the acceptance of this card, where my name and rank are neatly engraved for the satisfaction of all gentlemen who may render themselves worthy of my notice. Will you believe that the spalpeen refused to fight, and talked something about the law? I wished him good day—regretted I had mistaken his calling—the mistake being exactly the converse of Hamlet's, as I had conceived *a fishmonger was a gentleman*. I gave him no chance for his law, as I pushed on beyond his district before he had obtained the summons. But the fifty salmon were capital. I distributed them among all the poor cottagers as I passed along. Faith, it was many a day since any of them had seen such a meal, although living on the very banks of the river.—Did you see that rise?"

The intimation was enough. The fish had begun to stir, and the water was now clearing. We were within four miles of the town, which the major represented as bad enough at all times, but worse without notice. It was arranged, therefore, that Owen should push forward to apprise the landlord of our coming, and give the necessary orders. He was especially enjoined, if possible, to take with him a salmon, which was to be ready on our arrival. Owen pocketed his black pipe, and, charged by so important a mission, in which his skill as an angler was to be put to the test, with an air of offended dignity at the doubt implied, strutted over the bog, while the major and myself prepared our tackle.

The major's first throw instantly rose a fish, but he rose short. The same fish rose again at my fly, still short. Down went the major's rod, and, regardless of the recent rains, he proceeded to seat himself on the grass.

"Now, what fly do the wilful vermin want? A flood, and a light yellow golden pheasant not do for the epicurean villains?"

We produced the books, and, after a long examination and due balancing of probabilities, we selected a light blue hackle and gray wing. We were right; the first cast produced a salmon firmly hooked; he was my prize. In a minute, the major was fast linked to another. In the hilarity of the moment, the major hurled up his hat, as his fish steadily pushed up the stream.

I was not less exulting; but the moment of conflict I knew had not yet arrived. In due course, my fish conceived it more agreeable to travel downwards—a disposition I had no means of restraining—and, favoured by the strong current, had thought proper to adopt the railroad rate of travelling; I mean that rate expressed in the splendid schedules, about arriving here and there at such particular hours, but which schedules, and the columns they contain, have no further effect than that of disappointing elderly gentlemen who look for a hot dinner at 3.30, and get it cold at 5.20. My salmon had none of this irregularity; he pushed downwards in earnest, and not according to any schedule. In doing so—I could not help it, whatever my gallant colleague may say when he reads these pages—he crossed the major's line, whose fish was travelling upwards at the slow coach pace, checked the lines, and, I grieve to say, with such violence as to smash both. The remnants came up without trouble. The major looked at me, and I looked at the major.

  * * * * *

These asterisks express a pause—it was a long one. It is altogether wrong, and very wicked, to ejaculate,—and so is it

T

to write down apostrophes that have immediate reference to a state of misfortune not quite applicable to sublunary matters, but which exclusively belong to a particular extent of heat hereafter, and, therefore, I refrain. But I must record the fact that my gallant companion in arms did throw down his white hat—that he did stamp upon it, notwithstanding its intrinsic

I LOOKED AT THE MAJOR.

value as a hat—that he did commit devastation on the very small proportion of hair which remained at the back of his head, regardless of its inestimable beauty—and that he did then and there declare that I had no right—that it was wholly against the common law of angling, and, as he believed on his soul, against a particular act of parliament—to allow my fish to run down while his was taking the opposite direction!

There was nothing to be said; I had no excuse to offer; the fish was pertinacious, and the act of parliament referred to did not extend to him, however applicable to me. That was all I could urge; but if it had not happened that the major had some respect for me on other accounts, I verily believe our friendship had been from that moment at an end.

"That was the right colour," I observed, after some time, and looking cautiously at the major as he gazed on the stream in a certain inert state of intellect and bodily function. He looked towards me peeringly, as though he was examining the extent of my grief, expecting, doubtlessly, to observe a height of mental anguish which equalled or exceeded his own.

"It was a tolerable colour, by St. Patrick!" and he began to mend the disposition of his hat, by thrusting his hand rather energetically into the crown, and using other persuasives to a resumption of its original form. "You may say that; it was a tolerable colour."

I like to see a man recovering from a violent passion, the cause of which is irremediable. The indignation evaporates, but a strong pride remains, which will not allow the possessor to acknowledge that the cause was irremediable. The major had been unhappy but for the opportunity of casting all blame on me; and I ventured, therefore, to hint that the statute to which he had so learnedly referred really applied to himself, as it strictly forbade any person or persons whatever, under a penalty thereinafter named, holding, playing, drowning, or following any fish, whensoever it shall or may happen that another person, etc. The recitation of this act did not convince him; but it sufficiently soothed him to endure the renovation of the tackle with some coolness, although the knots were completed with some jerks, each being accompanied by a consignment direct to inferior regions.

We were presently surprised by a succession of leaps; four or five salmon at once cleared the surface. Our surprise and curiosity were soon satisfied; the nose of an otter was elevated, then another, and another. We were up in a moment; the rifle had been left with Owen. It was a brood.

"Pelt them with stones!" cried the major.

This I did with all imaginable industry, and succeeded in separating the young ones from the parents. The latter had gone down the stream, while the three whelps, unable to sustain themselves under water for so great a length of time, popped up their heads in exactly the most inconvenient places. The chase now began; as the young ones had started up the stream, we had no difficulty in keeping them in that direction. At length the three perched on a rock, and began to cry with the small voice of a cat; they were obviously in the wrong, and had missed the old ones, who were doubtless not far off.

The skill of the major was now in requisition; he had hastily tied to his line all the large salmon-flies he could find, and, at the distance of twenty yards, ere I was informed of his intention, covered the three whelps by a foot; they immediately started, and the major as immediately drew.

"Here's one at least," exclaimed he.

It was true; he had one of the otters fast; but the difficulty of holding him was not trifling. The fight was exactly in the style of a large and heavy fish; first he was down to the bottom of the pool, then, with the rapidity of lightning, he rose at another part where he was least expected. The contest was one of most singular dexterity on one part, and of strength and agility on the other. At length, the smaller of the two fishermen began to yield, and, in a few minutes, he was dragged by main force to the shore. I now assisted in the fight, but warily, as the little animal bit ferociously at everything that was put towards him. He died the death of honour; he was stoned to death, and crammed into the creel as the most remarkable trophy of expert angling.

It was hopeless to expect any success, at least within a considerable range of the river, the otters having taken down the stream; and I was by no means unwilling to dismount the flies, and go in search of comfort, a very attenuated portion of which had, for the last twenty-four hours, been our lot. In the triumph of his skill, my companion had forgotten the *contretemps* in which he affected to believe me so deeply implicated, and we improved in good-humour and courtesy as we shortened the distance to Castlebar.

The road was indeed a rough and boggy one; but, after the difficulties we had encountered by the river side, even this seemed tolerably direct; every second step did not, as before, give us one foot in the bog.

At length the turfy smoke of Castlebar met our view, and the exhilaration I immediately felt at the near prospect of food, raiment, and lodging, would not be repressed; strength returned to my previously tottering limbs, and my companion's heavy stump became more energetic.

The gorgeous beauty of the sun reflected on the glassy bosom of the Castlebar Lake, and the pure green of the mountains, regenerated by the late torrents, formed a cheering scene, to which the miserable huts we occasionally passed but ill responded. We had deemed that more extreme wretchedness than that we had hitherto seen could nowhere be found; yet the huts we examined, as we entered the county of Mayo, convinced us that the last and most meagre sustenance might be absent. Here, indeed, many of the cottagers, if they can be so termed, were without any article of food. Their small plots of ground, which were planted, from the damp nature of the soil had not yet matured the potato, which, in its early state, is watery and unwholesome.

Some of the poor creatures were huddled over the turf-fire, while other members of the family were begging around, even among those destitute as themselves. Starvation was in every countenance. There was neither spirit nor life in the eye of the forms which appeared at the hut-doors; the wife sat moodily nursing an infant, which found no nourishment in the squalid parent. The husband looked gloomily by the road side, as if waiting some impending outbreak.

The state of human creatures once reduced to this condition is fearful indeed. While their tenants are brought by a succession of absentee proprietors to the verge of human starvation, none are louder than those very absentees in soliciting the assistance of the English, and in promoting subscriptions for the relief of wretchedness which themselves have caused. Nor should it be forgotten, while these appeals are annually made to the sympathies of the English, that on few, I may almost say on no occasions, have the rents been remitted; so that the enormous amounts generously awarded by those subscriptions have literally found their way into the pockets of the landlords, they having first stripped the peasantry, by a ruinous rental, of all that should have resulted to their labours for sustenance, and the liberal contributions of the English furnishing that sustenance.

It is true that the inhabitants of these districts are idle; it is a common reproach to them. God help them! who is there to direct or foster their industry? Millions of uncultivated acres surround their miserable huts, on which the hand of man has never yet been exercised. No leases would be granted; there could be no remuneration for the labour requisite in the reclamation; and thus is a destitute population doomed to view the rank reed covering a soil which would, under a kinder destiny, supply all their wants, and create their content and happiness.

Nothing can be more unjust than the system of subscription, by which, from year to year, the unemployed population of Mayo is supported. It is not a subscription for the poor, but for the rich. It is an annual subscription towards the extortionate and monstrous rents which are demanded and exacted from the wretched beings who, unknown to other employ, must till the soil at any impost, or starve.

It is not in disregard of the value of freedom that I observe the readiness with which twenty millions of the public money were granted to a maudlin sympathy with the well-fed West Indian slave, while whole districts, in this our home-land, contain people hurrying to an early grave by the utter want of food. It is time that something be done. The sight of those peaceful, yet starving faces, which are presented at every hut, would affect the heart of a stoic: but the stoics who are the lords of the soil take good care never to behold them!

On our entrance into Castlebar, and on inquiring for the inn, we found that the town was really in a hubbub. It happened to be market-day, and groups of persons surrounded us. At last we were accosted by one of the country people, who seemed more capable of addressing the strangers than the rest, who informed us that our attendant, Owen, was in trouble—in truth, at that moment, in durance—for an offence of rather an extraordinary character. The landlord, who was of the roughest order, received us at the door.

"If it's your honour's man that's taken up, he has sent a dozen times to inquire for you, to clear him before the magistrate."

The major, who had contracted a real friendship for our humble attendant, was on fire.

"Who is the magistrate that dares to take up my man, without first informing myself? Och, it's myself will settle the matter without the law at all at all."

I could perceive, without much difficulty, that my friend was in an unlikely mood to become just then a very successful advocate. Leaving him, therefore, to the pocket-book from which he was selecting a card, with no very friendly intention towards the magistrate, I proceeded to make further inquiries, and learned that our Achates had been exhibiting himself in a state that would have offended even the ladies of the Connemara wilds—in fact, that he had been stopped in a state of entire nudity, running like a madman among all the people coming to market—that he had been seized, covered, and brought before the magistrate, to whom he gave so lame an account of our honours, that he had been consigned to durance till our arrival.

Our astonishment was immeasurable, and could only be appeased by the supposition that Owen's peculiarity of character had at length subsided into absolute madness. We forthwith proceeded to the rescue, the major burning with indignation, and determined to get up a fight with some one on this score. I succeeded, however, in prevailing on him to allow me to be the manager of the business; and, having sent up my name to the magistrate, we were immediately admitted. His account was that our companion had really been taken as described in the road; and that the people were fully impressed with the notion that he was deranged—a conviction to which he himself had arrived upon hearing the facts. For our satisfaction, he would send again for him, to enable him to give what explanation he pleased of the matter.

Owen was soon produced. At sight of us he forthwith brightened up.

"Och, and it's all right now, anyway! Your honours have got the salmon; I left him to be dressed; and is it myself would go to disappoint your honours of a breakfast along with a few spalpeen market people! I wonder what divil of a county this, that a man mayn't catch a salmon, because the river runs by the side of the road. But your honours will spake for me, and explain it, anyhow, to his nobleness the justice."

I requested permission to ask Owen for his own version, which being readily granted, the prisoner began:—

"It's clear, your honours will remember ordering me to catch a salmon, and go on before to the inn. Well, burn the rise I'd get, your honour, till I came within half a mile of the town; there I sees as fair a rise at the nathural as ever my eyes was blest with. Och! be aisy, sis I—is it there you are, and I wanting ye for my master's breakfast? With that, I makes a clane cast, and covered the beauty to an inch. Up he came—away went my winch, and I thought of my sowl he'd niver done running till my line was smashed. Into the river I pitches my rod—away run the fish, and away run I—and, faith, I'd enough to do to keep up, any way, for the stones and the bogs bothered my speed intirely. At last he stops; oh! sis I, it's my turn now, and with that I goes up towards my rod; off boults the fish to the other side the stream. There was nothing but a swimming or a ducking for it, and, to keep all clane and go dacent into the town like, I pulls off my bits of things, and swims over the river to the place where the wild brute had carried my rod. The divil a bit he stand a minute. Off went the salmon again; and it was then I had a run for it after the river, so, seeing my rod going doubts tide, and, finding the road alongside the river far best for running, to the road I went; and it's a pity your honours weren't there to see the sport—run salmon, run I, for a good half mile—there I caught my rod; and it's a good to the heart to see the way he played. But I soon landed my fish, and what do your honours think? In a fine country like this, a lot of spalpeens, without with your leave, or by your leave, or any politeness at all, seizes hould of me, crams an ould frieze or two over me, and brings me to be put to prison. 'Oh!' sis I, 'but I'm a free-born Irishman,' sis I; 'and there are two rale gintlemen that'll see me righted,' sis I; 'and what have I done?' sis I.—'Done?' sis they; 'haven't ye been running stark naked among the people, and them women?' sis they.— 'The divil a woman or man,' sis I, 'did I see at all at all'; and if your nobleness and honour will give me the book, I'll swear the same on my Bible oath this moment. What do they tell his honour, but that there were lots of women coming to market, and his honour believes 'em, maybe because I am a Catholic. I saw nobody all the time but the rod, and that was running swately."

I assured the magistrate of my entire conviction that Owen was innocent of any intentional wrong; and such was, I believe, the ardour with which he pursued the sport, that I did not doubt his declaration that he had seen nobody.

The magistrate was pleased to find that the affair was of no further consequence, and ordered Owen to be discharged, assuring him, however, that his being a Catholic had had nothing whatever to do with his detention or discharge, and in this declaration I joined; but the major, seizing the hand of Owen, and in the presence of the magistrate, declared his entire approval of the fisherman's whole course of conduct; "and, for myself, I'd follow a salmon into the very palace rather than lose him, any way. So, say nothing of being a trifle deficient in the cut of your surtout."

The major was now about to wax wroth in approval of Owen's conduct; and just as he was fumbling about for the card, on which was neatly engraved "Major ——, —th regiment," I thrust my arm within his, bowed to the man of authority, and we were at our inn before the gallant officer could determine in what way the proper insult ought to be conveyed to a magistrate. Owen was admitted to dine with us off the salmon which had been the cause of all his distress and degradation.

We were indeed weary, but had acquired in our peregrinations a perfect knowledge of what will be reasonably expected in a night up the mountains by the sportsman in Ireland.

CHAPTER XXII

A Curse against Preserves—Reasons for Condemning them—A Slap at the Peers—Apology and Reconciliation—An Irish Tory—After-Dinner Argument on Popular Education—Challenge—Preparations for a Meeting—Satisfactory Arrangement—An Old Acquaintance—The Spanish Legioner—His Last Trip—The Shipwreck—How to qualify for Exciseman—Belfast—Manufactures at Belfast—Last Evening in Ireland—Leave-taking.

"I'LL hold any man a dozen that this country will never prosper. I'll hold any wager, against any man, that, while all the rest of old Ireland is prospering, this will be the county accursed. What! I that hold his Majesty's commission—who have condescended to receive pay quarterly of as bad a set as—but never mind, it's a bad track we're in, and the sooner our marching order is beat the better for all anglers."

"What, in the name of Fortune, is the matter, major?"

"The matter! a set of rent-driving maniacs, that live upon gorse and subscriptions every spring——"

"Of whom do you speak?"

"Speak! who should spake of or to 'em——"

The major's countenance was swollen with indignation. Owen's, who accompanied him into the room, was by no means indicative of less, though of more subdued anger.

"Of whom do you speak, major?"

"Bring in the matarials—a good way to travel—Owen, some whiskey; here, gulp down your passion as I do, and let the horror of the place be eternal. Let 'em keep their bogs and their porther colour rivers, and drink 'em; it's all they have to drink four-fifths of their time. Presarve! oh, the divil presarve 'em, and keep all honest fishermen away from 'em. No wonder their mountains bring nothing; no wonder they call out starvation, and are hurried by droves to the grave for want of the food the miserable masters cannot furnish. Will you believe that in this county here, in Mayo—we'd scorn it in the south—the very renters of the weirs would scorn it—all is preserved, and the deuce a fly you'll be allowed to cast? Whiskey, Owen; keep your temper, man."

Owen kept his temper, and swallowed the whiskey.

"It's not long since but the whole of these tracts were free as air. The mountain eagle was not more unfettered than the stranger, who, with a rod, made way by the lakes; nay, it would go further; it would be odd, indeed, if the weary fisher did not meet some of the hospitality for which our fathers were celebrated. But now! The matarials."

The major was soothing himself by pottle-deep potations.

"Now, every scanty possessor calls himself a manor lord, assumes a royalty, issues an edict, and claims that for himself, or rather for nobody—since he can neither fish himself, nor will allow any other—which hitherto had been the only attraction such desert wastes afforded. Presarve! hadn't they better cry royalty over the broad sea, and tell us that's presarved—or over the air, and forbid us to breathe. Presarve! Heaven's name! what have they to presarve? Can these petty bog princes tell us that the fish are their property? do they score and name them?"

"Your honour sarved him right," said Owen.

"Right! and who would doubt it! a spalpeen keeper. Keeper! capital joke in the wilds of Connemara—up to your ankles in bog—squash every minute—keeper—Capit—d—n such keeping!"

The major emptied the second tumbler.

I now found that, while I had been endeavouring to regain

some of the freshness which my night's bivouacking and morning's walk had a little damaged, my two companions had sallied forth to the lakes, and that, in the exercise of the gentle craft, they had received a peremptory order to desist. The major's astonishment little qualified him for reasonable explanation, and he had therefore returned the intimation that the lakes were a preserve, by a polite assurance that the messenger should forthwith proceed to ascertain the exact depth of the pool he was fishing; and this would, in all human probability, have been the destination of the hapless keeper, but that Owen had stepped in between the threatening combatants.

Owen, indeed, had become the more immediate object of the keeper's rage, and had sustained divers blows before the major's heavy fist settled the affair, and gave, as I prognosticated, good cause for proceedings at law against our party.

I represented to my companion that the consequences might be serious; but it was impossible to make him comprehend any just reason why one man should not, on what he deemed a fair provocation, inflict personal chastisement on another. The pretence to preserve waters which had once been free to the world, was such a provocation, and, had it been the master instead of the man, I verily fear the major's want of personal control had been the same.

"What!" exclaimed he, "presarve in a country where the least attraction held out to foreign visitors is indeed a chance of its advantage? where every stranger more that visits it is so much added to the general wealth, and deducted from that amount which is sent to the absentees? Yet, in such a country, for a small-souled, petty proprietor to assume the dictatorial air which nothing but park walls ought to justify! yet whose park walls, if they should ever arrive at such a pitch of eastern magnificence, would be made of turf soaked in bog water, with here and there a block of granite for a gate.

"Thousands of fish come up and descend these rivers and lakes; they are destroyed by the otter and the wild bird. Not a hut offers the common shelter of a civilised country near the banks of the morasses that enclose them. What preservation is necessary under such circumstances? Summon the whole population of the district, and their collected wealth would supply nothing beyond a hazel rod and a coarsely spun fly. Who, then, are the strangers against whom such particular orders should be issued? those only who bring civilisation, and, in some instances, wealth with them: civilisation, I say, because their intercourse with so rude and barbarous a people as this, is calculated to soften the manners, and, perhaps, make other countries known to them. If *I* were a proprietor, not only should all strangers have full permission to amuse themselves, but I would stretch forth the hand of hospitality to encourage their visits.

"Anglers are never dangerous men. Show me a man devoted to the art, and I will show you a person whose feelings are well attuned to the exercise of the kindlier intercourse of friendship and affection. There would be no danger in showing hospitality to the angler.

"Where is now the hospitality of bygone days, when honest landlords held no peerage. What! a peer! The empty badge of an enslaved wretch, who sold his birthright for such a mess of pottage as an Irish peerage! A livery servant is the meanest and most contemptible of men; I hate the yellow and gold with which their monkey manhood is bedaubed: he is the walking monument of his own baseness and his master's pride. There is but one step lower in humanity: it is the peerage obtained by the hireling villain who betrayed his country's independence for so paltry and ignoble a bribe.

"Look at them. Who, what are the Pitt Union peers? Exiles—their domains in the hands of the receivers of the courts; or, if at home, the despised abettors of their country's ruin. That's a peer—an Irish peer—a Pitt Union Irish peer! Send for some gold lace, in God's name, tie it round his hat, and let him stand behind the chairs of honest men. That will be one step at least for their character. That's my opinion of the peerage; but I think less of the petty shades of shadows who call themselves proprietors."

The major had run himself out, and fortunately at that moment the servant presented a card. I foresaw the difficulty we were in, and entreated my companion to allow me to deal with the new-comer, promising most fervently to do nothing which should compromise the major's reputation of courage and dignity. On his retirement, therefore, I desired the stranger to be shown in.

He was a young man, of a somewhat military appearance, and presented himself with the utmost civility. I was the first to remark that I believed I could anticipate what was the cause to which I was indebted for the honour of his visit.

There had been, he feared, some misunderstanding on all sides. Nothing could be further from his intention than offering any obstruction to the fair angler, and his servant had mistaken his instructions; but one of our party could not, he thought, be excused in inflicting violence on the poor man, who was, in fact, doing no more than he conceived his instructions had directed.

The awkwardness of my situation was apparent; therefore I proceeded to acknowledge that the abstract assault was not to be justified, and that I should be most happy to offer to the keeper the reasonable recompense he should demand, and to present to my visitor the apology I thought was due to him.

Just as I had completed these arrangements satisfactorily, the major burst into the room, impatient to be made acquainted with the subject of our discussion. I introduced him, and the result was that both the belligerent parties were perfectly satisfied: Mr. S—— assuring the major that he was most welcome to all the angling he could find, under the fullest impression that I had used his authority in the apology I had presented; and the major accepting most graciously the permission thus given as a full apology for the obstruction he had met with.

It was not my business to undeceive either, both being perfectly satisfied with the conduct of each other; and, indeed, so pleased were the parties, that a warm and pressing invitation to dinner was on the spot given and accepted.

I congratulated myself on my skill at diplomacy, in having made two persons friends, who might have been very dangerous in hostility. Mr. S—— took his leave, and in a few minutes, Paddy, the keeper, was in attendance, ready to show our honours the best pools. I slipped a sovereign into his hand, and left him to stare at the wondrous luck which St. Patrick had brought him by means of a broken head, a matter he at no time would have felt as a great misfortune, and one that now, with its present concomitant, he would have been too happy to receive daily.

Our host's preparations were of the usual abundant order. His cottage was on the banks of the lake, which he had so carefully preserved, and presented a pretty sporting-box. The interior was indeed well supplied with all the means of rendering a secluded life agreeable. I must observe also that the preparations for the repast, to which we were invited, were of more than ordinary elegance; although the attendance was to be supplied by bare-footed trotters over the bog.

The numerous assembly in the kitchen betokened a rout for the dependants, one running in the way of the other, with the accustomed and "most admired disorder."

Our reception was cordial. Our host, himself an Irishman, possessed, I believe, of a patrimony more ancient and respectable than extensive, had figured in the records of hospitality; and in the course of a few years had managed to dispossess himself of an inheritance of considerable value. He had at last thrown open his house for a year to all comers, determined to place an honourable seal to the desultory extravagance, which was slowly but surely impoverishing his means. The end of the year brought the end of the rental; and his retirement to the lovely spot, which formed an island on the lake, was adopted with the view of recovering by seclusion the lost revenue. But even here his liberal habits pursued him; and though he was strict in the preservation of the fishing and shooting of the domain he rented, he was always ready to grant permission to any respectable applicants.

He was a Tory,—not of the vacillating and unsettled order, who sometimes rejoice in one name, and then eschew it for another, but a well-founded, honest, and intolerant Tory,—one who, with "Sir Charles" of honest notoriety, never could comprehend what the rights of the people could mean. He understood the privileges of *the order*, and the enjoyment of patronage; he knew also the full meaning of the supplies when properly appointed and distributed. But what the newspapers meant by the people and their rights, he could never be made to comprehend; and the difficulty he had found, while endeavouring to become enlightened on this point, had at last terminated in the very laudable resolution, should he ever arrive at the post of prime minister, of shooting down the masses like dogs.

There was not much to hope from the major's prudence, when Mr. S—— and his friend, well mustachoed, and both having the honour to hold Her Majesty's commission, bowed to each other in the dining-room. But the dinner treated not of war —the punch had commenced its inspiration, I congratulated myself on all being safe, and passed off, with some adroitness, the observation of my host, that the pest of the country was the Catholic religion, but that the worst of it was that all the people were Catholics, which Mr. S—— could by no means account for.

I replied, *sotto voce*, that it was very odd, and challenged my friend opposite to a tumbler. It was of no use; the word, the fatal word had caught the major's ear, and at the sudden gurgling which denoted the descent of at least a full pint, I was alarmed by the consciousness that the magic word had been effectual.

"It's a Catholic country we're in, sir," said the major.

"And a good country too," said I complacently.

"Good country!—I should like to see the one that's better, and I wouldn't lave this for it."

"The country is a fine country," said our host, "but it is ruined by the religion which seems to overrun it. Look at England! there the parsons are knowable people—men that decent persons may speak to—they are not always stirring up the poverty of the labouring classes to make them dissatisfied. What is the case here? every rascally vagabond is hand and glove with the priest; the priest instructs and directs him. What has the priest to do with instruction? people that have to work should work, and let education alone. It must end in the ruin of any country to be always teaching the people; they are too knowing already."

The major never argued well; it was by no means his forte. When he did express himself with a view to implanting conviction in the mind of another, it was done rather manually than logically, and the force of his position was rather established by the concussion of the fist and table than by any formula of verbal ratiocination.

"And why by St. Patrick shouldn't the people be instructed by their priests, since they can get no instruction elsewhere?"

The major made a pause; his fist was gathered up for the grand climax of the position he was about to establish, which waited only the reply of his opponent.

"That's the question I ask?" added the major with impatience.

Who could answer this question? It was unfair in the major to put it. The best reason I ever heard, even at a Tory parson dinner, or a public speechifaction, against the mischiefs of educating the people, was that they might, when servants, read their master's letters; and I believe it is on record, that one of our most talented early bishops recommended as the safeguard of the empire, the careful preservation of ignorance among the people, though he himself was, at that time, a "marksman." It was an unfair question, and there was no answer to it; but the friend with moustaches declared that it was very unpleasant to have fellows who ought to be digging affecting to know anything of books.

"I'd hang every priest," said our host, "that presumed to teach a letter to a peasant."

"And so would I," said the military friend.

The fist was ready, and down it went; the glasses rang a long and inharmonious peal.

"And the devil a priest you'd either of ye hurt, while I had an arm to defend him!"

This was plump in the major.

"You would hardly prevent me," said our host.

"Twenty of ye!" said the major; he was determined.

"Sir," said our host, with every indication of suppressed wrath, "after the apology you this morning made to me, I had not expected to meet such rudeness."

"Apology!—faith and if it had not been for the very proper one you presented me with, the devil a dinner I would have shared with you, here or anywhere!"

"Apology!"

"Apology!" re-echoed the major.

I was in the exact dilemma I had been fearing. It was useless to explain; neither would give up the conviction of having received and not given an apology to the other.

The grievances therefore were re-stated; the broken head of the keeper was again declaimed on; while the villainy of any man, in a free country, daring to prevent fishing on the open lake, met all the condemnation my friend's vocabulary could furnish.

The confusion of tongues was overwhelming—matter explanatory, condemnatory, and contradictory. It was hopeless to interfere; so the major took the last gulp at his tumbler of punch, proceeded towards the door, bowed with affected calmness, and assured Mr. S—— he should hear from him in the morning.

I bowed myself out also, resolved to attempt no explanation then, but fully impressed with the hope that I should effectually remove all the animosities of the parties in the morning.

I was deceived; with the morning came my friend in the moustaches, who claimed precedence in the message to the major. I assured him that I was perfectly prepared to make all reasonable allowances, if he were similarly disposed. To this I received so imperative a denial, that I became satisfied that nothing but the meeting was intended.

Nothing could equal the suavity of the lieutenant entrusted with this embassy, after he had obtained my appointment that we should be ready on the side of the lake in one hour from that time.

The major was stumping up and down his room, with his hands thrust into the very bottom of his pockets. He hardly perceived that I had entered; but my eye fell instantly on certain preparations, which were obviously made in contemplation of the probable result of the evening's conversation. On one table a pair of old horse-pistols newly rubbed up; the balls carefully deposited in an old horn, and the ramrod ready for the charge. On the other side were papers containing curious scratches, or marks which the major had deluded himself into a conviction that he had written.

"I am sorry," I observed, "to be compelled to say——"

"I'm ready, my boy—all right! It's myself will larrup the lot of 'em. But, there is one thing—if I should fall——"

"Entrust all to me, our time is short."

"Why, it's a grievous thing to have a boy's random shot through one's liver."

"Whatever be the event of the day," said I, taking the veteran's hand, "be certain that there are no instructions you may give me that will not to the letter be obeyed. If there be anything near your heart, I entreat you now to disclose it—perhaps family affairs."

"I have been upwards of fifty years bandied about this bothering world, and the divil a family affair I ever had."

"No relation to whom I could convey your last wishes?"

The major snapped his fingers, and assured me he valued not that simple evolution any living relation.

Still there was something which oppressed him. It was impossible not to observe, from his anxious eye and occasional changes of countenance, that some regret weighed on him. I pressed him to disclose it, and for some time ineffectually; nor was it till I had made all the necessary preparations for departure to the rendezvous, that he gave way to my importunity.

"You have pressed me to communicate my distress. I *have* a deep and insurmountable distress; but you cannot help me."

"At least I can endeavour to alleviate it, if it should concern others."

"Impossible; my distress is this. I have served through the Peninsular and American war, obtained my rank by work, and never spent an idle week at home in fifteen years. I am here reduced, and compelled to accept a paltry half-pay for my services, which has never yet been raised even to the nominal rank I hold. The sum is small, to be sure, and everything has its comfort—the smallness of it is some comfort just now. But the distress I feel that a rascally government should pocket the amount at my death, gives me a determination to shoot straight;—so now, my boy, come on! and we'll not be the last on the ground."

This being the only regret, I no longer sought the major's disclosures, but set forth, perfectly satisfied that no man was ever better prepared to meet the worst as far as his worldly affairs stood.

We reached the ground, and I must do my comrade the justice to say that cooler or more imperturbable courage was never displayed; nor was it long till the proof was demanded.

A bow from our friend in the moustaches showed that we

were really met in earnest; although I had great difficulty in believing such trivial causes should produce an effect of so serious a character to persons so lately in the enjoyment of friendly and hilarious communication.

I stepped aside with the second of our late host, and again demanded whether anything short of an apology would be satisfactory. An abrupt negative closed that part of the converse. I repeated, therefore, that if extremities must be resorted to, we might well understand the cause of the quarrel.

"There's no difficulty or dispute on the cause," said the lieutenant. "Your friend thought proper to break the head of my friend's keeper. No apology is offered, and it is clear some satisfaction must be had."

The belligerents took their ground. We had placed the pistols in their hands, and were in the act of retiring, that the proper signal might be given by the lieutenant.

"Hurush!" cried twenty voices, issuing from twenty persons, who in a moment jumped over the hedge:—"Hurush, and bind and secure 'em! Oh, it's a spalpeen's head that was broken, any way!"

Among the multitude, it was by no means difficult to distinguish the voices of Owen and the keeper.

"Oh, master dear," cried the latter, as he threw himself at the knees of S—— with all the genuine ebullition of feeling which is always the characteristic of an Irish servant:—"Oh, bad luck to Paddy Brady's head!—and that's my own—it's a whole head, any way. And, if it isn't, it's myself and Paddy Owen will fight it out. Long life to your honours, and we are the boys for a shindy!"

"Come along, Paddy Brady," cried Owen, as he seized the major's arms, with a full determination to allow of no combat in which he took no part.

The anxious sincerity of the poor fellow who had been the innocent cause of all the mischief, and the cool determination of Owen, were irresistibly droll. I met the eye of the lieutenant, who could no longer refrain from a smile. I gave way to a burst of laughter, while Paddy Brady descanted on the fact in language far too rapid for the best reporter to follow; the upshot of his dissertation being that his head had been most satisfactorily mended by a sovereign; while he heaped very profuse ill luck on his own destiny that had induced him to complain of a "thrifle of a crack, which was nothing to an Irishman at a patheern."

I looked at the lieutenant.

"Why, if the man is satisfied, I don't see that it is absolutely impossible to arrange," said he, confidentially.

"Enough!" I held forth my hand—it was frankly taken: the major and S—— bowed to each other at our intimation, and the affair terminated without the "apology."

A council of piscatorial war was summoned on the succeeding morning. We had found disasters enough in Connemara, and some of our escapes had not been without interest. The major's grand intention of visiting Ballina was much weakened by the specimen we had already found of preserving; and the full knowledge that one might as well be in Scotland (where the salmon are marked every succeeding day, and regularly trained to consider themselves no longer as *choses* in action, but as so many tenants already reduced into absolute possession) as in a country where the broad lakes are preserved, induced the major to forego his purpose of further prosecuting the tour of discovery into this unsocial tract.

On making inquiries for some mode of conveyance, I encountered a person of whom I had some, but an indistinct, remembrance. He was attired in respectable black, strutted with a military air, and smiled as he addressed me with all the ease of an old acquaintance.

"Is it your honour I see at last, and well and hearty? Faith and it does meself good to find you still in Ireland; and, above all, in the splendid country of Connemara. What shall I do for your honour?"

It was my old friend of the steamboat. I had fully recalled his features and manner before his address was complete.

"Faith and ye have good right to inquire by what manes I have turned gentleman at last! But it's cold talking in the streets of Castlebar. The wind cuts down the streets like a razor sent to shave off every rascally vagabond not well clothed, as all proper and respectable people should be. Why don't the people put on proper clothing for the weather, and accommodate their diet to their necessity? It is a difficulty not to be got over or explained. But if your honour will accept the comfort of the Black Lion here, I shall be overplased at the opportunity of thanking you for a past piece of friendship that I owe your honour for. The whiskey is capital."

I was so far interested in my early Irish friend that I readily complied with his wish, and was soon supplied with the "clanest throp imaginable."

My inquiries were soon made. The obvious change in the circumstances of the Spanish Legioner formed the first matter of question.

"It's the fault of the Irish themselves," said he, "that they don't do well in a country where the wealth only requires to be looked after. What did I get but starvation for my trip? What do I get by staying in my native country? Sir, it's meself that you see is appointed exciseman to a large district; and, by my soul, I mane to take good care of the duties."

"Appointed exciseman!" I exclaimed—"why, the last time I had the pleasure of seeing you, it seemed rather your business to avoid any particular intimacy with the officers of the revenue."

"Whisht! you are an Englishman, and a kind one. By St. Patrick! I may trust you well enough. You have a right to my history, because you may tache your children the way to achieve an excisemanship in Ireland. When I left you at the Valencia, the divil a rap I could muster. We went to sea that night with as pretty a cargo of tobacco as you would need to be happy with for a year. It was all carefully stowed when we saw you at

Cromwell Fort. It was soon got on board, and, before daybreak, buried on the shoals at the mouth of the Shannon. We had a night of it, you'll be sure; but our well-trimmed Kinsale boat mounted like a bird, and weathered the lights bravely. At —— we were again shipwrecked fishermen, and soon sold all the tobacco that was waiting only for our sending. By that gale of wind, which lasted two days, we cleared enough for a month's fine weather. This was a fine living, and I was delighted with the change in my condition. Not a gun fired at us, and abundance of whiskey, with a good *bed*, to be paid for handsomely. No straw dungeon or spokesmanship—both which I thoroughly despise—as also the honour of serving any imperial and Christian majesties who never pay but in stripes.

"While musing on the chance of the next trip, one of my comrades communicated that there was a chance, if it was well done, of our getting a good order; but secrecy was the word. I was the boy for a secret, so I betook myself to a big house, to which I had been directed, and was shown into a fine library by a lace-coated footman. Faith and I thought my fortune was come at last. 'Oh! oh!' cried I—'if one could but get domiciled in such a place as this, the devil a storm I'd again venture!' But there was no such luck for me at that time, so I bowed my best, and I had learned the bowing well in Spain, and began to converse with myself just as the door opened, and a little bald-headed gentleman, with a pigtail, entered. He shut the door in a perfectly distinguished manner, and motioned me to a chair. To be sure, I was hardly qualified to sit in the company of the likes—but there I sat, on a morocco chair, with the little bald-headed gentleman opposite, for all the world as though we were two privy councillors and the immortal Dan rading them a lecture.

"'You belong,' says the gentleman—who first helped me to a glass of real good whiskey—'you belong to the Kinsale boat?'

"'Faith, and it's myself, your honour, that has weathered the storm in her that has been blowing all the ships off the seas.'

"'I know it—you landed your tobacco last night.'

"'Oh, murther!' says I. 'I'm transported now, at any rate—here's a blow I'll never recover.' But, then, thinks I; 'tis odd before he sends me to gaol, that he should fill me with whiskey.

"'You needn't be alarmed.'

"'Not in the laste, your honour—sure when your honour's worshipful self says we landed the tobacco last night, it isn't me that says it—and so there's no splitting any way—and it wouldn't be manners to contradict your honour.'

"'Well,' says he, 'I know your crew well, and intend to employ you.'

"'Oh,' says I, 'it's all along of the good character we've got among the poor people.'

"'Yes, yes—I know the character you have—it blows now from the south-west—there will be a gale towards the morning. Do you dare venture out?'

"'Venture! faith we'll venture anywhere.'

"'I thought as much. About eighteen miles from the Head, you will discover a schooner, either this or to-morrow night. She will deliver to you some packages, which you must manage in the night to get on board your own vessel, and then run her up high and dry near the sand beach, between the Heads. That's all you have to do. But there is one thing more—if you should be discovered, you must never give any name. I'll manage, if you are silent, to see you safe through all difficulty, and will get any penalty mitigated, and furnish you with the means to pay it; so you must be secret, and hold out to the last.'

"Hereupon, I assured him that there was not the least danger of our breaking faith, while it was so clearly our interest to keep it, and with one tumbler more we parted, the little gentleman himself seeing me safe to the door.

"Having got our little vessel repaired, and duly stored with all variety of provisions, consisting of potatoes and red herrings, we beat out to seaward, with a stiff breeze blowing dead in.

We comforted ourselves with the remembrance that we could be shipwrecked at any time, and at any part of the coast we should please to take a fancy to, and when the wrecking came about, we could not be very far from the shore. Indeed, we could run her up high and dry, if there was anything like a surf.

"All that night we *fished* very carefully in forty-five fathoms water, and about eighteen miles from the Head. The bait was not particular, as it consisted only of a line and hook, and somehow the cod-fish took no particular fancy to it. So, that with the exception of the red herrings, we were not overburdened with the Friday's banqueting.

"All that night we had the pleasure of being alone, and the next we were visited by the revenue cutter, towards which we made, and very manfully solicited some prog. This we knew to be the best way of getting rid of her; for, if a boat at any time begs provisions of Her Majesty's cutter, or shows any symptoms of the crew being in distress, it is ordained, I suppose, by the government that the helm should be forthwith put up. This was the case on the night in question; for the crew on board Her Majesty's craft are kind-hearted creatures, and hate to see poor boatmen in distress!

"Not three hours after the cutter had parted company, we descried a sail. It was a schooner, bearing down upon us with all sail set. As she passed under our stern, she put her helm hard a-lee, and sprang up alongside of us in very seamanlike style. A rope was immediately thrown on board of our boat, and, though there was a roughish sea running at the time, we were dead alongside. There was nothing said—in fact, the people could say nothing but French, and that is the same as saying nothing:—'So, on with the packages!' cries I—and one after another—I thought they'd never end, about three hundred very nice white deal boxes, neatly screwed down, and directed to nobody. We shifted all the ballast, which consisted of sand, put the packages carefully at the bottom, and covered them well over. The schooner cast off, hauled close to the wind, and was soon out of sight.

"'What the devil will we do?' says I to my two comrades in the boat. 'It's morally impossible to be shipwrecked such a night as this. We can't reasonably be drowned with a fine beating breeze.'

"'It would be a scandal and a shame to us; for the coast-guard boat would be sure to come to our assistance in such a night if we were in distress.'

"So on we went, fishing with empty hooks, till in the morning the cutter again appeared in sight. We cracked on all sail, and endeavoured to pass under her stern. The crew knew we were come begging, so they put up their helm, and walked away from us in the most easy manner imaginable.

"'It's a thought of my own,' says I; 'if you don't agree to it, don't! but I should like to see, just for curiosity, what the deuce can be in those pretty boxes.'

"'Quite proper,' said both my crew; 'we ought to know the cargo we've got, for fear of offending the law in ignorance.'

"'Nothing more sensible ever observed—I know the law,' says I—'magistrates' law—and they say that we have no right to do the things that's illegal, although we don't know it. Therefore we are bound to know it; so haul the foresheet to windward, and put the helm fast down—she'll ride like a duck, while we obtain the proper information.'

"To this both agreed; and we were not long in getting up a case, or in smashing it. Of all the long-necked bottles it was ever my good fortune to see whiskey in, these were the longest. Off they went—phiz!—one after another, all froth and bubbabooism.

"'Capital whiskey,' says Pathrick, my comrade.

"'Glorious,' says I; and a bottle never gave a wry face. Oh! it would have done the hearts of the cutter's crew good to have seen how comfortable we were—helm up—dead in upon the land—pipes lighted, and a smart breeze. This was a shipwreck the likes I never before heard of; and, I believe, a happier crew never approached the lee-shore with the certainty of running on it. It was dead dark. Just as we were debating on the propriety of further making ourselves masters of the legal effect of our cargo, smash went the boat's head against a range of rocks. The force of the shock would have roused a dying or a dead man—and it did rouse us; but we could not get up—some unaccountable influence held us at the bottom of the boat. But, not knowing myself that the feeling was general, I took the command at once, and gave orders that were unquestionably of the best.

"'Up and be doing, you spalpeens!' says I; for nothing assists soldiers or sailors, under your command, so much as swearing at and calling them hard names. This I learned in Her most Christian Majesty's most Christian army. And so I began in the regular way. 'Up with ye, spalpeens, and the devil give life to ye, for a set of short-pipe-smoking villains, when the vessel's on the rocks! Have ye no fear of death before your eyes?' This last I said to terrify them.

"Pat Murphy only takes his pipe out of his mouth for a moment. 'Git up yourself, and see how you like it,' says he. 'What d'ye bother about death? sure we're only being shipwrecked, and what else would ye have us do?' says Pat. And on he went smoking, as if he was in one of the smoky comfortable cabins ashore.

"With that a sea takes the boat in the stern, lifts her clane over the reefs, and one more, catching her on the quarter, sent her twenty yards up the sands, and broke right into her.

"'By St. Pathrick! this is drowning,' says I, 'and not shipwrecking at all.'

"'Drowning?' says Pat Murphy; 'the pipe's out, so now for a rale move.' But he couldn't move when he tried.

"Another sea washed clane over us. 'Over the bows,' cried I, as soon as the surf fell back, 'over the bows!'

"It was slow work that same. I think I fell ten times in

getting forwards; and as to Pat Murphy and the boy, if I hadn't given them a shove, they would never have escaped the boat at all. As it was, Pat fell upon his head in the soft sand, and went up to his middle in it, just like a bed of mortar. The boy and I pulled him out as well as we could. As soon as Pat had wiped the sand from his mouth and eyes, he didn't thank us for the trouble we took, but sent us, without the priest's blessing, to the infernal regions for shipwrecking him in sand.

"'More whiskey with the long necks,' cried Pat. 'More whiskey,' cried I. 'Whiskey,' said the boy; and just upon that our heads all turned round, and we couldn't, for the soul of us, help the most audacious robbery that ever took place. Twenty fellows, for all the world as if they knew we were there, jumped on board the boat, handed out the cases, slung them across each other's backs, and disappeared in a jiffey. Of course I couldn't guess who they were, but I thought they were very respectable thieves — they did their business so cleverly.

"After all was gone, they popped us on hurdles, and carried us off, I couldn't imagine where; and I didn't long try to find out, for the effect of the sea water makes one drowsy, and the motion of the wattle sent me fast asleep.

"That was our shipwreck. In the morning I woke, and found myself in a comfortable bed, and a doctor and the little old gentleman with the bald head and the pigtail standing over me.

"'Poor man,' says the doctor; 'he may take refreshment now if he likes.'

"'What will you take?' says the kind little gentleman, wagging his pigtail.

"'Oh!' says I, 'I'm not particular—but a small drop of the same clane whiskey out of the long necks.'

"Ah!' says my friend, 'I understand him; a little broth or gruel, doctor.'

"'By all means,' says the doctor, and left me.

"A little whiskey was soon produced, and I never felt better.

"'You had a successful voyage?' says my friend.

"'Capital—only we were robbed of all the cargo.'

"'Yes, those robberies generally happen on these occasions. You need not distress yourself about it. I am quite satisfied with your exertions, and mean to provide for you. Now, what comfortable little situation can I get for you?'

"Comfortable situation, thought I. What if I ask for a farm?

"A farm wouldn't do; it would be a great temptation to me, as my kind friend assured me, and would certainly, if it happened to be on the coast, lead me into trouble.

"'I am afraid,' said he, 'that when once these evil habits of smuggling have been successful, nothing cures them but one method. Your conduct, young man,' says he, with all the feeling imaginable, 'has been very irregular, and you have really, in the eye of the law, been criminal. There is danger also of yourself, at some unhappy moment or other, accusing yourself. I shall, therefore, take the only effectual means to prevent that. You must be silent, for your own sake—and you must cease to smuggle, as your business and profit shall be to prevent it. I have now thoroughly tried your skill—of which you must be silent, or instant dismissal would be the consequence. I have it in my power, through great interest, to recommend young, active, and talented men to the service of the excise. You have all the qualifications which it was my bounden duty to investigate before I sent any one for the appointment. You are selected.'

"'An exciseman!' exclaimed I—'I am the happiest man in existence.'

"I was soon rigged out—you see, sir, how improved my exterior is since I had the honour of seeing you when dressed in Her Majesty's most Christian ten pounds' worth. I have money in hand, and am proceeding to the general office for due instalment in my government duties. Sir, I am most happy again to have met you. I am surprised only that you have not made your fortune. Patronage, sir, is the thing in Ireland. Any man that can get patronage is a made man; but patronage isn't got by going about in the straightforward way that every poor man can go—that will never do—patronage of the kind I enjoy, sir, is gained by real services—and I am a made man!"

I heartily congratulated my companion on the change of fortune which had befallen him; and I could not help thinking, as I reflected on the man's history and recalled his remarks on the all-powerful influence of patronage, that in Ireland, as elsewhere, the straightforward services of honesty and truth do not always ensure it. It is but justice, however, to remark that, in this instance, I thoroughly believe the government was never served by a more dauntless and, excusing the errations of his necessity, a more honest officer. I believe he is now in the service.

The major had tried the lake again during my long absence, and was little successful. His indignation had not cooled against the inhabitants of a preserved country, and I could perceive that Owen's spirits gradually declined as his lengthened absence from his sick mother had increased his anxiety for her safety. He had regularly made small remittances to her, which had been kindly acknowledged by the priest to whom they were addressed. It was resolved, therefore, that the major and Owen should accompany me to Belfast, and there take the Cork packet.

The next difficulty was the conveyance. A car, the only alternative, was obtained—the pony having been long since abandoned; and, by a forced march, we reached Galway in time for the Tuam mail.

Our journey will be uninteresting, as we lingered nowhere, and it is no part of my business to make any but a piscatory road-book. My readers, therefore, ought not to be disappointed if I proceed at once through the beaten track, without notice of those particulars which do not appertain to the sports the country affords. Misery, rags, and poverty, however, still met the eye; deformity and disease presented themselves at every post; and the pertinacious importunity with which their claims were enforced constituted a severe impost on our loose change. But this kind of begging, which is perfectly systematic, will be found only in the more populous towns; wretchedness in the country is more modest, and certainly less obtrusive.

Belfast is no longer Ireland. The proximity to the Scottish shores is at once perceived; there is a bustle and an activity which declare a commercial enterprise, unknown in other Irish cities. While Dublin is half untenanted, and while the pretence to grandeur is mocked by the empty rows of houses and the squalid poverty of its listless and idling population, in Belfast every nook seems to boast its occupant, and every occupant his employment.

Belfast is a new town, one of the present century, and speaks in its prosperity a lesson which the Irish landlords do not understand, nor can be taught. The manufactures of linen and cotton goods have rendered the population of this district prosperous and happy; wages are fairly remunerating, and the rent of land is much less than in the degraded districts through which I had so lately passed. Other and more remunerating employment, for an increased and increasing population, has been found, than the mere culture of the land—the lowest of all human employment—and the competition for the tenure is consequently repressed.

The last evening in Ireland was passed amid real regrets; and, though the enlivening sallies of the major, and the affectionate attachment of Owen, should have tended to create cheerfulness, I felt that I was leaving a people and a country which had become greatly endeared to me. To the sportsman its freedom and wildness constitute attractions which the more cultivated and prosperous countries present not. It is just to say, that a more obliging and hospitable people will nowhere be found.

The farewell of the major was sincerely responded to, as I stepped into the Glasgow packet. The steam was roaring, and the bustle of the coming passengers and luggage was confounding. Amidst the din, however, which all this created, I contrived to make an intelligible promise to visit the north next summer.

Ireland, farewell! Thy wildness and thy beauties have touched me; and, when I behold the aristocratic display which everywhere covers England, I cannot but exclaim, "I love the land of mountain and of flood!"

THE END

www.ingramcontent.com/pod-product-compliance
Lightning Source LLC
Chambersburg PA
CBHW030302240426
43673CB00040B/1035